Oversold and Underserved:

A Financial Planner's Guidebook to Effectively Serving the Mass Affluent

Oversold and Underserved:
A Financial Planner's
Guidebook to Effectively
Serving the Mass Affluent

Marc S. Freedman, CFP®

The Financial Planning Association (FPA) is the membership association for the financial planning community. FPA is committed to providing information and resources to help financial planners and those who champion the financial planning process succeed. FPA believes that everyone needs objective advice to make smart financial decisions.

FPA Press is the publishing arm of FPA, providing current content and advanced thinking on technical and practice management topics.

Information in this book is accurate at the time of publication and consistent with the standards of good practice in the financial planning community. As research and practice advance, however, standards may change. For this reason, it is recommended that readers evaluate the applicability of any recommendation in light of particular situations and changing standards.

Disclaimer—This publication is designed to provide accurate and authoritative information in regard to the subject matter covered. It is sold with the understanding that the publisher is not engaged in rendering legal, accounting, or other professional service. If legal advice or other expert assistance is required, the services of a competent professional person should be sought. —From a Declaration of Principles jointly adopted by a Committee of the American Bar Association and a Committee of Publishers and Associations.

The views or opinions expressed by the author are the responsibility of the author alone and do not imply a view or opinion on the part of FPA, its members, employees, or agents. No representation or warranty is made concerning the accuracy of the material presented nor the application of the principles discussed by the author to any specific fact situation. The proper interpretation or application of the principles discussed in this FPA publication is a matter of considered judgment of the person using the FPA publication and FPA disclaims all liability therefore.

Financial Planning Association
4100 Mississippi Ave., Suite 400
Denver, CO 80246-3053

Phone: 800.322.4237
Fax: 303.759.0749
E-mail: FPApress@FPAnet.org

www.FPAnet.org

Copyright © 2008 FPA Press. All rights reserved.

ISBN: 0-9798775-2-0
ISBN-13 978-0-9798775-2-0

Manufactured in the United States of America

This book is dedicated to the following people:

1. *To my incredibly dedicated wife, Laura, who has given me the courage to be passionate about my beliefs, to be the voice of reason when I (periodically) stick my foot in my mouth, and for being a jack of all trades among our household of five children.*
2. *To Mindy, 12; Ilana, 10; Jerry, 8; Noah, 6; and Corey, 5. Your smiles, your inquisitiveness, your energy, and your love are reasons you've made fatherhood the greatest volunteer profession I could have ever imagined.*
3. *To my parents, Phyllis and Barry Freedman, who have proved to me time and time again that community service builds character and that through those life experiences, we can better mentor, lead, and guide others.*
4. *To my team at Freedman Financial who have been periodic proofreaders, listeners to my stories, and my life preserver when I couldn't be in more than one place at a time.*
5. *To our clients, both present and those who have passed away, who proved to me that great financial planning can happen when trust, integrity, open dialogues, and great stories remain constant components of the relationship.*
6. *Finally, to all of those financial planners who know that personal success is indeed possible by serving the mass affluent community—and not having to elephant hunt for the high net worth market, this book is for you. I assure you that the mass affluent are so glad you've chosen to serve them.*

About the Author

Marc S. Freedman, CFP® is president of Freedman Financial, a Peabody, Massachusetts, community-based, financial planning and wealth management firm. He is a second-generation financial planner.

He has served as a national member of the Board of Directors for the 29,000-member Financial Planning Association (FPA) from 2000–2003. Most recently, he was appointed chairperson for FPA Boston 2008, FPA's national conference. He was named to this post on the heels of his successful leadership as the 2006 chairman for FPA's national conference in Nashville, Tennessee and is a charter member of the Foundation for Financial Planning.

He speaks both internationally and domestically on trends in the financial planning profession and practice management issues. Over the past couple of years, he has addressed international audiences in Singapore, Germany, Austria, and the Netherlands.

A periodic guest on Fox25 Morning News, Marc is regularly quoted in national media outlets, including the *Wall Street Journal, Reader's Digest, Money Magazine, Business Week, USA Today, Washington Post, Fortune Magazine, Journal of Financial Planning, Financial Planning Magazine, Investment Advisor Magazine, Registered Representative,* the *Boston Globe* and the *Boston Herald.*

Marc has made it his personal crusade to educate the public, and those who hold themselves out as financial advisers, on the enormous differences between investment advice and integrated financial planning. His stories enlighten those who will truly listen.

In 1986, Marc traveled with the international music and educational organization Up With People. In 1998, he was awarded the Harry Ankeles Community Service Award for the City of Peabody.

A graduate of Peabody Veterans Memorial High School and a 1989 graduate of Babson College, Marc is married to Laura and has five children, Mindy, Ilana, Jerry, Noah, and Corey. Marc is an avid fan of the Boston Red Sox and the Wonderful World of Disney. It is his lifelong dream to dress as a Disney character in the Magic Kingdom for just one day—after that, he'd happily retire as a tour guide or guest relations cast member.

Freedman Financial
8 Essex Center Drive, Third Floor
Peabody, Massachusetts 01960
978-531-8108
www.freedmanfinancial.com
marc@freedmanfinancial.com

About FPA

The Financial Planning Association® (FPA®) is the membership organization for the financial planning community. FPA is built around four Core Values—Competence, Integrity, Relationships, and Stewardship. We want as members those who share our core values.

FPA's primary aim is to be the community that fosters the value of financial planning and advances the financial planning profession. The FPA strategy to accomplish its objectives involves welcoming all those who advance the financial planning process and promoting the CERTIFIED FINANCIAL PLANNER™ (CFP®) marks as the cornerstone of the financial planning profession. FPA is the heart of financial planning, connecting those who deliver, support, and benefit from it.

FPA was created on the foundation that the CFP marks best represent the promise and the future of the financial planning profession. CFP certification offers the public a consistent and credible symbol of professional competence in financial planning. And FPA benefits the public by helping to ensure that financial planning is delivered through competent, ethical financial planners.

FPA members include individuals and companies who are dedicated to helping people make wise financial decisions to achieve their life goals and dreams. FPA believes that everyone needs objective advice to make smart financial decisions and that when seeking the advice of a financial planner, the planner should be a CFP professional.

FPA is committed to improving and enhancing the professional lives and capabilities of our members. We offer a variety of programs and services to that end.

Table of Contents

Appendix: *Forms & Templates*

Foreword

By Barry M. Freedman, CFP®

I feel privileged to have been more than just an observer of the evolution of financial planning practices these past 40 years. My four decades of service to the profession and Marc's 18 years have provided us with the opportunity to actively manage the growth of a practice. Through our affiliations in the industry, and attendance at countless industry meetings, we have learned the "how to's" by observing and adapting our unique style in a practice that primarily serves the mass affluent. Over the past several decades, I've seen our firm mature from selling product to consultative selling to basic financial planning to fee-based advisory and now to our own version of life-long relationship planning for a client base that is moving through what Ken Dychtwald calls the "power years."

A recent survey by Financial Research Corp. reveals that the sweet spot in the marketplace is the "Power Boomers" (40–60 years old, with at least $100,000 in investible wealth). I believe that the independent financial adviser is best positioned to work with this demographic, since he or she can offer face-to-face time, something most savers crave but which is too expensive for large firms to effectively provide.

Over the years, we learned to develop some standards and core values that helped us build a client-focused business model. In this book, Marc will take you through our history of practice management and development over our combined 58 years of experiences. You will learn how to:

1. Focus your practice on a market that is best suited to your style.
2. Build lifelong client relationships.
3. Leave the prospecting business to door-to-door salespeople.

Methods of compensation are not nearly as important as the perpetual relationships you create with those you serve. Whether you are commission-based, fee-only, fee-based, a NextGen-er, a student, an experienced adviser, an employee of a broker-dealer, wholesaler, or product/service provider, there is much to be learned from Marc's observations of "the old way," as well as the development of new ideas, practice techniques, and thoughts of what could be.

In Section I—How Financial Planning Changes Lives—An Introduction to Serving the Mass Market, Marc will explore the importance of planners honing their leadership and business management skills in order to guide this highly underserved and oversold market segment, the mass affluent.

In Section II—Get your Head In the Game—Practice Management Tips to Help You More Effectively Serve the Mass Affluent, Marc will challenge you to examine every aspect of your business's five senses so that the mass affluent find comfort and trust in your approach to serving their needs.

In Section III—From Start to Implementation—Crafting a World Class Financial Plan for the Mass Affluent, prepare for a journey that invites you to examine each aspect of your role in the financial planning process. Marc will share tools and techniques that have worked effectively in our practice and encourage you to make each client experience both unique and memorable.

In Section IV—From Simple to Spectacular—Marketing and Practice Management Techniques that Retain the Mass Affluent Client, Marc will present a collection of actionable and proven strategies that will position you as a lifelong trusted partner in the financial planning lives of people you serve.

Finally, he ties it all together with a top ten list of essential keys to building lifelong client relationships.

To say that I am proud of Marc's work would be an understatement. At this young stage in our profession's growth, there are very few of us who have had the opportunity to see the dream of business succession (especially within a family) actually accomplished. In addition to Marc's work in the practice, he has taken the rather unusual step of looking at the macro factors affecting our industry as we move forward into serving the aging mass affluent as they move through their power years.

While young in years, Marc has had the opportunity to observe a financial planning practice over many years, and keen observation is one of the greatest developers of wisdom. Marc's unique vantage point and vision should serve to help countless others in their searches for efficient and successful careers.

Introduction

HOW I GOT STARTED IN THIS BUSINESS—A NON-TRADITIONAL JOURNEY

When I graduated from college in 1989, I wasn't aware that financial planning was a profession—and then one day, almost two years after matriculating, I learned that my father was, in fact, a financial planner—and had been since 1968.

The path that lead me toward a career in financial planning has been non-traditional, to say the least. I wasn't hired as a trainee at a large financial institution or insurance company. Instead, I was mentored by my father, Barry M. Freedman, CFP®, and I served an apprentice-like role for the better part of two years before I ever gave any type of financial planning advice to a client. Here's my story.

Upon graduating from Babson College, Wellesley, Massachusetts, with a bachelor's degree in marketing, I worked as a manager for a popular seafood restaurant. While my friends had weekends off, I was busy catering to the whims of tourists, local patrons, and a host of weddings and bar mitzvah parties that we held in our function rooms. I soon learned that maintaining a work schedule dramatically different from my peers and family was something I simply didn't enjoy, so I set out to find a job that allowed me to work at times that aligned with my personal life. I soon left the restaurant business and went to work as a salesman for one of my closest friend's father's paper distribution company. One of their niches was selling Chinese food take-out containers throughout Massachusetts. If you wanted to know where to find the best chicken and cashews, moo shoo beef, or hot and sour soup, I definitely had the inside scoop. Yet, selling to restaurant owners through the kitchen's back door and dodging barrels of pre-cooked pork fried rice wasn't exactly what I had envisioned when I graduated from college.

About one year into my career at the Atlas Paper Company in Woburn, Massachusetts, I decided to re-ignite one of my many passions, singing, and began moonlighting as a karaoke host in downtown Boston. At the time, karaoke was all the rave in Japan and it was just beginning to gain momentum in the States. Every Sunday and Tuesday evening I would work the bar scene at Seaside, a trendy eatery in Boston's Fanueil Hall Marketplace. Yes, it was back to working a couple evenings a week—but sometimes it's the price you pay for love.

Aside from having the opportunity to interact with a vast cross-section of co-eds, tourists, and business folks, on this particular Tuesday evening, March 5, (9:45 p.m. to be exact), a beautiful dark-haired woman entered the area where I was hosting my weekly show. She was out with one of her co-workers, and we were immediately drawn to one another. She asked if I'd be interested in singing the song "Summer Nights" from the movie "Grease" with her. The duet we performed that night forever changed the direction of both our lives. You see, later that evening as we talked to one another during a break in the karaoke performance, she asked me for my last name.

"Freedman," I said.

Immediately recognizing that she had found a Jewish guy in a bar (something every Jewish parent insists will never happen), she said, "My last name is Weinstein. Do you want to get married?"

I had never imagined that I would be proposed to within the first three hours of meeting Laura. You see, within 4 months we were engaged and 14 months later we were married.

So there I was at the age of 23, preparing for my wedding day and working for the Atlas Paper Company. Fortunately, I had expanded my product offerings from selling Chinese take-out containers to providing packaging solutions for local sandwich shops, convenience stores, and delicatessens, and, in rare instances, selling printed shopping bags to local retailers. That was pay day when I landed one of those accounts, let me tell you.

As Laura and I approached our wedding day, we sat together

one afternoon and began talking about our future. I was truly fortunate that we could openly share perspectives on children, religion, family histories, where we'd live, and what we hoped to do together—but when the subject of money came up, Laura said something I'll never forget. She asked, "Are you sure you want to sell paper products for a living? Do you imagine this being the career for us—for our family?" While I might have hoped to achieve "ownership status," at Atlas Paper, in reality the lines of leadership were already in place.

I knew what Laura was leading toward. She knew that any marriage needs the basic emotional connections and fundamental shared beliefs, but to fulfill tangible wishes and dreams, a breadwinner's household income in excess of $30,000 was something we'd need. In reality, my personal financial habits were terrible—hers on the other hand were grounded, responsible, and mature. I never saved my money, I spent it and accumulated debt. To this day she still jokes that she was engaged to my father rather than me. After all, he loaned me the money to buy the ring, and I was still paying him back well into the first year of my marriage.

And then, from out of nowhere, she asked the question I had never even considered.

"What does your father do for a living?"

Honestly, I was tongue-tied. I really didn't have any idea. I knew it had something to do with money, I knew he worked long hours. I knew he worked on weekends and I knew he made enough money to support our family. Throughout my childhood, my parents provided both my brothers and I with the opportunities to travel with them, have cars when we graduated from high school, and they covered our costs for college with the exception of a $10,000 government loan that my parents ultimately paid off for me when I got married.

"Ask him out for lunch," she suggested. "Talk with him. Could it really hurt?" With some trepidation and a flurry of butterflies in my gut I made the call to my father.

I met my father at the Sylvan Street Grille, in Danvers. When we were kids, this restaurant was a local clam shack with a very popular miniature golf course next door. I recall being dropped off on many a Saturday afternoon with my brothers to have lunch and play golf so that my parents could run errands around town. Now here I was in a remodeled, family-style, booth-filled "grille" about to ask my father a question I should have known the answer to long ago.

Although I am certain that Dad wasn't quite sure why I had asked him to lunch, something told me that a little bird had whispered my intentions in his ear, because he was clearly prepared for the onslaught of questions that followed.

I told him that I wanted to better understand what he did for a living and, if he was interested, pursue whether working in a firm such as his was even a possibility.

We sat at lunch for well over two hours. I remember Dad saying that he worked with people in our community. His enthusiasm was infectious. He told me story after story about how he connected with people and how he guided them with ideas on how best to use the financial resources they had so that they could lead more fulfilling and meaningful lives. He told me that the most exciting part of the job was that every client situation was different, and there had never been a time when he felt that he had learned it all.

He told me how important it was for him to attend association meetings, expand his wealth of knowledge, and be active in the community, so that not only his face but the reputation of the firm was always known and respected. He told me that when you make a visible difference in the lives of people you serve, the sense of pride is everlasting. He also impressed upon me how important it was for him to share what he had learned with others in the profession. In doing so, he believed that others would favor him with wisdom and ideas. My dad had a passion that was easily contagious and it was an enthusiasm that he had a hard time containing. Frankly, I don't think I had ever seen my father so excited.

In the back of his mind, he said that his quiet hope was that one of his three sons would look to come into the business. This day had finally come and I could see that he held a swelling sense of pride. He could smell the prospect of a business succession plan and was determined to mentor and train me with care and integrity. My two younger brothers, Jeffrey and Drew, would never have a desire to seek employment in the firm, yet their unique entrepreneurial spirit launched them into successful careers of their own. Today, Jeffrey runs "Small Army," an advertising agency on Boston's trendy Newbury Street and Drew has built "The Boston Bodyworker," a notable massage therapy and neuro-muscular treatment center with two locations in Boston.

Maybe it was too many iced teas that afternoon, but we both agreed to give this a shot. In 1991, the traditional route for becoming a financial planner was through formal training programs offered by a host of large financial institutions. While it included a well-managed curriculum, it typically required a trainee to find their own clients; usually through cold calling, so that they could hone the skills they learned. Dad decided that if I was to become a financial planner, he wanted to mentor me his way. I trusted and followed his lead.

Almost immediately after our lunch meeting, my father put on his manager cap and insisted that I pass the Series 7 Securities license examination before beginning employment at his firm, Freedman Financial, a Massachusetts Registered Investment Adviser. At that time, our securities business was offered through LPL Financial Services, yet from 1968–1987, my father had been affiliated with IDS/American Express, an institution, that he says offers a formal training program into this profession that is second to none. His only resistance for sending me into their training program was guilt. He knew that after completing the corporate training program I would leave IDS/AMEX (at the time) and begin working at Freedman Financial. He had great respect for his old firm and he didn't want to jeopardize the good will and great relationships he still held with his former colleagues.

For the next eight weeks, I studied for the exam. I moved back home with my parents to save money—after all I had to pay for my upcoming honeymoon and had already accumulated about $2,500 in credit card debt. I still worked at Atlas Paper, but my head was clearly focused on passing this test. I was promised that I could submit my resignation immediately after I passed the exam and start as a full-time employee at the firm. On June 26, 1991, I passed the Series 7 on my first attempt. I never imagined how passing that exam would become the launching point for a career that extends into its 18th year. It is a career that I love, appreciate, and am humbled by each and every day.

Fulfilling his promise, Dad welcomed me into the office on June 27. As I entered the 850-square-foot office that was Freedman Financial, I noticed that Marie, my dad's secretary, assistant, office manager, and jack of all trades for what became 28 years, had prepared employment paperwork for my signature. In addition, applications to enroll in the Certified Financial Planner (CFP) Certificant program were mixed in the pile. It was clear that dad was serious about my commitment to ongoing education, yet it also showcased his proactive knowledge of the profession. You see, on July 1, 1992, the multiple choice/essay test approach for obtaining the CFP designation was changing to a new format.

I'm not sure whether the current test is easier or harder than the one I took, but I do know that my father's proactive planning to have me enroll for this highly esteemed certificate was a clear indication of his commitment to me—and I was not about to let him down.

For the next two years I was my father's sidekick. I listened, I took notes, and I talked with our broker-dealer's back office. I communicated with mutual fund and insurance companies. I completed every application, posted every detail about a client's financial situation into our financial planning software, and became the go-to guy for the construction of spreadsheets, graphs, and new templates and forms.

I am convinced that had I gone to work for a large financial institution, I would have never been able to learn these practical skills. Instead, I'd likely be thrown to the wolves with expectations of gathering clients and meeting sales quotas first. Because of my father's dedication to mentoring me, I learned that while technical skills could be taught, lessons of leadership, offering advice, and remaining focused on placing a client's interests first was something you learned through observation first. Anyone can learn the technical terminology and rules governing any profession, but skills of relationship building, effective communication, creativity, and practical problem solving are lessons that are best learned in the field and from watching them in action. For two years, that was my training program.

After two years in the business, my father allowed me to talk with a prospect and start building my own client base. Yet it was through this apprenticeship experience, that I learned what it really meant to be a financial planner. I learned how genuine financial planning changes lives. I learned how to provide advice, wisdom, and guidance to the mass afflluent—a segment of our population that remains indebted to the power of financial planning.

I was given the opportunity to explore the possibilities of serving clients without walls, without management pressures, and without sales quotas. My father gave me the unique opportunity to see the world of financial planning evolve through the eyes of our profession's founding fathers and great leaders, both past and present. Through his commitment to advancing the profession, mentoring others, and volunteering as a steward for our professional association on local, national, and international levels, he inspired me early in my career to do the same. I served on FPA's Board of Directors from 2001–2004. I have chaired three FPA national conferences and have served on task forces, advisory councils, and committees for our association for almost 20 years.

Oversold and Underserved: A Financial Planner's Guidebook to Effectively Serving the Mass Affluent

With 40 years of stories from my father and lessons I've learned on my own, I feel confident that our experience in serving the needs of the mass affluent client not only works, but it leads to lifelong relationships. In 2007, dad retired from the firm, but still remains an active and vocal advocate for serving the financial planning needs of consumers around the globe. In doing so, he has handed me the reins to manage our local practice and keep genuine financial planning at the cornerstone of every action, conversation, and relationship we have with our clients. My promise to him and the community that helped us develop the skills needed to be genuine financial planners is to share the lessons we've learned and perpetuate the stories, templates, examples, and techniques to impassioned planners who seek to deliver a better financial planning experience to their clients.

Through our combined experiences, we know that the mass affluent population craves financial planning services that extend beyond investment advice. Whether you are a new planner, a seasoned veteran, or what Ben "Colin" Coombs refers to as "a rat in the barn," I hope that you'll enjoy the stories, perspectives, and new ideas that are scattered throughout the book. I welcome your feedback, your criticism, or an animated dialogue over a beer by the pool. I hope that this book inspires others to share their stories and their beliefs, because the planners of our community need to contribute to the body of knowledge that advances the financial planning profession.

Enjoy!

How Financial Planning Changes Lives—
An Introduction to Serving the Mass Affluent

1 | *Why I Wrote This Book*

I am honored to be called a financial planner. With each passing day, people around the world have found peace of mind by simply embracing the genuine guidance and leadership of financial planners. If you have picked up this book, I suspect that you are a practicing financial planner, a supporter of financial planning services, or someone who hopes to transform your business into one where financial planning is the foundation of your client relationships.

I began my financial planning career in 1991, and from the very first day, I've been amazed at how each planner maintains a passionate belief about the best way to build a client base. Over the years, consulting firms and business management coaches have stressed the importance of identifying target markets. While that may sound obvious if you are just starting out in this business, what if your client base is already diverse? Are you more apt to continue building a potpourri of client types and styles, or would you spend the time to find client similarities that exist already? The majority of us gravitate to conferences and education meetings with hope of finding a brand new market segment to solicit. If you're like most planners, the temptation of finding the next undiscovered niche is more appealing than addressing the mess that already exists in your book of business.

Over the years, I have noticed that too many planners have built client mixes that could best be compared to an old 128-count box of Crayola crayons. Open the box and not a single crayon looks the same. Some are sharp, some are blunt. There are some we certainly rely on more than others. There are others we have used once, but for the most part, sit in the box collecting dust. Why do we find it so hard to throw away crayons we know we'll never regularly use? Why do we keep them in our box with the ones we like using? What's the chance your client base resembles a box of crayons?

I happen to believe that some of those underserved crayons in your box represent clients who could hold the key to your personal financial success. That's right, hidden in your existing client roster is a subset of clients that has been forgotten. I call them the mass affluent, and they are a population of consumers who have been oversold and underserved. Too often we tend to confuse this segment with the middle market, but that's far from who they are.

HOW WE DESCRIBE THE MASS AFFLUENT
The mass affluent are people who:

1. Save more than they spend.
2. Seek to invest for their futures.
3. Worry about funding college education, but in most cases, will not impoverish themselves because they can cover costs through savings strategies, loans, and/or personal income. In addition, many aren't opposed to their children paying some part of the education costs.

4. Worry about how they will replace their paychecks when retirement approaches, but in most cases, they will need to be encouraged to spend *more* money in retirement.
5. Have a greater desire to leave a legacy to their children, not to charity.
6. Have household incomes between $75,000 and $175,000.
7. In retirement, seek to spend between $4,000 and $10,000 per month.
8. Will have between $500,000 and $1.5 million in investable assets upon retirement.
9. Maintain a net worth (including property and liabilities) between $500,000 and $2.5 million.
10. Would never consider calling themselves high net worth investors or millionaires.

I couldn't imagine the above list of people being considered part of the middle market.

HOW WE DESCRIBE THE MIDDLE MARKET

Admittedly the differences between typical middle market and mass affluent households are not as easy to recognize. They are both gainfully employed. They face pressures from children and parents, and they enjoy taking periodic vacations and periodically eating out. In many cases, middle market clients and mass affluent clients share a significant overlap in household income. Yet I believe that middle market clients also carry strains from life decisions they have made.

Often, they:

1. Face mounting credit card, auto, and personal debt.
2. Are unprepared or underprepared to fund education costs.
3. Are blue collar, union workers, and assistant managers.
4. Require a dual income to cover expenses.
5. Are continually trying to "keep up with the Joneses."

6. Are susceptible to fragile employment conditions.
7. Have a pessimistic outlook on their future retirement.
8. Have slim possibilities for inheritances.
9. Need to tend to both children and aging parents.
10. Face significant financial solvency challenges from rising health care costs.

Consider the following research. Recently, Russ Allen Prince and Associates published a book entitled *The Middle Class Millionaire*. The book was based on surveying middle class Americans with investable assets between $1 and $10 million. Yes, they called them "middle class." How do you think Americans would feel if they were told that this statistic represented the middle class? Do you think when politicians are lobbying for votes from the middle class, this is who they think they are talking to? Could assertions like these be a reason why such a disconnect exists among what the Financial Planning Association refers to as "the Heart of Financial Planning," those who need financial planning (consumers), those who deliver planning services (financial planners), and those who manufacture products and business-building solutions that support the profession (financial institutions)? I think each group described holds certain perceptions and beliefs about the needs and services available in the mass affluent marketplace.

So why haven't we spent more time carving the mass affluent out from the middle market? I simply don't believe that the mass affluent has been properly segmented. In my opinion, the mass affluent seem to be stuck in a world where they want financial planning advice, yet what they buy is primarily investment advice.

My personal suspicion is that most planners' client rosters contain a certain percentage of mass affluent clients. These clients are loyal. They respect your advice and, more than anything else, they are willing to financially open up to you, in the hope that you'll build a plan that you will monitor and manage for them together. But here's the big question. Can planners effectively build a successful business by exclusively serving the mass affluent? I know it can be done—and you can do it too. In fact, that's why I've chosen to write this book. I want to share some insight, habits, and first-hand experience about this largely untapped market and encourage you to understand the enormous opportunity in serving the mass affluent marketplace.

WHY ARE THE MASS AFFLUENT UNDERSERVED?

As I've traveled the country and talked with planners, I've learned that the mass affluent community seeks advice on a wide array of financial planning issues. While they generally have investable dollars, they also want to explore how their money will affect their lives. However, many of the financial relationships they maintain are built on investment strategies, performance comparisons, technical analyses, and tactical repositioning. These clients feel like the planning element of the relationship is missing, yet they struggle to articulate it because their current adviser calls the existing narrow relationship financial planning.

While the mass affluent may be underserved, they are oversold. We see too many of these clients visiting our office with stories of how they felt like a small fish in a big pond. They had been initially solicited by representatives who were well-intentioned, but at the end of the day, the representatives had an obligation to meet product quotas and sales projections. These clients felt an initial sense of security aligning their business with a big name firm, but when it came to having their financial planning needs addressed, the relationship would fall short. In fact, when it was time to do serious financial planning, they'd tell us that they couldn't imagine using their current advisers to help them.

Representatives from these big companies are generally compensated at payout rates between 25 and 40 percent. And while they may express a desire to work in a fee-based environment, they need to capture three to four times as many assets as independent financial advisers to receive the same compensation. As a result, the big-firm representative needs to focus on one of three items:

1. Heavily prospect to gather assets. After all, a $500,000 fee-based account at 1 percent yields less than $2,000 per year (25–40 percent payout) to this adviser, when an independent adviser can annually earn $3,500–$5,000 (70 to 100 percent payout) on the same $500,000 account.
2. Include annuities, brokerage securities, and alternative investment products in the client implementation strategy. These products generally pay commissions of 4–7 percent, and serve as a nice one-time compensation supplement.
3. Focus on building a higher net worth client base that could deposit minimum assets in excess of $1–$2 million.

Registered representatives who choose to build a client base with mass affluent clients need to have hundreds of, if not a thousand or more, relationships to earn a living that rivals the compensation levels of the top producers in the office. In doing so, service standards to their clients are diminished dramatically, and ultimately, the client begins to search for a different, more personal relationship.

Some registered representatives have chosen to buck this trend and focus on delivering genuine financial planning services to all of their clients. Ultimately, these reps run the risk of falling short of sales goals and reduce their likelihood of earning greater payout rates from their firm. It's unfortunate, but when so many layers need to be paid in a large firm, success relies on building scale, not on developing deep individualized relationships. Ultimately, representatives at these big firms must decide to accept their roles as average producers who deliver exceptional service, or to seek relationships with other broker-dealers or custodians, so they can be compensated for the wisdom and advice they deliver.

On the other side, there are planners who choose to build an independent boutique practice. They may affiliate with a broker-dealer, or they may choose to become Registered Investment Advisers. For some, a mass affluent client can become their first "big" client, and they over-serve his or her needs while neglecting too many other existing client relationships. Generally, the adviser finally sees the opportunity to get adequately paid for financial planning services including tax planning, cash flow management, asset allocation, insurance solutions, and basic estate planning. This big client becomes the test case for new financial planning software, and they are first to be considered for alternative investment strategies, annuity products, etc. They also seem to be the client who is regularly pursued for referrals. However, over time, this client begins to realize that his or her financial situation bears little resemblance to the majority of relationships this adviser has built.

Financial planners know that it's best to serve their most profitable clients, yet too often, we find that smaller independent adviser firms have one to five clients that generate more than 20 to 40 percent of the annual revenue to their office. We believe that concentration of revenue and the business risk associated with it is quite dangerous.

We believe that advisers who seek to serve the mass affluent market should build client relationships where no single household accounts for more than 2 percent of the revenue to the firm. Nor should they build a client base that lists their largest client's accounts producing 1/1000th of a percent of annual revenue.

WHAT MAKES THE MASS AFFLUENT MARKET SO ATTRACTIVE FOR FINANCIAL PLANNERS?

People in the mass affluent market are becoming more and more educated about the elements of financial planning. They know that there is more to financial planning than investment advice, and they are expecting an expanded host of services from you.

They want to work with a planner who cares about their overall financial well-being, not just the money they can manage. They want advisers who will communicate with them in a warm, empathetic manner and show genuine interest in helping them achieve their goals and dreams.

Financial planners who position themselves to serve clients by delivering ongoing advice and offering tangible solutions to meet their needs are destined to maintain high retention rates. In our experience, planners will not starve by serving the mass affluent—they will thrive. In 1991, our firm served over 500 households and our net revenue was about $300,000. Today, our firm serves 350 mass affluent families. Our revenue in 2008 will exceed $1.8 million, with 91 percent coming from recurring investment advisory fees. With a staff of five people, we're making a fine living while maintaining an average retention rate in excess of 98 percent over the past five years. And if our firm could make this transition, so can you. The only difference is that you can do it in much less time than it took us—and I'm going to show you how.

I believe that financial advisers who build practices centered on meeting with clients in person have a much greater opportunity to understand the emotions and resistance clients have toward making decisions in their financial lives. Choosing to primarily engage clients by telephone, over the Internet, or through the mail stretches your ability to establish a connection and extends the time it can take to build a foundation for lifelong relationships. That's not to say that financial planning services can't be provided electronically, telephonically, or through the mail. In fact, it's likely that some of your clients wouldn't ever want to meet face to face. But when you are serving the mass affluent, I believe that the greatest opportunity to build relationships occurs when financial planning is delivered in person. As a result, we've concentrated on targeting our efforts so that most of the clients for our firm live within a 15-mile radius of our office.

Mass affluent clients are best served when the relationship builds through the conversation, not projections and analyses. Without a doubt, it is significantly harder to deliver financial planning in person. You need to "perform" on the spot in the event a client wishes to tweak their goals or question your findings. But once you overcome the pressures that every individual in a leadership position experiences—and make no mistake, a financial planner is in a leadership position—you'll find that the rewards are substantial. They will generate ripple effects that lead to referral opportunities from your clients and stronger, tighter relationships with those you serve.

Mass affluent clients want to view you as a leader in their lives. They want to work with you professionally, but they also like seeing you active in the community. They enjoy bumping into you at the local coffee shop, restaurants, the movie theater, and the grocery store. They love telling their friends that they work with a financial planner, and they are quick to make introductions when they are with acquaintances.

The mass affluent community has needs that extend beyond traditional financial planning training. They want to rely on you as an adviser. They will seek wisdom from you in areas that include purchasing a vehicle, moving into a retirement community, talking with their children about money, and selecting the right withholdings on their W-4s. More than anything, they want to know that you're willing to offer guidance on non-financial issues pertaining to their life's goals, as well as quantitative knowledge when it comes time to crunch the numbers. There is an enormous demand for these services, and this market segment wants it from you.

This book is written to celebrate this highly underserved group of people, with the hope that you will recognize the importance of genuine financial planning, and how you, as a financial planner, can build a business and a stream of revenue that will allow you to focus more on planning for your clients.

What if the mass affluent is not the market for you? What if your niche is more specialized or you expect it to remain undefined? Can you benefit from this book? Absolutely! No matter the size of your client base or the length of time you've spent in this profession, I am certain that you will find tools and techniques that will make you a better financial planner.

Within the pages of this book you will find wisdom and resources that will help you...

1. Identify existing target markets within in your practice.
2. Transition your business from transactional methods to ones that focus on delivering ongoing value and service for a fee.
3. Learn how genuine financial planning can be delivered as the foundational principle of every relationship you maintain with clients.
4. Build marketing strategies that accentuate your best skills and make the most of hidden gems that exist in your practice today.
5. Better communicate your value proposition to clients and prospects.
6. Become immersed in the profession of financial planning so that you can both change the lives of the people you serve and ground your core value and beliefs to make growing your practice easier than ever before.

As we close this opening chapter, I want to share one of my greatest frustrations with you and make a pledge that I hope you'll hold me to if ever our paths cross.

I find that when attending practice management sessions at conferences, or reading books about building a business, the speaker/author will pepper their narratives with ideas on "What you should be doing." Instead, it has always been my hope that they would say, "Here's how we do it. Feel free to use these ideas and examples so that you can enjoy the success we've found by implementing these concepts in our office." That's my pledge. In return, all I ask is that someday, you'll "pay it forward" to someone else who might just look to you as their mentor.

Finally, I hope that as you read this book, you will share the honor I feel each day as a member of the world's most important profession.

2 | *Why Leadership Matters in Financial Planning*

OBJECTIVES

1. Explain why leadership development is essential for financial planners
2. Convey the importance of listening to your heart
3. Encourage you to ask tough questions

WHEN FINANCIAL PLANNERS ARE VIEWED AS ADVICE PROVIDERS OUR PROFESSION GAINS GREATER NOBILITY

What's the second most important thing (the first being health) in anybody's life?

Make no mistake, it's money!

Not that you have to have an enormous amount of it, but money will dictate everything that you do in your life. So why do people struggle with recognizing the fact that money needs a level of personal (and possibly professional) attention equal to the care and dedication we give to our health care needs?

I think the real reason is that most people are embarrassed. They were never given financial planning training in school, and their greatest point of reference for handling money is observing their parents' money habits, or by hearing from friends, neighbors, and relatives about money-saving deals, a great software program, or financing tool. Personal finance is a taboo topic. In fact, I believe people are willing to tell you their full medical history, right down to the goriest of details, but will make up stories, disguise the truth, or simply stay silent when it comes to money.

As a financial planner, you are likely the first person to ask deep-rooted money questions that people want to answer, but they need your assurance that they are in a safe, confidential environment. They are fearful that you'll talk down to them. All they really want to know is that you care and you'll listen. Consumers seek a leader who is willing to show them a guided path, but human experience has programmed skepticism and fear of deceit in their minds. It is your responsibility to build their trust by offering sincere education and a big-picture perspective on how to envision their financial goals and dreams.

THE TRANSFORMATIVE POWERS OF LEADERSHIP THROUGH FINANCIAL PLANNING

Like it or not, your clients view you as a leader in their lives. As a financial planner, you are in the enviable position of empowering people to examine their financial lives in ways they never imagined. In these times of economic uncertainty, your client leadership skills are needed more than ever. It's time to heighten your understanding of the significant responsibility you accepted as a planner, and make sure that both you and your clients know that your leadership is something they can count on. Because when they do, you've earned a client for life.

Financial planners transform people's lives. In fact, I believe that when the process of financial planning is delivered to clients with authenticity, integrity, honesty, and compassion, the profession of planning elevates its relevance.

The moment you decided to be a personal financial planner, you placed yourself in a position of leadership. Leadership is one of the hardest disciplines to attain because it is nearly impossible to find courses designed to help financial planners in this area. It is incumbent upon you, the professional associations with whom you affiliate, and those who serve as your mentors to continually offer courses, discussions, and workshops on building authentic leadership skills—without them, you lack a critical tool in the lifelong client relationship-building process.

THE FINANCIAL PLANNER AS A LEADER

Genuine financial planners inspire clients to envision their dreams. They know when to play devil's advocate. They know when to ask just the right question, and they know when they need to keep their mouths shut and simply allow a client to think, talk, and consider alternatives. Great financial planners also give advice—*and they are willing to put that advice in writing.* They pride themselves on their ability to guide clients through myriad of potential outcomes, present arrays of perspectives, and raise clients' confidence so they feel as though they made smart decisions.

Too many financial professionals rely on training manuals, sales idea pieces, scripts, articles written by others, and frankly, their own personal biases when steering a client towards a solution. When you talk to your client in a manner that fosters trust and allows for the exploration of possibilities, your skills as a leader distinguish you as a planner who can become revered by the clients you serve. You'll find some ideas for how to develop these skills later in this chapter.

In the end, lifelong relationships require you to focus on patience, wisdom, and guidance so much more than analytical training and computational skills. Lifelong clients must view you not only as their financial planner but as their champion. It is *your* responsibility to vigilantly create an environment where clients feel that you've heard them.

As you journey through the chapters in this book, you will find examples of leadership in action. With each client story you read, consider whether your approach to serving a client's needs would be similar or different from the example. Leadership comes in all shapes, forms, and sizes. It is your personal responsibility to find the style that best serves you. Without leadership, clients are left to wander on their own, and they will simply view you as a conduit to helping them execute strategy. Remain focused and guide them with wisdom and care.

A TIME WHEN LEADERSHIP WAS NEEDED MOST

In March 2000, the most prolonged bear market in most financial planners' lifetimes began. After years of double-digit positive returns on portfolios, the role of a financial planner became fuzzy. Many financial planners watched their aggregate assets under management dwindle along with their ongoing fees.

We, too, felt the financial hit, and each time the phone rang, I wondered if it was a client calling to cash out, yell at us, or simply question the investments in his or her portfolio. Yet, strangely enough, the phone rang as normal. No one yelled. Only two clients requested to cash out their accounts. Not a single client moved their portfolio to another investment adviser, broker, or financial planner.

Like many financial planners, we spent those three years communicating with our clients and reminding them about the value of long-term planning. We always wondered whether the notes we sent were effective, but lack of responsiveness left us with an unsolved mystery.

A DIFFICULT QUESTIONS IN CHALLENGING TIMES—"WHY DO YOU STAY?"

After numerous sleepless nights, stomach churning, and anxiety, we sought answers through our advisory council. With our next meeting scheduled for fall 2002, we thought that talking with our clients might help address our unanswered questions—and frankly, give us the therapy we needed.

As the dinner plates were cleared that evening, we explained that we had only one agenda item to discuss. I took a deep breath, looked to my father for a nod of support, and proceeded to frame the question I dreaded to ask.

"For the past many years, it has been our pleasure serving your financial planning needs. Yet I need to be candid with you. As you well know, the stock markets in general have continued to precipitously drop. We have all read stories of hysteria at stock brokerage firms, day traders finding new careers, and people commiserating in coffee shops over their lost fortunes. But in our office, we have been worrying too. We've been worrying about your states of mind when you open your monthly statements. The balances in your portfolios have dropped further and further and optimism is clearly not rampant these days. We think that we've done our very best to share our honest perspectives through a series of letters, e-mails and review meetings. Yet we wonder whether it has been enough.

"In truth, only two clients have closed their accounts. They haven't left us to hire another financial planner; they simply couldn't stomach the gyrations in the market and they have chosen to position their assets in certificates of deposit.

"So that leaves us trying to better understand our clients' perspectives on this challenging market environment. Tonight, we'd like to capture some perspective. Simply put: Why do you stay?"

The room sat silent for a moment, and the fear and anxiety I anticipated in the eyes of our clients didn't appear. They were calm, even-tempered, and almost still. Finally, someone spoke. He had been a client of ours for only a few years. All he knew through our office was negative investment performance, because he had joined our firm just after Y2K.

"Where *else* would my wife and I go?" he asked, "It's not your fault that markets have fallen, and honestly, I couldn't bear living with the losses had I sold out."

True enough, but it wasn't quite the comforting message we were looking for. Nor did it express a sense of confidence in our services and efforts over the past couple years. That was until Mr. Waterstone stood and addressed the group.

MEET THE WATERSTONES

As I was about to respond to the previous comments (though I wasn't quite sure what I would have said), I was "saved" by another client. Roger and Janet Waterstone joined our firm in 1996 when Roger retired from a large employer in Massachusetts. For the past several decades, Roger had managed their investment portfolio on his own. Periodically, he consulted with a friend who was a stock broker and also a member of their church. Occasionally, upon the recommendation of the broker, he would purchase a few mutual funds and a couple of annuities. For the most part, though, the bulk of their wealth was held in the stock of his employer, his 401(k) plan, and a Vanguard portfolio. His wife, Janet, was a frail, small woman who accompanied Roger on all client meetings, yet she never spoke. As Roger, age 72, cleared his throat, he rose to his feet slowly. He began speaking in an almost uneven way. Clearly he was a bit nervous, and he looked back to Janet for assurance as he proceeded.

"Marc," he said, "the reasons we hired your firm in 1996 are completely different from the reason we maintain a relationship with you today." He continued, "When I approached retirement, I knew that I didn't want to be held responsible for providing for our family's next paycheck. I had managed money on my own for years, but I knew that if I wanted to fulfill Janet's and my retirement goals, I couldn't be monitoring investments and figuring out where to draw money from my accounts. Your firm provided us a comfort that extended beyond just investment management. You gave us an impression that you'd continue to manage our income needs and draw money from the most tax advantageous locations. But, like I said, the reason we stay today is different from why we hired your firm years ago."

A heavy pause hung in the room for a moment. I wondered what would come next. Roger looked back again at Janet, whose eyes had begin to fill with tears. Emotions began to creep into Roger's voice, "Two months ago I was diagnosed with cancer." He paused for a moment, looked down to pace his breathing, and then glanced again at Janet, who reached out and grabbed his hand.

"My doctor has informed me that my life expectancy is less than 12 months and I am scared." He continued with a renewed strength and confidence in his voice. "The reason we stay today is because while Janet and I sat at our kitchen table last month, contemplating how she would manage to live her life after I was gone, she said to me, 'Don't ever fire the Freedmans. Who else will I turn to when you're gone?'"

I didn't quite know how I'd respond to such a personal expression of appreciation in a setting among 12 other client couples, so I let him continue to hold the floor.

He reminisced for a moment about some of our previous meetings and conversations from years ago, and reminded me that Janet would never speak at any of our review meetings; yet, she always talked with him after our client reviews. She regularly expressed an appreciation for his delegating his financial planning and ultimately hiring a financial planning firm that she trusted as much as she trusted him.

Janet indicated that after Roger passed away, she would need to rely on us for details as simple as writing a check, managing expenses, purchasing a vehicle, and helping her sell her home so that she could move into an active 55-plus community. He told us that she would need our guidance and leadership more than ever, because she would likely carry the emotional burdens for her children and grandchildren.

The room held still and Roger quietly sat back in his chair. Not an eye was dry and we all knew there was no reason to press harder with our question. Do you think anyone was thinking about the volatility of the stock market after Roger's story? Instead, we were all humbled by his openness. His story is an example of why we need to be leaders for our clients. We need to keep them focused on what matters most in their lives. At the end of the day, market volatility seems so insignificant when we're forced to face life's largest hurdles. As a financial planner, you hold your clients' respect more than ever when you give them a sense that you can be a leader in their lives.

As financial planners, our greatest value to our clients comes from our advice and compassion during difficult times. Your responsibility to deliver better performance or temper emotions in irrational times is nothing compared to the effect you will have on the lives of the "silent partner," when you can uncover the unspoken emotions about money that clients have difficulty expressing. It is this voice, in times of crisis, that crystallizes our value as financial planners in the lives of clients and their extended families.

So why do your clients stay with you in difficult times? What would it take to ask them? I suspect the answer you receive will be different from anything you could have ever imagined.

THE POWER OF LEADERSHIP THROUGH FINANCIAL PLANNING

An expression of leadership doesn't only appear when people are at the most difficult points in their lives. Sometimes leadership emerges when you ask a client a question they never anticipated. Sometimes it appears when you raise an undiscussed issue that you know could lead to fireworks in the conference room, but being willing to take the risk best serves the interests of your client.

Leadership can appear in all forms, but it is most effective when it is supported with authenticity and sincerity. You don't need to have a powerful voice, be the highest paid person in the room, or wear the fanciest clothes. Leaders come in all shapes and sizes. They are found in financial planning offices throughout the world, and they are respected by the clients they serve.

Who are the leaders in this profession that you respect? What makes them leaders in your eyes? Do they ask provocative questions? Do they listen more intently when the conversation gets more complex?

Some of the greatest leaders I've admired have taught me the following:

1. **You're not as smart as you think.** Great leaders surround themselves with people smarter than themselves. They are always learning, always listening, and are always willing to imagine new possibilities.
2. **Patience works, persistence hurts.** Great leaders are willing to give people the time they need to work through difficult questions. Pressing for answers or seeking immediate solutions can lead to missed possibilities.
3. **Ask the tough questions.** Leaders know that when uncomfortable issues are purposely avoided, it is impossible to develop an open and honest relationship. Have strength to lead the dialogue through uncomfortable conversations.
4. **Stay curious.** Leadership is a skill that needs refinement, practice, and continual development. Find authors, mentors, and advisers who will challenge your thinking and motivate you to hone your craft.
5. **Read.** Leaders are continually seeking tools, expressions, and ideas that help them better inspire others. Be vigilant about reading books on leadership. Despite being busy, leaders find time to develop their skills.

Here are a few books you might consider:

- *Authentic Leadership* by Bill George
- *True North* by Bill George
- *Inspire! What Great Leaders Do* by Lance Secretan
- *The Corporate Mystic* by Gay Hendrick and Kate Ludeman
- *Squirrel Inc.* by Stephen Denning

What leadership traits do you have that will make you the most trusted person in your client's life? What commitments will you make to personal leadership development to ensure that you are serving your clients and even your family as well as you can?

SUMMARY

1. Include leadership development as part of your professional development.
2. By incorporating leadership skills as part of your role as a financial planner, you can change people's lives.
3. Trust your instincts and attempt to uncover issues that may be preventing a client from telling you the whole story.
4. Identify stories that reflect how your leadership has led to building better relationships. Write them down. Tell them to others. Be proud of your accomplishments.

3 Why Argue Over Compensation Models when It's Advice that Matters?

OBJECTIVES

1. Share a perspective on why arguing over compensation models makes no sense.
2. Consider whether advisers should be compensation neutral when it comes to financial planning services.
3. Identify two dominant camps in the world of financial planning

All financial planning services will be delivered in accordance with the following standard of care:

1. *Put the client's best interests first*
2. *Act with due care and in utmost good faith*
3. *Do not mislead clients*
4. *Provide full and fair disclosure of all material facts*
5. *Disclose and fairly manage all material conflicts of interest*

— Standard of Care—as adopted by Financial Planning Association Board of Directors, August 2008

I believe that the method by which a planner is compensated holds little bearing on his or her integrity and commitment to serving a client's needs. In fact, I believe that a client would never even raise the issue of compensation methods if she felt that her planner was delivering advice in a manner that placed her interests first.

Nevertheless, continued advice and service require compensation to the adviser. When financial planning is viewed as a free service, it diminishes the value of both your credentials and the profession at large. Too many planners fear that clients won't pay for advice. Trust me, that is simply in your head. Rational people pay for services that deliver value. If financial planning is about improving the quality of a person's life, shouldn't that be considered a pretty significant value? The bigger question is whether you can articulate your value in the eyes of people you serve.

WILL THE MASS AFFLUENT PAY FOR FINANCIAL PLANNING?

They absolutely will. However, if financial planning is viewed as simply reviewing an investment portfolio and making a recommendation for a new and improved strategy, then a client would be a fool to pay for *that* as a financial planning service. That is a sale. The way in which advisers seek to be compensated for services is completely up to them. But transactions are not what financial planning is about.

No matter your compensation method, commit to deliver all the facts regarding how you're paid up front. Allow the client to fully understand the costs involved. Never try to sell yourself as the "low cost" alternative. Consumers who want quality advice don't expect bargain basement prices. Your knowledge, guidance, and leadership is worth it. Stand behind your compensation structure, and never be ashamed to let a client know what you're getting paid.

In our practice, we tell our clients up front that initially, we wear two hats. The first is to objectively serve their needs as a financial planner. We explain that we charge a fee for financial planning before any strategies are implemented. Our minimum fee is $1,500 and it's based on an hourly rate of $200. We generally provide a client an estimate of our fee (which ranges between $1,500 and $4,000) at the conclusion of our initial meeting. Our plans are written objectively and with generic advice so that a client can implement the strategy anywhere they see fit. They are under no obligation to hire our firm for investment advisory and/or transaction based-services.

Our second hat comes in after the initial financial plan is presented and paid for. Then, we present implementation strategies that we can handle on behalf of the client. In fact, when we do establish a fee-based advisory relationship with a client, we tell them we believe that 30 percent of our asset management fee will cover the costs for our investment advisory services—the balance pays for upkeep of their financial planning needs along with additional value-added services delivered by our firm. In Sections II, III, and IV, we will broaden your understanding of these services and benefits you might consider delivering to your clients.

INTERNAL BATTLES OVER COMPENSATION METHODS

Too often, I find that those in the fee-only or fee-based world suggest that planners who seek to be compensated via commissions can't deliver authentic financial planning services. In some circles, commission-based planners are viewed in the same category with used car salespeople. On the other side of the spectrum, the commission-based community views the investment advisory world as touchy-feely, spiritual types who believe that until "Kumbaya" is sung, financial planning can't even begin. As a long-time professional in the financial planning community, I can tell you that both perspectives are at the extremes of financial planning. If planners expect to change the lives of the people they serve and make our profession one that earns admiration and respect from the public at large, we need to embrace our strength in diversity and celebrate how multitudes of business models allow for financial planning to reach every corner of the Earth.

Despite being able to call ourselves financial planners, business too often uses that term as more of a marketing tool, rather than a professional distinction based on placing the client's interest first. For instance, there are many commission-based advisers who will seek to capitalize on continued sales opportunities from existing clients. These transaction-driven planners have a financial incentive (though it's not always the primary objective) to capitalize on a client's dissatisfaction with the performance of an investment, and offer an alternative solution. In many cases, the new sales opportunity yields a *certain* commission to the planner and an *uncertain* return for the client—though the story that supported the sales transaction rarely suggested the uncertain possibility. But how are these planners any different from some fee-only (and fee-based) advisers who are solely interested in asset gathering? This group focuses on building a large, recurring income stream and leaving the management of money up to outside managers. Their involvement in the ongoing tweaking of a clients investment portfolio is negligible. Instead they espouse the use of private money managers whose sheer names add panache to the sale, but in the end, it's about gathering more assets and earning a larger collective fee.

In both cases, these advisers are compensated well, but their dedication to serving the financial planning interests of a client is significantly less than their passion to build a financial empire.

Remember when your favorite local restaurant knew your name as soon as you walked in the door? You knew all the chefs in the kitchen and the bartender knew your choice of beverage. Your friends and neighbors all met here and your kids found their first jobs as servers, dishwashers, and busboys. On weekends when a line was out the door, you knew that you could walk up to the hostess and they'd seat you before many others. Then, all of a sudden, the lines shrunk, the quality of food was inconsistent, and the personnel changed as quickly as the weather. This popular restaurant decided to expand its success and open locations all around the state. The people you knew were now trying to acquire a new clientele in a new city. The head chef was now managing a revolving door of newly hired chefs and the owner was busy trying to franchise his success and cash out.

As our businesses have grown, no matter whether we sell on commission or charge fees, the challenges that come with growth are inevitable. Every planner faces the dilemma of how to manage service standards in the face of change. Managing a growing business while serving the individual needs of our clients' comprehensive financial lives is no easy task. The moment we lose sight of that, the walls can begin to crumble.

My guess is that many of you who are reading this book are tasting that flavor of success, but before you get too carried away with the rewards that follow, it is important to reflect on what got you to where you are today, and what changes are needed to keep you grounded.

For instance, if you're collecting a sizable annual fee from your clients each year, what commitment are you making each year to serve these advice-based clients better? Have you found that your passion to find new clients has been tempered by your enthusiasm for retaining existing clients?

When your business's revenue is predictable and your model focuses on client goals and objectives instead of client sales and opportunities, you'll find that conversations with your clients will be easier. They will be deeper, more compassionate, and revealing and clients will be more emotional and involved. When you do this and do it well, business—the right kind of business—will walk in the door.

TWO DOMINANT CAMPS IN THE WORLD OF FINANCIAL PLANNING

A few years ago, David Yeske, a financial planner in San Francisco and former chairman of the Financial Planning Association, offered a metaphor for financial planning that remains an ah-ha moment for me. Many planners have modified the metaphor, and I think the example below clearly illustrates the distinction between the two dominant camps in the world of financial planning.

Imagine, for a moment, a pie (you can pick the flavor). Camp (Pie) Number One features financial planners who view the foundation of the pie (the crust) as financial planning. It doesn't matter which slice of the pie is removed from the dish, the "financial planning crust" supports each serving. Each slice of pie represents a subset of financial planning, such as investment management, distribution planning, capital needs analysis, cash flow management, tax planning, estate planning, etc.

Camp (Pie) Number Two features those who view the pie crust as wealth management. In this case, investment solutions serve as the crust—financial planning, tax planning, estate planning, college planning, etc., become slices in the pie, and every client conversation carries a foundation that supports an investment conversation. So who's right?

If you're still a little fuzzy on the metaphor, let me try to explain it in different terms.

Simply explained, the two camps break down like this:

1. There are those who market themselves as financial planners and deliver balanced levels of service in all areas of their client's financial well-being—wealth management stands as one slice of the pie.
2. There are those who market themselves as financial planners yet primarily offer wealth management strategies as their core service—financial planning stands as one slice of the pie.

- *Which camp do you represent?*
- *In a few years from now, would you imagine yourself in the same camp?*
- *Have you seen business migrating from one camp to another?*

DO SOME PLANNERS WEAR SHEEP'S CLOTHING?

A few years ago, I attended a FPA annual symposium. About 300 people sat in a room to listen to a speaker offer his perspective on the future of the financial planning profession. At the start of the presentation, the speaker asked the group to raise their hands if they thought they were "pretty good" at managing investments for their clients. About 80 percent of the hands in the room elevated. He then asked, "How many people feel they are very good at managing investments for their clients?" About half of the hands in the room dropped. He then asked, "How many people view themselves as being exceptional at selecting investments for their client's portfolios?" Only one hand remained in the air.

Honestly, I think that had the question been asked in a different room with people who weren't their peers, more people would survey the landscape and hold their hands up high, knowing they wouldn't run the risk of being taken to task by a peer or competitor.

The speaker asked this gentleman to stand, and began asking him questions. The gentleman responded with a vocabulary of analytical wisdom that would surely lull to sleep the brightest of actuaries. The gentleman further explained that he ran a very small investment advisory shop with about $10 million dollars under management from 45 clients.

Ever since that day, I've often wondered why people who believe they are the very best managers of investments continue to hold themselves out as financial advisers. If financial planners truly believe they can create investment strategies better than most, what are they doing running a financial planning business? Why are they spending time prospecting for new clients? Why are they busy writing financial plans and selling investment products? Shouldn't they be sending résumés to the financial institutions of the world and securing portfolio manager slots?

Have you ever stopped to think about what a portfolio manager of a mutual fund earns? What about an investment banker? The *lousy* ones have earnings that average in the high six figures. These managers are supposedly the very best in the world at picking securities.

That's the reason so many people have chosen to outsource the money management functions in their offices. They partner with either private money management firms or full-time independent research firms. This allows the adviser to spend more time communicating with his or her clients, develop financial projections, and focus on the larger goals or objectives set forth by the client.

Financial institutions dedicated solely to managing investment portfolios full-time hire teams of professionals composed of highly skilled analysts and research specialists who have great incentives to succeed. Wouldn't you admit that this type of team is better organized and more focused, on a day-to-day basis, to manage the investment slice of your clients' financial planning pie? Do you really believe that you can deliver investment results that equal or exceed the skills of these specialists, while managing the financial planning needs of your clients, marketing for new business, and managing the operations of your firm? Is it possible that your business could be even stronger if you aligned with partners and presented yourself as a company who has a leader like yourself orchestrating your clients' symphony?

There are a growing number of large independent financial planning firms who maintain a corporate infrastructure that supports Certified Financial Planner professionals, Chartered Financial Analysts, portfolio managers, attorneys, tax professionals, and others as part of the overall team. Typically, these firms are positioned to serve a more affluent and highly sophisticated client. Advisers who serve the mass affluent market must determine the extent to which investment management and portfolio design will serve as a core service performed in-house. If you position your business as a financial planning firm, your clients should expect that the core services provided are financial planning focused.

The mass affluent marketplace is seeking professionals
whose relationships with them are built on a financial planning
pie crust. They don't have financial resources to rely on multitudes of service professionals to "try out" or "spread the wealth
around." They are looking for a trusted adviser in you. They want
someone who will deliver advice for life. They want someone
who will always use a formula for financial planning that represents a strategy that includes every aspect of their lives when
any recommendation is offered.

Think back to the two camps we talked about earlier in this
chapter. If both camps are allowed to exist under the umbrella of
financial planning services, the institutional world (those who
support financial planning) will continue to have difficulty serving
our needs. Despite their good intentions to build financial planning symposiums, marketing tools, and intellectual capital, they are
faced with challenges as planners insist that the information doesn't
apply to their needs. If our profession doesn't rally around a reasonable definition for what financial planners do and how financial
planning is integrated in the lives of consumers, we run the risk of
consumers, the media, large institutions, or even worse, our government, defining it for us.

Perhaps it's time to explore a minimum definition that supports
financial planning in its purest sense. The next chapter offers a
glimpse at a possible solution.

Consider the following questions about the core services you
deliver to your clients:

*What is it about your business that you love to do more than any-
thing else? Is it tactically selecting the very best investments for your
clients? Is it cultivating collaborative strategies that help clients better
envision their financial futures?*

Give yourself a moment to reflect on these questions and ask
yourself what you're passionate about every day. If being a financial planner is your calling, the rest of this book will feed your fire

and unleash you as someone who can serve clients with integrity, compassion, and leadership.

When your business has value, you work differently. You treat your clients, your employees, the people in your community, and your family differently. Simply put, you care! Value creates ownership and personal pride emerges from ownership. What is the value of your business? To what extent do you own it? If it had a greater value, would you treat it and those you serve differently?

When the *process* of financial planning serves as the glue that ties your client relationships together, your method of compensation will never be the most important thing about you.

Fortunately, organizations like FPA support a compensation neutral position. Fostering the value of financial planning and delivering advice that places the client's interests first becomes paramount. Compensation methods become simply a means to an end—and nothing more. I hope someday that our profession can move beyond the bickering, finger-pointing, and deep segregation and agree that clients' interests are placed first when an adviser's desire to serve the long-term needs of a client becomes the cornerstone of the relationship, not the belief that the adviser's compensation method diminishes his or her ability to serve a client well. Whether it's commissions, fees for assets under management, annual retainers, or hourly rates, no one solution will ever indefinitely prevail in the marketplace. You need to find a style that aligns with your values and it is a journey every adviser should explore. After all, we all need to be true to ourselves.

SUMMARY
1. You need to be able to explain financial planning and demonstrate that your firm is structured to support this philosophy.
2. There are two significant camps in the world of financial planning. As a profession, we have a difficult time emerging when wealth managers who market themselves as financial

planners focus more on the investment component of a
client relationship and not on the collective pieces of the
financial pie.

3. Your commitment to a client's financial planning needs
   is greater than ever before. Looking within yourself to
   identify your core passion is the key to success in fulfilling
   your life's work.

4 A Financial Planning Formula for the Mass Affluent

"Financial planners are in on all the juicy intrigue that goes on between people and their money."

—*Lee Eisenberg, author of* The Number

OBJECTIVES
1. Introduce the characteristics of the formula for financial planning
2. Explore the value of having a single formula

Could there be a magic formula that embodies the delivery of financial planning?

It has taken a long while, but finally, "financial planning" has become a recognizable expression among those who need, those who deliver, and those who support financial planning. Yet, for a term like "financial planning" to be regarded as one that can stand on its own and not be viewed as a subset of investment management, we need a minimum benchmark so that everyone can identify when financial planning is delivered or when it is a variation of *something else.* Fortunately, the CFP Board of Standards and Practices created a six-step process to help us understand developing a financial plan:

1. Identify goals and objectives
2. Collect data
3. Analyze data
4. Develop a plan
5. Implement strategies
6. Monitor the plan, make necessary adjustments

While I wholeheartedly endorse this staged approach when building a financial plan, I don't believe that it is the best descriptor for the "ing" part—the financial plann*ing* function. I believe we need a clear formula so that anyone (the public and providers) can state with conviction, "*That* is financial planning." This is the reason I have attempted to build a formula for financial planning. I have built this formula with the mass affluent client in mind. While I believe it could translate well in any market group, my thinking and presentation below are intended to benefit the mass affluent population—and those who serve them.

INTRODUCING THE FORMULA FOR FINANCIAL PLANNING

I am far from a "quant" guy. So I decided to combine my background in marketing with a collection of financial components in the hope that I could create a simple enough formula to be understood by anyone. The formula acknowledges the importance of both the quantitative and qualitative sides of financial planning. It incorporates both the human condition and realities of pure finance. It also attempts to place a balanced emphasis on the elements of a planning relationship. I hope the formula will ultimately be viewed as a primary reference point that planners rely upon when they begin to wonder whether their advice leans more heavily toward one particular subset of the equation and unintentionally neglects to include the other important parts.

The formula is:

Discovery	**(Goals, Challenges, Successes)**	**+**
Capital Protection	**(Family, Health, Life, Legacy)**	**+**
Wealth Management	**(Net Worth, Net Cash Flow)**	**+**

$=$ **Financial Planning**

I believe that for clients to say they received financial planning, they must feel confident that the planner:

1. Asked questions about their goals, challenges, and successes. (*I call this discovery.*)
2. Explored how effectively clients have elected to protect their family, health, life, and legacy. (*I call this capital protection.*)
3. Discussed issues that affect the quantitative elements of their financial life, with particular attention to how changes in cash flow, market volatility, inflation, and other factors will affect the client's expectations. (*I call this wealth management.*)

What is your general impression of the formula? Is it possible to deliver financial planning when you focus solely on wealth management (WM) and ignore discovery (DY) and capital protection (CP)? What if you focused solely on discovery (DY) and (CP) capital protection? Are you doing financial planning now?

Think about these other formulas and consider some of the outcomes:

Discovery + Capital Protection → (yields) Estate Planning, Risk Management, Charitable Planning
Discovery + Wealth Management → (yields) Investment and Cash Flow Management, Wealth Accumulation, Income Planning
Capital Protection + Wealth Management → (yields) Insurance and Investment Sales
Discovery (all alone) **→** (yields) Therapy, Leadership, Advice

Therefore, could the collective components of discovery plus capital protection plus wealth management be an equation that defines financial planning?

FP = DY + CP + WM?

Let's dig a little deeper into each segment of the formula:
Discovery (DY)—Financial planning needs to start with a conversation that explores a client's relationship with his or her money. Failing to address these issues prior to implementing any strategy puts your credibility as a planner at risk. Think about it. If someone were to ask, "Have you placed your clients' interests first?" would you be able to confidently answer this question with integrity? If you neglect to understand their goals first, how can you suggest a strategy that serves their needs? As a financial planner, is it really possible to make implementation recommendations without fully understanding how they affect everything else in the client's life?

To effectively serve the needs of the mass affluent, it is inexcusable to make recommendations before asking about and agreeing upon their goals and objectives. Clients who choose not to share this information are probably best served in transactional environments because they are more apt to make impulsive decisions.

Generally, you should expect that discovery questions will address at least these basic issues:

1. Long- and short-term goals
2. Personal and financial successes in life
3. Challenges your client faced and those they may expect to encounter in the future

Sometimes, conversations surrounding the discovery process can get quite personal. Frankly, that's where the leadership component comes into play. If you are unwilling to ask the important questions, you're likely to have a relationship with your clients that rarely gets to the heart of the matter. The best financial planners know that challenging your clients with provocative questions ultimately leads to uncovering the core of our clients' true financial plans.

Goals + Successes + Challenges + Opportunities
Goals (Gl), Successes (Sc), Challenges (Ch), and Opportunities (Op) are examples of the subsets that are part of the discovery portion of the formula for financial planning. The deeper you dig into your clients' connections with their money, the better they will be served. Never stop asking your clients about their hopes, wishes, and concerns. I can't stress enough how important it is that you explore the discovery segment of the formula before *ever* offering solutions for your clients' quantitative needs.

Essentially, the discovery component of the financial planning formula becomes *the* cornerstone every time you converse with your client.

Capital Protection (CP)—A primary goal of successful financial planning is to help clients achieve a greater quality of life. Insurance planning and risk management advice serve as the "peace of mind" component in your relationship. Financial planning must include continual guidance, advice, and sound strategies in areas that affect:

1. Life risks—Premature death, long-term disability, or even having to care for a family member could have drastic

implications on your clients' ability to achieve their life's goals. What conversations and strategies do you introduce and monitor to deliver peace of mind solutions?

2. Family's risks—Divorce, second marriages, children with special needs, and marriages that can alter a family's estate plans can all affect the ways in which you protect your dreams from being derailed. What guidance will you offer when it's time to protect the family from spendthrifts, the financial complexity of blended families, and those who may not have the ability to manage money on their own?

3. Wealth risks—Changes in inflation, personal spending, employment, market conditions, tax law, and more will affect your clients' ability to achieve their financial goals. What risk-minimization techniques will you employ to smooth out the choppiness when detours in your planning occur?

4. Legacy risks—Unless they plan to spend their last dollar on the day they die, it is imperative that clients prepare for the transfer of their wealth, their personal property, and possibly the guardianship of their offspring. Ensuring that a client's wishes are explored, documented, and reviewed is essential for planners.

Think of capital protection as the glue that adheres the emotional components in your clients' lives to the analytic side of their financial wealth. When capital protection issues are addressed and maintained, clients share confidence in their ability to protect their family, their health, their income, their wealth, and their legacy.

Death, disability, medical costs, and long-term health care are typical items that clients worry about, but that I don't believe we, as planners, spend enough talking about—especially as years pass in relationships with our clients. Your clients want direction and guidance on these matters. They seek your leadership and expect you to raise questions and offer ideas for protecting these points of vulnerability. Financial planning cannot be delivered without the implementation of capital protection strategies.

Wealth Management—*(growth – inflation (Net Worth – Net Cash Flow))*

growth(g) – inflation(i)—As the projections and analyses of planning strategies come into the conversation, planners need to continually review the net assumed growth rate used for a client's total aggregated net worth. Building projection models based on net growth of a client's overall wealth is significantly more valuable than crafting strategies that focus more exclusively on the performance of individual investments and/or accounts.

Multiplying your client's net projected growth rate by their net worth plus net cash flow, you can truly begin to show a client the changes in their financial wealth. We all know that costs increase; but with proper planning, so too will your client's net worth.

Net Worth (NW)—This is a snapshot of a client's life. Without having a clear picture of the comprehensive assets and liabilities of a client's financial status, is it appropriate to implement investment strategies for them? Moreover, as a financial planner, you have a responsibility to verify your client's data within the net worth statement. Never allow your clients to simply tell you what they have. How can we both "know our client" and "place the interest of our clients first" without having a mutually authenticated representation of our clients' financial positions?

Cash Flow (CF)—This requires a careful assessment of how a client uses their financial resources to cover expenses, taxes, and ongoing savings. Exploring the choices about where clients draw funds from to cover costs is incredibly important for assessing their ability to either increase or shrink the overall value of their net worth. It enhances your ability to build better planning scenarios.

You can serve as your clients' champion when you have a solid handle on how money is used in their lives—and how it could affect their ability to achieve goals.

Taxes—So where are taxes in the formula? I believe taxes are an important component of a client's ability to achieve financial peace of mind, but they can generally be found inside the expense area of a client's cash flow (and tax sheltering can be found in the net worth component). With good planning, taxes must be addressed as internal factors that planners consider when addressing each client issue. We have found that clients generally think about taxes as something they pay or a refund they receive in April. Planners need to look at taxes from several angles. Whether it is a calculation of your tax witholding on a pay stub, consideration on the taxes due from the sale of securities, or deciding whether to select a tax-free, tax-deferred, or fully taxable security for your client, taxes are part of the process. In other words, they are an important factor in the formula, but simply one of a number of factors that planners must consider in the process.

Discovery	(Goals, Challenges, Successes)	+
Capital Protection	(Family, Health, Life, Legacy)	+
Wealth Management	(Net Worth, Net Cash Flow)	+

= **Financial Planning**

So what do you think? Does this formula define financial planning? Does it avoid the minutia and keep you focused on the bigger picture?

If the general population were each given this formula on a laminated card, do you think they would have a clearer sense of what they could expect from a relationship with a financial planner? As a financial planner, do you deliver these services? Is there something missing from the formula? Is it fair to call something financial planning without addressing one of the three primary components of the formula (discovery, capital protection, wealth management)?

And for all of you quants, here's a marketing guy's more technical interpretation:

$$FP = Dy(G+C+S+O) + CP([l + f + w + lg]) + WM (g - i (NW+Ncf)$$

ANOTHER PERSPECTIVE ON THE FORMULA FOR FINANCIAL PLANNING

Consider a more graphical way to explain the formula for financial planning. If you view the discovery side of the equation as qualitative issues and the net worth and cash flow components as quantitative issues, capital protection serves as the buffer that adds peace of mind to your client's ability to achieve their goals in the event of an unexpected personal tragedy.

Goals + Challenges + Successes	My Family + My Life + My Wealth + My Legacy	Assets – Liabilities Money In vs. Money Out
QUALITATIVE	←——————→	QUANTITATIVE

The above formula is far from scientific, but *can fully integrated financial planning be delivered without including all of the above components?*

As I said earlier, I think planners have focused their expertise on the wealth management side of the formula. Planners, in general, are working harder at weaving the discovery element into client conversations. But all too often, we find that the capital protection component is either a forgotten conversation or one that gets delayed to another financial professional. Without the inclusion and ongoing review of capital protection issues, you place yourself and your clients at risk. Certified Financial Planner professionals have an obligation to place the interests of their clients first. Neglecting to include strategies that address the importance of capital protection is an area we need to better incorporate into our practices.

THE FORMULA FOR FINANCIAL PLANNING AT WORK

Just imagine how empowered your clients would feel if they could articulate the following statements about the relationship they had with their financial planner. Here are a few examples. "My planner...

1. Revisited my goals and objectives with me. I continue to be excited about my future and have a vision of where I am going."
2. Asked me new, probing questions about recent challenges and successes in my life. She made it so comfortable for me to tell her anything about money."
3. Revisited the rationale for the protection vehicles I have in place. I know that if something unexpected happens to me, my family will be protected and financially secure."
4. Updated my overall net worth statement and showed me how much it has changed. I view my financial world from a much different perspective now that he has taught me to look at my net worth as opposed to the individual mutual funds in my portfolio."
5. Asked about my current cash flow and talked with me about a few major expenses I will have this year. I know that she will help me select where best to draw money from when I need it, and consider the most tax-appropriate strategy for me."
6. Examined my tax return and offered me a couple ideas on how I could position money more wisely. I am so happy he helped me change my payroll withholdings."
7. Introduced me to a new investment that seems to align with my goals. I am so lucky to have a financial planner who really wants to understand my whole financial life, and is willing to offer advice to me whenever I feel I need it."

If a client left your meeting with peace of mind around these points, would you have honored the formula for financial planning? Could you image regularly visiting with your clients when only a fraction of your time consists of discussing investment returns, asset allocation, hypothetical reports, Monte Carlo analysis, or a new product idea? A planner who focuses only on segments of the formula for financial planning risks not fully understanding a client's needs. Without forcing yourself to reflect on the formula, it is easy to get wrapped up in micro issues, such as the components of a client's portfolio or a long-winded discussion about the current return on a particular investment.

When we get too comfortable with our client relationships, it's easy to forget about, or completely neglect, new goals that your clients need to explore. We tend to drift back to the quantitative side of the equation and forget about the emotions. Just imagine how intrigued your clients would be if they knew the bulk of your conversations assured them you would rely on the formula for financial planning.

PLANNER EXERCISE—SEEING FINANCIAL PLANNING FROM THE CLIENT'S PERSPECTIVE

Imagine, just for a moment, that you weren't a financial planner. You knew very little about the profession, but you knew you needed to seek advice from someone. Prior to your initial consultation, you did an Internet search on the words "financial planning" and came across the formula for financial planning. You chose to print it out and have it accessible as a reference point for your meeting. You also read that the CFP certification seems to be the gold standard of planners in the profession, and you decided to select five CFP certificants to interview. Based on the formula for financial planning, read the five examples below and determine which ones would be offering financial planning to you.

EXAMPLES:

1. You are meeting with a planner for the first time because

you've just received an inheritance. During your 30-minute visit, the planner offers an investment strategy and a recommendation for your consideration.

2. You are seeking long-term care insurance protection because you've recently watched a parent suffer in a nursing home. The planner prepares a proposal for long-term care coverage based on what you told him you could afford while you wait.

3. You are seeking advice on how best to save money for your child's education costs, but the planner is more interested in exploring whether your 401(k) plan allows for in-service rollovers. The planner has clearly dismissed the primary reason you scheduled the appointment.

4. You visit with a planner and they ask you about your goals and objectives. Because you've never explored them before, the planner shares some rules of thumb and offers to build you a financial plan based on these rules.

5. You're visiting with a financial planner for the first time and instead of listening to why you are there, they jump to conclusions with answers to your questions before you have had a chance to fully share your thoughts.

Can you think of any financial planners who might represent any of the above five examples? If these examples truly exist (and I assure you, they do), how can the public accurately understand financial planning?

Delivering financial planning effectively takes an enormous amount of practice. Admittedly, it is much harder to offer financial planning than it is to sell a solution to a client. But when you gain the skills to deliver a well-balanced conversation with your client, you not only earn a client for life, but you've secured another raving fan who will espouse the virtues of your "different" approach. More than anything, this improves the public's understanding of how financial planning can be effectively delivered.

Throughout the next sections of this book, we will apply the formula for financial planning to the overall client experience. At the beginning of this section we talked about how the mass affluent are oversold and underserved. This market segment, while truly appreciative of a professional who can deliver solutions to their issues, is more likely to build lifelong relationships with someone who is willing to:

1. Discover their dreams, reflect on their successes, and tackle their challenges.
2. Build peace of mind by protecting their lives, families, wealth, and legacies.
3. Analyze the intricacies of their financial life and offer solutions to help them achieve success.

The methods of compensation that you use to deliver financial planning to the mass affluent are not nearly as important as giving them the assurance that your firm is committed to the planning formula. Whether you choose to work solely as a fee-only adviser, or as someone who might deliver both commission-based solutions and/or fee-based advisory services, the mass affluent market is asking for your help. I promise that if you allow the formula for financial planning to serve as your guide, no one will ever question whether you are a genuine financial planner.

Section I was about introducing why the mass affluent are oversold and underserved. In addition, we supported our case with core elements that every financial planner must embody (no matter the clientele they serve) to best meet their clients' needs. They start with:

1. Leadership skills
2. A commitment to the pie called "financial planning"
3. Using a formula for financial planning that transparently aligns you and your client with clear expectations from a planning relationship

As we move to Section II, we will focus on communication skills that encourage you to more effectively connect with you clients. In addition, we will help raise your consciousness about how to remain aware of impressions clients and prospects form about you and your firm before you ever open your mouth.

SUMMARY

1. The formula for financial planning is a new tool for helping planners identify the cross section of issues needed to craft strong financial planning relationships.
2. It is critical that planners heighten their knowledge of capital protection issues and raise them as forefront issues in the overall scheme of the client relationship.
3. Allow the formula for financial planning to serve as your guide. Your clients will better understand your role as a financial planner and will be able to better articulate the elements of financial planning.

Section II:

Get Your Head in the Game— Practice Management Tips to Help You More Effectively Serve the Mass Affluent

5 | *Are You Ready to Serve the Mass Affluent? Getting to the Heart of Your Clients' Expectations*

OBJECTIVES
1. Impart the importance of relying on your firm's values
2. Share the story of the Greens

Are you in the right frame of mind to deliver financial planning services? If a prospect were to walk into your office stating exactly what they'd like you to do for them, would you immediately act on their request or would you insist on digging deeper? In other words, when you meet with clients, do you lead the conversation or are you letting them lead you?

The mass affluent seek your listening skills as much as they seek your leadership. In most cases, they describe what they want without a true understanding of what's possible. It is very common for them to provide answers they might think they're supposed to

65

give. You need to try to read between the lines. You need to ask probing questions that open their eyes to possibilities they may have never imagined. For instance, when a client says they are looking for a better return on their investment, do you simply ask, "What has your investment return been in the past?" Might you ask why they don't believe their investment's return was good enough? Do you respond to their question by analyzing their portfolio, identifying the lousy performers, and offering a recommendation for a better allocation of investments? Or do you try to understand what returns are necessary to achieve the goals and lifestyles they want in the future?

Many mass affluent clients lack the experience or vocabulary to ask for the services they would like to receive from you. Instead, their limited understanding of what financial planners do prevents them from exploring the expanded role you can play in their lives. The questions they ask you generally revolve around investments simply because they are uncertain about the breadth of services you offer. Mass affluent clients welcome your thoughtful questions, and they are open to exploring a much a broader perspective with you.

Consider the following conversation we had with a prospect: Paul and Patricia Green inquired about our firm in early January 2006. Their relationship started with what Paul thought would be a brief telephone call to schedule an initial consultation, but instead, it was the beginning of a lesson he never quite expected.

Paul explained that his financial planner of more than seven years had recently passed away, and he and his wife were looking for another planner to take over their accounts. He had been referred to our office by his neighbor, who remains a long-time client of our firm. Paul was quick to mention that he really wasn't in the mood to be shopping around; he was looking for someone who could take over where his last financial planner left off.

As we continued our phone conversation, I learned that his planner provided him with quarterly performance updates of his investments, scheduled quarterly meetings to review the investments, and typically made tactical changes to the investment portfolio a few times each year.

The bulk of the Greens' money came from personal savings. Over the years, Paul and Patricia actively participated in making suggestions for changes to their portfolio by calling their planner, listening to new ideas, and collectively researching trends, sectors, and economic statistics. The Greens thought they were doing pretty well, and they hoped we could continue to deliver the same service and statistical reporting they had come to expect.

"Can you help us?" Paul inquired.

I thought for a moment, and then said, "It sounds like you really respected the advice and relationship you had with your adviser."

"We really did," responded Paul. "We got to know him so well and we were devastated to learn of his death. I'm not great at keeping spreadsheets and doing analysis like he did, but I think we're doing well and I don't want to stop the momentum."

I wondered what made Paul use the words "I think," when mentioning the performance of his investment account.

Paul went on to tell me that it looked like X fund was up 15 percent, and that Y fund was up almost twice as much.

During our conversation I asked Paul a question that caught him off guard. I said, "Paul, it sounds like you're generally pleased with the performance of your investments, but I'm curious. What are some of your family's goals for the money, and how certain are you that your current investment allocation is aligned to achieve these goals?"

"Huh?" said Paul.

"As financial planners, we believe that it is our obligation to gather a collective understanding of our clients' overall short- and long-term personal goals, and then align their resources in a manner that helps them envision the possibility of achieving them. To what extent did you explore these issues with your financial adviser?"

Paul responded in a manner that expressed both curiosity and defensiveness. "My financial planner never asked me questions like what you're asking. We were just interested in getting the best return possible on our money. Isn't that everyone's goal?" He added, "Isn't that what financial planners do? Isn't that what you do?"

At that moment, I had to make a decision about the direction we would take with this prospect. I knew nothing more about him than the cursory information he had already shared, but I suspected that the financial planning relationship with his planner was relatively shallow. It revolved around making ongoing changes to his portfolio—changes that were made as much to validate the planner's service to the client as they were to assure the client that there was always something better to buy.

"Paul," I said, "while I am delighted that my client referred you to our office, I suspect the services you are looking for from our firm may not exactly fulfill the objectives you've detailed."

I continued, "As Certified Financial Planner professionals, we believe that in order to deliver genuine service to our clients, it is incumbent upon us, as well as mandated in our professional code of ethics, to develop a comprehensive understanding of our clients' overall financial resources, goals, dreams, and concerns, prior to implementing any financial strategy."

I waited for a response on the phone. There was silence and I wondered if Paul was just holding the phone in the air and allowing me to talk without him having to listen to my rhetoric. Instead, what followed surprised me.

"I'm still listening…are you saying that your firm will take a look at the big picture of my financial life?"

"Yes."

"You'll give me advice in areas that cover more than just the investments I've been holding with this planner?"

"Yes."

"Will you help me understand all these insurance policies I've accumulated, my 401(k) allocation, my wife's annuities, my debts, and my taxes?"

"Yes. That's what financial planners do for their clients. In our case we will offer you tax planning advice, but we won't prepare taxes for you."

"Well, why not?"

"While many very good financial planning firms offer this service, we believe that to deliver consistent financial advice to our clients year-round, we would need to have a dedicated team focused on preparing tax returns for our clients. Without it, we believe there would be a significant drop-off in our service standards from January to April, and at our firm, we don't believe it would be best for our clients. We are happy to work with your existing tax preparer or provide you with a list of accountants we've gotten to know and trust in the community."

"And this is included as part of your services, right?" said Paul. "My planner didn't charge me for any of his services—he said that the investment companies paid him."

At this point, I began to get a better picture of the type of client Paul could be. I explained to Paul that he was welcome to visit our office for a complimentary meeting and that we would send him one of our information kits for both him and his wife to review. But more importantly, I insisted that Patricia and Paul attend the first meeting together, and that during their visit we would explore how best to pursue a potential relationship with them.

I further explained that our firm's minimum financial planning fee was $1,500, and that it was our policy to prepare a comprehensive analysis of a client's total personal financial situation before implementing any strategies.

Honestly, I thought for sure he would thank me for my time and end the conversation right there and then. Instead, he told me he had always wondered if a financial planner could give him a "peace-of-mind snapshot" of his financial situation, but thought planners just handled investments and he would be responsible for the rest.

"Let me talk it over with my wife," he said. There it was, I thought. The dreaded "I'll talk it over with my wife and get back to you" line.

I thanked him for sharing his situation with me, and we exchanged pleasantries. But just as we were about to hang up, Paul asked, "On second thought, is it possible to schedule an initial appointment for later this week?" His wheels must have really been turning during our conversation. "I'll be sure my wife will make it."

I put Paul on hold and asked Cathy, one of our client service specialists, to gather the necessary data and information on the Greens, to hand-deliver a kit to their home, and to schedule a meeting.

When you talk with a prospect over the telephone, is it your style to answer their questions, or professionally challenge their statements? It is likely that this prospect was destined to become a client if we simply agreed to take over the relationship they had established with a previous adviser. Yet the client's impression of what a financial planner did was significantly different from the role we believe we played in our clients' lives. To what extent do you transform your style to accommodate a particular client's needs and beliefs? Would you feel more confident about the long-term relationship you had with clients if you could deliver financial planning services through the same lens of integrity, character, and style with each client you served? What would it take to get there?

The mass affluent marketplace is full of people with differing understandings of what financial planners do. The formula for financial planning introduced in Section I offers a framework that opens the eyes of these consumers. When the mass affluent find an individual who is willing to address their comprehensive financial issues and raise questions they never imagined could be objectively answered, I assure you, they will be forever grateful.

SUMMARY

1. Seek to fully understand a prospect's questions before ever offering a recommendation.
2. Don't be afraid to question a prospect's understanding of your services. Often, their impressions of planners are far different from the services you offer.
3. Never allow a prospect to steer your ship. Know your values and be purposeful when discussing your business's practices.
4. Have a clear understanding of your client's objectives and be able to express the methodology your firm uses to help clients develop a plan.

6 | *The Importance of First Impressions When Serving the Mass Affluent*

OBJECTIVES

1. Discuss how planners can improve first impressions by remaining aware of the five senses.
2. Impart the importance of having an information packet that describes your firm and your services.
3. Highlight the importance of managing distractions and positioning yourself so the client focuses on you.
4. Introduce the importance of knowing your core values.

Have you ever considered how important first impressions become when attempting to establish a lifelong relationship with a client? How you choose to position your firm, your process, your staff and, of course, yourself is key, and prospects make note these choices before you ever say hello.

RELYING ON THE FIVE SENSES TO CREATE POSITIVE IMPRESSIONS

When I think of the five senses, my mind reverts back to my elementary school days. But understanding how sight, touch, hearing, smell, and taste affect our lives is probably one of the most foundational skills we ever learn.

Let's explore how your clients' five senses create impressions of you and your firm before you ever say hello. For purposes of this example, let's assume that all prospects and clients come to your office for appointments.

Items a client *sees* that create impressions about you and your firm:

1. Where is your office located? Is parking accessible? Are the grounds well maintained?
2. Are there clear signs directing them to your office? Is your office handicapped accessible?
3. Is your office neat and clean? How is it decorated? What plaques, pictures, and awards appear on the walls?
4. What color are your walls?
5. What furniture have you selected?
6. Who greets your clients when they arrive at the office? How are they greeted?
7. What reading material is available in your waiting area?

Items clients *hear* that create impressions about your firm:

1. What music plays in the office while clients wait to see you?
2. What office chatter do your clients hear while waiting to see you?
3. What time does the cleaning service visit (vacuum) your office?
4. Can clients in your waiting room hear conversations you are having with other clients?

Items clients *touch* that create impressions about your firm:

1. Is your furniture dusted and clean?
2. Are your coffee cups comfortable to hold?
3. Do you serve water in a bottle or in a glass with ice?
4. Is your reading material well-kept?

Items clients *smell* that create impressions about your firm:

1. Does your staff eat lunch at their desks? Could the aromas of onions and garlic be lingering?
2. Do you consciously create a positive aroma in your office?
3. Does your conference table smell like it was just cleaned?

Items a client *tastes* that create impressions about your firm:

1. What candy, snacks, etc. are available for munching?
2. How fresh is your coffee?
3. Is your water cool or room temperature?
4. Do you make tea available?
5. Do you offer both regular and decaf coffee?

These items speak volumes about your firm. Whether you want them to or not, clients begin forming impressions about you the minute they plan to visit your office. One way to ensure that client impressions begin positively is to hire a "director of first impressions" for your office.

Our current director of first impressions (DFI) performs a number of important functions in the office, yet she knows her primary responsibility includes ensuring that every aspect of our business connects our firm to our clients through our internal objective: "*To Exceed our Clients' Expectations by Paying Attention to Detail.*"

Admittedly, I did not create this objective—the folks at Disney World did. The only exception is that their statement replaces the word "clients" with "guests." If you've ever been to Disney World, I bet some of your most significant memories revolve around the service, the atmosphere, or simply the "magic" of Disney. We wanted to create that same experience in our office.

Imagine that a new prospect walked in your office door right now. What first impressions might be made? Are client statements and reports scattered around the office? Are you dressed to impress? What pictures are hanging on your walls? Has the furniture been dusted? How is a prospect greeted when they enter your office? Answers to these questions are left in our DFI's hands. Failure to make an exceptional first impression affects her performance review. After all, shouldn't it be part of the gatekeeper's job to make you look good?

The moment a client walks in the door of our office, they are immediately greeted by our DFI. Regardless of whether she is on the phone, working on the computer, or busy completing paperwork, she realizes that the most important person to connect with is the one who's looking back at her. Normally, she will get up from her desk and assist our clients with their coats. She will ask if she can get them coffee, tea, etc., and then encourages them to make themselves comfortable. In fact, we post a beverage menu in a fancy table frame on one of our side tables.

When she returns with the beverage, she makes pleasant conversation and shares a story or two. The work on her desk and her pending phone calls are put on hold while a client is waiting to visit with our planners. Once one of our planners has greeted the client and brought them into the conference room, our DFI heads back to her desk and attends to her other work.

It's important to note that everyone in your office should hold a responsibility of exceeding your clients' expectations by paying attention to detail—it's just that the DFI generally makes it happen first.

When you are building a relationship with clients, it is essential to remain aware of both the tangible and intangible surroundings that can affect your clients' abilities to remain focused on you. By reminding yourself of how the five senses create impressions, you will stay in your clients' good graces.

CREATING POSITIVE IMPRESSIONS ABOUT YOUR FIRM IN ADVANCE OF YOUR FIRST MEETING

How do you formally introduce your firm to a prospect? When it is time to schedule an initial consultation with a prospect, what, if anything, do you deliver to them in advance? What expectations should a prospect have about how they will spend their time with you?

I have always found it fascinating that so few financial planners have taken the time to develop a personalized introductory kit about their firm. While many planners will spend oodles of money on marketing systems, direct mail campaigns, and advertising techniques, rarely do you find a planning firm that spends money on its image. When you have a personalized introductory kit, a prospect can take the time to learn about your background, your experiences, your process, and your expectations.

An introductory kit should include the following items:

1. A personalized brochure—This document provides an overview of your firm and your services.
2. A planner biography—This one-page document should include a photograph and description of the planner's experience, as well as personal information. Each bio should also include a head shot in the upper left-hand corner with the person's face looking toward the body of the text.
3. A fact finder—often referred to as a questionnaire. This document will allow your prospect to begin organizing their thoughts (and data) in preparation for your meeting. Note: I find that too many planners believe that clients won't fill out the fact finder before an initial meeting. That belief, in my

opinion, is an insecurity of the planner. Nine out of every ten new prospects we meet arrive with either a completed fact finder or significant supporting data.

4. Part II of your ADV—If you are a registered investment adviser (RIA), you are required to submit Form ADV annually to regulators. Part I of your ADV is for regulatory use only. Part II should be made available to your prospects in your kit.

5. Privacy notice—This document states that you are committed to client confidentiality.

6. Financial planning contract—This contract is used to engage a client in your financial planning services. Clients should have ample opportunity to review this document before hiring your firm.

7. Business card.

Additional information you may include: press clippings about you and/or your firm, current newsletters, a kitchen magnet, etc.

You will find examples of several of these documents in the appendix.

Planner Exercise: Here's an idea to gauge how other planners in your community are introducing themselves to the public. This summer, hire an intern and ask them to create a list of 100 individuals who hold themselves out as financial planners. Once you review the list, ask your intern to prepare an e-mail that inquires about the services of a financial planner and asks for more information about how their firm operates. The e-mail should include a request to have them send information to their home address. I think you'll be quite surprised by how few planners actually have something to send to a consumer. You will likely find that many planners will suggest that your intern visit their Web site or contact the office directly to schedule an initial appointment. Our experience tells us that less than 10

percent of the planners our interns solicit actually have personalized information about their firm and how they engage clients in the
financial planning process. In Section IV, Chapter 18, we will share
the details pertaining to this competitive analysis.

Therefore, if you have been on the fence about whether to craft
an introductory kit, I'd strongly encourage you to build one. You'll
be in a very small minority, and you'll be making an impression very
few financial planners present.

ONE MORE THOUGHT ON YOUR INTRODUCTORY KIT
Just When You Think You've Figured It Out...

Drew has been a friend of mine for over 30 years. Drew is one
of those guys who has known exactly what he wanted to do
with his life since he was in elementary school. It was his goal
to work in advertising. I remember when his father got him his
first job in the mail room of a mid-sized agency, but now he is
the president and COO of a top ten agency in Boston. One afternoon, Drew called my office and asked me to send our firm's
introductory kit to his in-laws. I had known them for well over
12 years, and knew they were planning on moving from their
home in Cleveland to a town near my office. As far as I was concerned, this was a slam-dunk client. I had every expectation that
they would establish a relationship with our firm. In fact, they
had mentioned to Drew that they were planning on ending the
relationship they had with their broker of many years in Ohio,
and wanted to work with someone who would offer comprehensive financial planning services.

About a week after we sent our kit in the mail, I received a call
from Drew, who said that his in-laws received the package but they
were overwhelmed with all of the information we sent. They simply
didn't know what to do with it. The thought of reading through all
of the propaganda scared them so much that they just tossed the
folder in the trash.

How could this be possible, I wondered? Each year, as I mentioned earlier, we completed our own internal market research. We knew that we had a great-looking kit. It had personal information about our firm. It included articles where we had been quoted. We included personal biographies, a wonderful fact finder, an ADV, our newsletter, our core values and beliefs, and much more.

So we were thinking that we had the best information package around, but could it be possible that people found it intimidating? Maybe all those advisers who were building successful practices and sending nothing to prospective clients knew more than I thought.

A few days later, Drew offered me this suggestion. "Why don't you include a one-page document that introduces the kit? Just call it 'How to Prepare for Your Initial Consultation.'" Could something as simple as a one-page document clear things up?

In my wildest dreams I could have never expected the comments that followed from new prospects expressing how refreshing it was to receive a package in the mail that not only shared the details of our business, but also advice about how to work with our firm.

You will find the document that now introduces our disclosure kit below.

How to Prepare for Your Initial Consultation
Thank you for this opportunity to introduce our firm to you.

Hiring a financial planner is an important decision in your life and must be built on a foundation of trust. We seek solely to build lifelong relationships with our clients, and the enclosed Core Values and Beliefs sheet embodies our commitment to you.

Generally, an initial consultation lasts 60 to 90 minutes. This confidential conversation is complimentary to you, as we believe it is critical that you find a financial planning firm that not only listens well and asks the right questions, but one that you believe will meet (and hopefully exceed) your expectations.

During our meeting, you can expect us to ask questions about your goals, dreams, and aspirations. Please begin thinking about what's important to you and how your quality of life could improve if X, Y, or Z were addressed.

The enclosed information kit has been designed to help you gain an overview of the services and background our firm offers, but even more importantly, it allows you to begin organizing quantitative components that affect your personal financial life. Please review the questionnaire carefully and try to complete the form in advance of our initial meeting.

You may also find it helpful to bring the following items with you:

1. *Your most recent tax return*
2. *Current investment, insurance, and bank statements*
3. *Employee benefit booklet(s)*
4. *One month's pay stubs*
5. *Endorsement pages for life, disability, auto, homeowners, and personal insurance*
6. *Any estate planning documents, such as wills, trusts, powers of attorney*

On behalf of the entire team at Freedman Financial, thank you for your inquiry. We look forward to building a long and successful financial planning relationship with you.

Please contact us at your earliest convenience to schedule your complimentary initial consultation.

I guess those advertising guys really do know a thing or two. Drew's simple idea was not only a wonderful enhancement, but his honesty was a constant reminder that no matter how successful our business becomes, we need to continually reevaluate and be open to criticism and suggestions.

TANGIBLE TECHNIQUES THAT LEAVE POSITIVE IMPRESSIONS

Setting the Mood

Do clients love coming to your office? Is it warm? Is it cozy? Is it the respite where clients want to tell their stories? Do they slow down? Do they want to listen? Think about what it would take for you to make a few incremental changes in your own office to make clients feel at home.

Rather than leaving our walls "doctor's office white," we bought two gallons of paint and covered it with "Sedona red." Instantly, our conference room turned from a board room to a living room. Almost without exception, every prospect who walks into the conference room makes a comment on the warmth of this room. Try it. Buy a can of paint and put it on your walls. Watch how quickly your mood will change.

We always meet with our clients in our conference room. There's a wireless mouse and keyboard hidden in a drawer at the end of the table. This is generally where the lead planner sits. Clients are given the choice of where they sit. An LCD projector is mounted in the ceiling and it projects onto a five-foot by six-foot screen. Presentations are delivered interactively, such that both viewing the screen and face-to-face dialogue occur. Today, these projectors run less than $1,500. A wireless mouse and keyboard cost less than $100. These minor investments in your business not only raise the professional appearance of your office, they eliminate having to worry about sharing your LCD monitor with a client and forcing them to squint as they attempt to follow your presentation.

When clients visit you at the office, it's important that you control the meeting. Remember, one of the key disciplines of exceptional financial planners is the leadership role they play in their clients' lives. Make sure that clients are looking at you and you are looking at them during conversations. Do your best to prevent them from having wandering eyes. One simple technique is to use a pen and paper and refer to pictures, numbers, or diagrams periodically. Ask your client to point, react, or add to your drawings. This connects them to the meeting and gives you signals that they are listening to you.

When it's time to demonstrate something on your computer screen, let the client know where they will be looking and give them time to absorb what they see. It is very easy to move through analyses quickly because you know what you're going to talk about next. Give your client time to catch up, and when you're finished using your screen, use a hot-link key so that your screen goes black. This will bring the attention back to you and the conversation you will have with the client.

FINAL THOUGHTS ON MAKING POSITIVE IMPRESSIONS WITH THE MASS AFFLUENT

I believe the mass affluent client is best served when you meet with them face to face. E-mailing, the Internet, talking on the telephone, or relying primarily on written communications diminishes your ability to sense your client's emotions, respond to the inflections in their voice and measure nonverbal characteristics. When clients visit your office, you control the distractions. Make sure your cell phone is turned to vibrate mode. Insist that your staff not disturb you. And most importantly, make sure your meeting room has access to hard candy, a box of tissues, pads of paper, and pens, not to mention chairs that are free of annoying squeaks and squeals. When you maintain a welcoming, comfortable office, clients will look forward to spending time with you. It's an impression that clients remember.

WHY THE LIFE YOU LIVE MAKES AN IMPRESSION ON THE CLIENTS YOU SERVE

If money is so important in people's lives, why do we as financial planners seem to allow clients to schedule meetings with us like they schedule automobile service and late-night errands?

Several years ago we realized that financial planning (and money more specifically) was probably the second most important thing in people's lives, health being number one. Some might say that family should be number two, but I'd bet that if you excluded health-related family issues, it would easily slip to number three or even further. Simply put, *money rules.*

Money is what allows people to fulfill many of their life's dreams. Do you position yourself as the professional champion positioned to help them achieve these goals? If so, you need to *stop* allowing your clients to dictate your schedule.

Several years ago, we concluded that holding evening appointments or scheduling meetings over the weekend just didn't feel right. To us, it seemed to be a contradiction of our core values. In fact, if you think back to the five senses discussion at the beginning of this chapter, you'll begin to understand how we were able to come to what appears to be an extreme decision with absolute clarity and comfort.

What are your office hours? Does it vary based on your clients' scheduling needs? Is your weekly calendar built around your clients' schedules or yours? Who gets scheduling priority—existing clients, new prospects, vendors, wholesalers, lunch invitations, family, or personal activities? Could you prioritize them?

What would happen if we asked this question of your spouse? *Yikes!*

The point is that your business is only one component of your life. Your family and your personal interests are as important as the quality-of-life issues you help your clients achieve. To what extent are you willing to commit to developing a balance between your work and your personal life? If you've been struggling to find this balance, what would it take to make it more realistic? Perhaps it means developing boundaries in your business's overall operations to ensure you can find time for you and your family.

You may scoff at this idea, but I bet your family would throw you a party if you were committed to finding more quality time with them.

Perhaps the following set of questions will help give you a better sense of priorities in life. Which set could you more easily answer?

Question Set #1
1. Who is the vice president of the United States?
2. Within 200 points, where did the Dow Jones Industrial Average close last night?
3. Who are your mentors?
4. Who is Jack Bauer?
5. What are the makes and models of the past three vehicles you've owned?
6. Name your three closest friends.

Question Set #2
1. What did you give your child last year for his or her birthday?
2. Where do your children turn for life advice?
3. What are three things your spouse/partner enjoys doing with you?
4. What are three reasons you decided to get married?
5. How much is a school lunch?
6. Who is Hannah Montana?

It's rather obvious that Question Set #2 is more focused on family issues while Question Set #1 is focused more on your issues. While not all of the questions may apply to your situation, I hope the exercise above gives you pause to think about the things that matter most in your life.

Mass affluent clients respect planners who have values. Needing to leave work early to coach your son's baseball team or having to arrive late at work because you need to read a story to your second grader's class earns you respect from your clients. It shows them that, as much as you're interested in helping them achieve a better quality of life, you are equally committed to achieving a balance between your work and your family. When the mass affluent see this quality in you, they want to emulate it—not run from it.

If you are truly interested in serving the mass affluent from a position of integrity, I would suggest that the best model for building relationships with these folks is to work with people locally. These people need you to look into their eyes and they need to see the sincerity in your face. We have chosen to build a community-based practice where 90 percent of our clients live within a ten-mile radius of our office. Perhaps that's impossible for some, but for those who live in heavily populated states, it's easier than you could ever imagine.

Our office building is located in the parking lot of a major shopping mall. When financial planners ask us how it's possible to build such a local clientele, I encourage them to look at the parking lot of any shopping mall in their community. I ask them to consider how many cars belong to a client of theirs. The remaining hundreds, if not thousands, of cars are prospects who probably live in the surrounding community.

In today's world, there is a significant shortage of financial planners to fill the public's appetite for financial planning. You need not look much further than your own community to find a collection of prospects that meets the mass affluent profile.

CONTROLLING DISTRACTIONS

Can you deliver your best work or expect the best of responses from your clients when your mind (or theirs) is drifting in 95 other directions?

I recently spoke on a panel at a conference in Nashville in front of more than 500 attendees about the financial planning process and how our firm keeps it alive during each meeting we have with clients.

My scheduled breakout session was scheduled to begin at 4:15 p.m. and run until 5:30 p.m. The conference began at 8:30 a.m. with an opening general session and, throughout the day, as at most conferences, attendees bounced from one session to another.

As I looked out into the audience, the faces that had begun their day with great anticipation and enthusiasm were showing signs of wear. That normal white noise of conversation was barely present, in fact, many were using the time prior to the session to read a paper, take a brief nap, or simply play a game of Brickblaster on their Blackberry.

As the moderator turned the microphone over to me, I began my presentation:

"Let me ask you something. How many people here are tired?"

A grumble of laughter modulated through the room, though there were still others with their heads buried on their desks and others engaged in electronic games of "Bejeweled."

"Come on, a show of hands. Be honest. It's been a long day today, hasn't it?"

The nods and smirks were something I'll never forget. You see, each person was desperately tired, yet as dedicated professionals, they wanted to soak up whatever nuggets of wisdom they could gather from the panelists.

"It's 4:45 right now. How many people here offer evening appointments with clients? Quite a few of you, right?"

In fact, all but a handful of hands rose in the air.

"How do you think your clients feel when they come into your office to listen to you present a plan? How do you think clients feel when they open the front door of their home at the end of a long day at work, knowing that the next hour or so will be filled with having to think, consider, and follow your presentation or questions?" I asked. "They're probably feeling the same way you're feeling right now."

The laughter certainly woke anyone who was napping and forced the Blackberry users to pay attention and listen.

When is your optimal working time? Have you ever considered what your clients' best time to make decisions might be?

To hold a client's attention on matters surrounding their financial and personal life, you need to control the outside distractions, rather than allow the client's distractions to control the meeting.

Think about how many times a client is interrupted due to a ringing telephone, a barking dog, the kids crying, or the dinner burning. What about the doorbell ringing? When you hold meetings in your office, your staff can be your gatekeepers and the distractions are limited to whether or not your clients choose to respond to their cell phones.

If you are to be viewed as a leader in the eyes of your clients, you need to be looked upon as someone who has the ability to set boundaries and live by them. Leaders do this. Do you?

As you consider whether building a local financial planning practice makes sense for you, here are a few "nevers" I propose for building a local practice for mass affluent clients.

1. You should *never* go to a prospect's home for an initial consultation or review appointment, unless of course this client is too frail to travel or has a disability that prevents them from leaving the house. Remember, when you visit a client outside of your office, they control the distractions—you don't.

2. You should *never* visit clients in their offices. Once again, they control the distractions.

3. *Never* work weekends. You are entitled to time off. Clients find time to visit with their doctors, dentists, and attorneys during the week—shouldn't your role as their personal financial adviser be held in such high esteem? Whose fault is it if your client doesn't see it that way?

4. *Never* work evenings. How alert are you and your clients at the end of the day? Financial planning is serious business and it requires everyone involved to be fully engaged in the conversation. Babysitters, television shows, committee meetings, and family time are all distractions that add to the weariness of the end of the day. Be mindful of them.

When you set boundaries and rules, you convey how serious you are about which clients best align with your firm's values and which ones don't. There are plenty of financial professionals in the industry. If you want to truly deliver genuine financial planning advice, find clients who connect with your values—don't simply take anyone for the sake of building your client list.

We're always telling clients that genuine financial planning leads to the improvement of people's lives. If you as an adviser are making that statement, I would challenge you to examine both your life and the lives of your employees and ask yourself whether these lives are reflecting that shared belief. After all, these are what impressions are all about. When you can align your personal life with your business life and showcase the same level of awareness on how people's feelings are affected by both the tangible and intangible actions we deliver, you are in a wonderful position to deliver advice and serve people well.

SUMMARY

1. The power of first impressions will affect the way clients view you. Consider appointing a director of first impressions to focus on serving the five senses.
2. Make sure the values you convey to your clients about life and work reflect the values you and your staff live.
3. A collection of mass affluent prospects is closer than you think. Consider finding clients within your community and you'll be amazed at how successfully you can build a local practice.
4. Build boundaries for your business and be proud to state what they are.
5. Do your best to control any distractions during a client meeting.

7 | Lessons for the Initial Consultation— Interview Experiences that Convey Your Values and Boundaries

OBJECTIVES

1. Learn tips and techniques to engage clients in effective conversations with you
2. Identify the process needed to convey that clients are being heard
3. Explore client stories and examine methods for responding to client inquiries

INTERVIEWING EXPERIENCES THAT SHOWCASE YOUR VALUES AND BOUNDARIES

The free initial financial planning consultation remains the most common form of personalized introduction into understanding your prospect's goals and objectives. This first meeting has become the entry point into understanding a prospect's motivation for seeking your advice. It is also the opportunity to determine whether this prospect is a "good fit" for your firm. Presented properly, it provides a prospect a no-obligation conversation to share stories about their financial situation and for you to explain your firm's process.

LESSONS FOR THE INITIAL CONSULTATION

If your practice is similar to most, the length of an initial consultation typically runs 60–90 minutes. There are some business coaches who insist you should complete an initial meeting in about 20 minutes. After all, they say, your time is valuable and how much of it should be given away for free? If your goal is to grow your client base quickly, take the advice of these coaches. If it is your sincere goal to build life-long relationships, *slow down* and enjoy the conversation.

During the meeting you should be prepared to:

1. Find common ground and connections between you and your client.
2. Spend more time on qualitative than quantitative data.
3. Listen to what prompted them to visit you:
   - Why do they think that *now* is the right time to consult with you?
   - What experiences have they had with other financial professionals?
4. Ask how they have handled money in the past.
5. Describe your process and how it is delivered to the client.

At the conclusion of any meeting you should be prepared to:

1. Restate to the client the most important goals and objectives you heard.
2. Tell the client the next steps your firm will take after the meeting.
3. Tell the client what their ongoing expectations should be.
4. Share your processing timeline.

It is your role to set the tone of the meeting. It is your responsibility to create an environment that allows the prospect to feel comfortable with sharing the story of why they are meeting with you.

One strategy that shows off your resourcefulness is to do an Internet search on clients' names before their arrival. Usually, some story will appear that highlights an award they've won, a road race that posted their finishing time, stories about their children's achievements, and more. Be careful that you don't come across as a private investigator, but as someone who seeks to learn more about them and is deeply interested in helping them imagine goals that may align with their interests.

Present yourself in a manner that lets your clients know they have been heard. Try using probing open-ended questions that encourage more than one-word answers. This gives prospects an opportunity to further explain themselves and adds color and texture to their personal story.

For instance, offer probing questions and statements that start with "Tell me more about what you mean when you say…" or "Let me be sure I heard you correctly. Did I hear you say…?"

One of the most powerful questions I've ever heard comes from Dan Sullivan, a highly regarded coach who trains financial advisers on how to interview clients. He refers to the following question as "the R-squared" question: "Imagine you have been working with our firm for three years now. What would need to have happened for you to feel great about our relationship?"

When I've asked this question, many people initially respond with a statement that refers to improved performance of their portfolio. Use this opportunity to ask, "Is there anything else you would hope we could accomplish during that time?" If a client can only think of improving their investment performance and has a difficult time offering examples that focus on goals, objectives, peace of mind, etc., you should proceed carefully with this client. Be certain that they can benefit from the services of a financial planner. If investment performance is their sole objective, perhaps they are better served by an investment professional or stockbroker.

Be conscious of how much time you spend talking vs. how much time you spend listening. Listen to the way your clients ask questions and be mindful of the way you present concepts. One way to remain conscious of how much time you talk instead of listen is to invite another member of your staff into the interview. While they may be there primarily to take notes of the meeting, you can arrange nonverbal cues to help alert you when you begin dominating the conversation or losing the attention of a client.

Be very careful that your questions aren't suggesting a certain outcome. Instead, allow for your points of conversation to be framed in a manner that allows a client to explore his or her thoughts more deeply.

HOW NOT TO CONDUCT AN INITIAL INTERVIEW
Recently, a couple shared a story with us after they had agreed to sign on as clients of the firm. It seems that they had interviewed two other planners before deciding who they would hire. While one of the other planners impressed them, another turned the couple off immediately. They told us that the line of questioning during the initial interview went something like this:

Planner: *I'd like to start our meeting by telling you how we've helped other clients like you. Okay?*
Planner: *You said you've inherited some money. How much money are we talking about?*
Planner: *You do plan on retiring, don't you? At what age, 65 or sooner?*
Planner: *Have you given much thought to the amount of money you'll need in retirement? Generally our rule of thumb is….*
Planner: *Do you have children?*
Planner: *Are you aware of how much college costs today?*
Planner: *How much money do you think you'll need to pay for their education costs?*

Planner: *Oh, they're older. What do they do for a living? Have they ever worked with a financial planner before?*

Planner: *Did you know that the way I can focus my attention on serving the needs of my clients is to insist that they provide me with referrals? Could I get the names and addresses of your children?*

Planner: *So, what was wrong with your previous adviser?*

In the example above, the client was most disappointed that the planner never took a breath to listen to what they had to say. There was a sense of presumption before the client ever had a chance to provide answers.

How did those questions feel to you? This line of questioning clearly puts a client on the defensive. Many people feel that assumptive questioning conveys arrogance, presumptions, and simply an uncaring attitude. This planner was rushing them through the interview so he could get to his story and how he could help the prospect.

Can you think of a time when you were involved in an interview where the interviewer made assumptions about your situation before you ever gave any answers to the questions? Do you know any planners who conduct their interviews in this manner? Perhaps you were trained in a manner that encouraged you to focus more on the interview script than on listening to your client's answers. When we ask questions of clients without pursuing additional exploratory questions, it is possible that we make gross assumptions about a client's real goals and objectives? I think so. Without a strong commitment to ongoing questioning, we run the risk of not placing the interests of our clients first.

For some planners, probing may be uncomfortable, but without asking follow-up questions, can you really know your client?

MEET THE VINCENZOS

Rose and Stephen Vincenzo had been long-time New Englanders who raised three children in a modest-sized home. Rose (age 65) retired from General Electric after working 38 years as an administrative assistant. Her annual salary never approached $50,000, yet she managed to amass over $1.2 million in her 401(k) plan. Her husband Stephen, 71, a maintenance worker for a publicly-traded company, earned no more than $40,000 a year in his working lifetime. Despite their modest earnings, they lived in their home mortgage-free, helped pay for their three children to attend college, and personally saved close to $250,000 in assorted mutual funds and certificates of deposit. Rose was also holding $1.2 million in GE stock in her former company's 401(k) plan (her lone investment in the plan).

For decades, Stephen managed all of the household expenses and maintained a handwritten spreadsheet listing, in great detail, how money was being spent monthly. In fact, Rose had joked that she would need to itemize her expenses to Stephen when she ran out to the convenience store to buy some milk and eggs. Their income stream consisted of about $20,000 in combined Social Security and roughly $30,000 in dividends they drew from Rose's 401(k) plan. Over the years, they had methodically reinvested the interest on their CDs as well as the dividends earned on their assorted growth and income mutual funds. Stephen insisted that drawing upon any additional funds would affect their ability to sustain their lifestyle.

When Rose and Stephen arrived at our office for an introductory meeting, it was clear that Stephen did not want to have any part of a personal finance discussion with a total stranger. Rose, on the other hand, had been persuaded by her son-in-law to visit with a planner. She wanted about $5,000 more per year so that she could feel comfortable giving her nine grandchildren a "nice gift" at Christmas. Not once had either of them considered the income power available to them.

Most financial planners will immediately see a variety of financial planning issues that needed further discussion and exploration. Owning a single stock in a 401(k) plan, asset allocation concerns, considerations for better use of their financial resources to increase their desired income stream were all quantitative issues that could easily be explained and delivered as solutions for the client. But as we listened more intently to Rose and watched Stephen become less and less involved in the conversation, it was clear that if our objective was to build a lifelong relationship with the client, we'd need to dig a bit deeper and focus more intently on the real issues affecting them. It would have been easy to offer a few strategies for the clients and move on to the implementation phase of the planning process, but we had a hunch that they had never been asked to identify their personal financial wishes, hopes, and dreams. While Stephen wasn't quite in the mood to discuss feelings, it was clear that Rose liked the direction of our questioning.

A tool we use on this occasion comes from George Kinder, a highly regarded and progressive financial planner who wrote the book *The Seven Stages of Money Maturity*. Admittedly, many planners find more comfort in expressing solutions to quantitative issues than they do leading a qualitative discussion designed to touch upon a client's feelings. But to deliver effective financial planning, I think you need to be skilled at both. Kinder's famous "Three Questions" are a conversational tool that has helped open dialogues between spouses as well as client and adviser. While I'll admit there are times when it's tough to roll out these questions on a first meeting, a skilled financial planner knows the right time and place to ask them. Our meeting with Rose and Stephen was a perfect venue.

Question #1: "Rose, I'd like you to imagine for a moment that you have all the money you've ever wanted. What would you do with it?"

"Oh, that's easy," she said. "Travel."

"To where?" I asked.

"Oh, I don't know. Anywhere. I've been to Florida a couple of times and attended a family wedding in Chicago, but besides that I really haven't left New England."

"So given the opportunity to travel, since you have all the money you ever wanted, where might 'anywhere' be?"

"Stephen," she asked, "where would you want to go?"

"I like it at home," snapped Stephen. "Besides, what would we do with the dog?"

"Rose," I said, "let's talk about what you want for a minute. If you could travel, where would you go? Remember, with all the money you needed, you could fulfill your life's dreams."

Rose began to offer up European countries, U.S. states, and national parks, but it was clear that she really wasn't dreaming; she was simply exploring a few top-of-mind ideas that popped into her head.

I went on to question #2: "Imagine you've just visited your doctor and he's told you that sometime in the next ten years you will die suddenly. The only thing for certain is that for the first five years, you will enjoy extraordinary health, but beginning in year six, you could die at any time. What would you want to be sure you accomplished?"

"Well, I'd want to be sure I got a chance to spend quality time with my grandchildren. Would you like to see some pictures?" Rose had already opened her purse and had the translucent accordion of photos out.

"Put those away," barked Stephen. "He doesn't want to see pictures of the kids. He's got other important people to see—people who I'm sure have a lot more money than us." Little did Stephen know that if we were to place this client's assets under our management, their household account would fall into our top ten.

I decided to proceed with the third question, because I felt that we were falling a bit off track, and I could see that Stephen was growing more uncomfortable with the questioning.

Question #3: "Imagine you had 24 hours left to live. Is there anything you'll regret never doing?"

And then it happened—it all came together for Rose. "I know what I want, but I could never afford it," she said humbly.

"That's right, Rose. These questions are ridiculous. He's talking to us as if we are millionaires," said Stephen, who seemed to already know what Rose was thinking.

"Shut up, Stephen," snapped Rose. "Shut up," and then she began to weep.

"I need to say what's on my mind. Stephen, I worked so hard at my job and every day I was amazed at how much money I accumulated at GE. Stephen, tell me something—what do you think a millionaire is? Because I think we are millionaires, yet I don't know how to act like one, because—and I love you with all my heart—you've always made me feel poor."

The silence hung in the room for a long time. I knew it was my place to keep my mouth shut and just watch what would happen next. A few moments later, Stephen apologized to Rose. It was clear at that moment that Rose ruled everything about their family except the money side. Rose had accumulated more money than Stephen, had been the matron of the family, and had led each and every one of their Italian gatherings. Clearly, Stephen believed his only role of significance in the family was the control of the household finances. Expecting him to relinquish this was a wish of Rose's, but seeing it happen was another thing.

Another moment passed and Rose finally began to share her dream. Though she believed it to be impossible, she had always imagined planning a week-long vacation for her entire family at Disney World in Orlando, Florida. It would include 18 people—their three married children and their spouses, ten grandchildren, and of course, Rose and Stephen.

Rose finished by looking at her husband and saying, "The dog would stay with your sister."

By asking questions and giving our clients space to both reflect and colorize their answers, the emotions that became attached to their dream heightened our realization that if we could help Rose achieve her goal, perhaps she could feel more empowered to have more open conversations about money with Stephen. Our meeting ended with us agreeing to include this "far-fetched" wish as part of our goal-planning analysis.

About four weeks later, the Vincenzos returned to participate in our financial planning presentation. Stephen's mood was significantly different from the first time we met. In fact, he was intrigued enough to recognize that there were other ways to manage their money, and potentially deliver a larger income stream. His greatest surprise came when they learned the amount of money Rose would need to draw from her 401(k) plan upon reaching age 70½. While no one knew what the future earnings on a $1.2 million portfolio would be, it was quite clear that if they continued drawing only the dividend each year, the required minimum distribution could easily exceed $60,000. This shook Stephen and Rose both, because they admitted to not knowing what to do if ever they received such a large sum of money. While we talked about methods that could more evenly spread income to them, what happened next became the turning point in the lifelong relationship we now maintain with the Vincenzos.

We explained that, during our analysis, we sought the guidance of a travel agent and asked them to create a proposal for what it would take to bring the entire family to Disney World. This included an estimate on airfare costs, a mid-priced hotel on Disney property, and park-hopper passes for their entire stay. The cost, which included an estimate on food, was about $25,000. Our next step was to show Rose and Stephen how it was possible to deliver this money to them from their existing portfolio whenever they wanted it. And the final step was to suggest that they begin contacting their children to identify a date when all of them could join them in Orlando.

It took almost 18 months from the day we made that presentation to the day they took the trip, and it's now more than six years since Rose and Stephen fulfilled a lifelong dream. In fact, they've fulfilled a few more dreams. Each year, the Vincenzos call us from their winter place on Cocoa Beach, Florida, to express their appreciation for opening their lines of communication about money and allowing them to live their dreams. Stephen, even more than Rose, regularly expresses gratitude for teaching them how to spend the money they had accumulated in a manner that has forever changed their lives. As you may imagine, the Vincenzos are raving fans. Yes, their wealth is managed, but through the transformative powers of financial planning, their personal lives have been changed as well.

Through this story, were you able to gather the integrative conversation that wove both qualitative and quantitative questions together? By periodically asking provocative questions, we were able to better grasp the issues affecting this client couple. And more surprisingly, with little nudging, they were willing to share more than they had ever planned on disclosing during our initial consultation.

Questions for discussion and/or further exploration:

1. How might have you handled the Vincenzos if they walked in your door?
2. How much time would be spent talking about the risks of owning a single stock as opposed to a better-allocated collection of investments?
3. What parts of the client's story would be of greatest interest to you?
4. How much technical analysis effort was needed to encourage the client to move money under our management?
5. Why would or wouldn't the Vincenzos be good clients for you?

HANDLING UNCOMFORTABLE SITUATIONS IN AN INITIAL INTERVIEW

Imagine, for a moment, that during an interview, a prospect states that this is the husband's second marriage. How much time should you spend exploring the history of the husband's first marriage? Might it be an uncomfortable conversation? Perhaps, yes—but it could also be quite revealing. Could the answers that come from this conversation affect the way you might offer recommendations for their investment portfolios?

What types of responses might your client give if you asked:

1. Could you help me understand whether any financial commitments remain from your first marriage?
2. Are there any alimony, child support, or special expense payments that could affect your cash flow? For how long?
3. Are there adjustment factors attached to changes in income, age, etc.?
4. What type of relationship do you maintain with your ex-spouse, children, current step-children?
5. Have provisions been made within your current estate planning that could affect your financial planning outcomes?
6. How were beneficiary designations addressed during your divorce? What changes have been made to reflect your current marital standing?

By asking open-ended questions, you give the prospect a moment to pause and offer a thoughtful answer. In the case of the second marriage questions, we find that the other spouse feels more connected to the conversation when they know that questions about each other's pasts will be important elements in understanding their ability to imagine their future together.

But when does probing go too far? Some have suggested that financial planners walk a delicate line when questioning clients about their personal issues and then offering advice about how to improve their quality of life. I believe that planners must find their own comfort level with how far they are willing to probe and the extent of advice they are willing to offer. Planners are not in a position to offer medical or psychological advice, but we are accustomed to identifying issues that need attention and recommending our clients to professionals who specialize in areas where we believe our clients might need assistance. In the end, whether to take our advice is up to the client.

Part of what makes a good financial planner great is the confidence to ask questions and offer suggestions. It's a delicate business and a lesson I learned early in my career.

ADVISER OR THERAPIST?

It was a 10 a.m. appointment. Marie, our executive assistant and "jack of all trades," offered Jim his choice of a beverage. She took his coat and hung it on the coat rack. Back in the early 1990s, all client meetings were held in my father's office, as opposed to now, when all of our meetings are held in our state-of-the art conference room.

Both Dad and I came out to greet Jim. He was a 34-year-old drug salesman for a large pharmaceutical company. Jim explained that his wife, Joanne, needed to stay at home with their three-year-old son. It has since become our unwavering position that financial plans will never be presented before a comprehensive conversation with both spouses is complete.

After proceeding through the pleasantries, Dad asked Jim to explain what brought him to see us. It's important to note that Jim was sitting on the innermost chair, across from my father's desk. I sat beside him. If Jim had needed to leave our office, he would need to ask me to move or practically climb over me to get to the door. We didn't have the largest of offices back then.

Jim told us that he had been working for the same company for about six years. He had seen his income increase from $50K in year one to its present rate of $160K. He traveled quite a bit, and besides having a nice income, his expense account gave him additional opportunities to entertain clients and dine at locations he never imagined when he was just breaking into this business.

Jim had two children, ages three and seven. College accounts totaling about $10K each were invested in a couple of mutual funds. He had about $180K in his company 401(k) plan and had recently stopped funding it because he felt his family needed the money to cover expenses. Joanne, who had worked as a nurse before having children, also had a 401(k) plan with her previous employer totaling about $65K. Beside the $250K mortgage they held on their $350K home, Joanne had a couple of thousand dollars remaining on an auto loan.

The primary reason for Jim's visit to our office was that he was expecting a $30K bonus. Joanne, who paid all of the family's bills, was looking to use the money as an added contribution to the kids' college funds. She had already built an emergency fund with about $50K and she had Jim set up his paycheck so that $200 each month would be split and allocated to each of the kids' college accounts.

With Joanne having so much involvement in the family finances, my father asked how it was possible that she wouldn't want to attend this initial meeting. I'll never forget what happened next.

Joe told us that he hoped that we could keep this conversation private, as he had read in the disclosure kit we send to prospects in advance of our meeting that we would always maintain confidentiality regarding conversations with clients. He hoped we'd be able to schedule a secondary "initial conversation" with Joanne after today's meeting. She didn't even know he had scheduled the appointment.

"I sense there is much more to talk about than what we've discussed," proposed my father.

In Jim's words, "It's really not that big of a deal."

He then told us about how he had been handling some personal financial issues without Joanne's knowledge. Because his use of money was under her watchful eye, he hadn't told her about the raise he received earlier that year, or the one six months prior. He had been allocating all of his raises to a separate personal checking account to pay for things he wanted to do.

"My wife was hell-bent on building an emergency fund and it limited my ability to go out with friends and do things I had been used to doing before we had all these added expenses," he stated.

For a while, Jim was using this extra money to buy new clothes, play golf, extend business trips, and pay the expenses on a nicer car.

He then confided, "I've finally come to realize that I need to talk with my wife about this issue, and as a result, I'm planning on telling her that my raise is $15K rather than $30K."

We learned that he had gotten a bit carried away with spending. Two years ago, Jim applied for a credit card, which was now carrying a $10K balance.

Jim sincerely hoped we would not tell his wife about the credit card debt during the next meeting.

"I'll find a way to pay off the debt on my own," he said. "Joanne would probably leave me if she knew of the credit card balance I was carrying."

Jim was willing to pay our $1,500 initial financial planning fee. He hoped that during our next meeting, we would listen intently to his wife's goals and objectives (along with his) and build a plan that showed them how to balance their current spending pattern with the need to fund their children's education costs and a retirement lifestyle in the future.

In years past, they had looked forward to their $4,000–$5,000 tax refund. They relied solely on Jim's company for life insurance coverage and there was the near-term possibility of an inheritance from Jim's mom of about $250–$500K. His mom was widowed about five years earlier. At age 74, she was having a series of health problems, and her long-term forecast seemed bleak. Jim was one of three children. He expected that all would be solved once his mom passed away, but for now, he wanted us to approach the next initial consultation with his wife on his terms.

How would you have handled this situation? Would you have scheduled a secondary appointment with Joanne? Would you have honored Jim's secret? Would this be a good financial planning client for you?

As I sat and listened to my father ask more questions, and saw Jim share more and more about himself, it was clear that, with every discussion point, there was more to learn about the couple's financial and mental well-being. I was curious how Dad would handle this conversation. Surely, I thought, he would encourage Jim to invite his wife back for an initial consultation so that he could listen to the couple's goals.

What happened next surprised me.

With Jim confident that we'd go along with his request, Dad simply said, "You don't need a financial planner, Jim. You need a marriage counselor."

I thought for sure Jim would bolt up from his seat, offer my father a few obscenities, climb over my chair, and head for the exit.

But that's not what happened.

Instead, Jim sat in silence for a good minute or two. So did my dad and I. After a lengthy pause, and some reflection, he began to talk. "Barry, you're right. As much as I'd like to begin long-range financial planning, I do need to figure out a way to better communicate with my wife. I appreciate your honesty and your frankness. I didn't realize it was what I was looking for today, but somehow you've opened my eyes. Your perspective is valid and I think I just might take your advice." There was another pause, and then he continued. "But Barry, would you be willing to meet with both of us once I get these issues resolved?"

My jaw dropped. Had Dad become a therapist without my knowledge? No. What he did was listen. He offered a direct perspective, presented a provocative statement, and allowed the client to make a decision that suited him best. He placed the client's interests first. What I learned was how important it was to showcase our values and be willing to lose business if the relationship didn't feel right.

About four years later, Joanne called our office to schedule an "initial" interview. Though we had never met her before, she had referred two other friends to our firm over the past two years. During this call, Joanne indicated that Jim would be joining her and that their relationship was stronger than ever. In fact, she thanked us for giving Jim the courage to tell Joanne what she said she had known all along.

In the instance of Jim and Joanne, how might have you handled the situation?

1. Would you have suggested that Jim needed marital help before proceeding with financial planning?
2. What other questions might you have asked to determine whether this client was a good fit for you?

Your integrity as a financial planner is your badge of honor. Only when you ask the tough questions are you able to place the interests of your client first. Financial planners take risks by daring their clients to explore their financial lives in ways they may never have considered. Use your leadership skills, ask genuine questions, and live with personal integrity—clients want that from a genuine financial planner. Yet there are prospects who will view you differently. When you confront a prospect who has a different expectation from the services you deliver, how will you address it with them?

IS IT ABOUT THE MONEY OR YOUR VALUES?

Financial planners are reasonable and patient people. They recognize that one of the most dangerous things to do in an initial meeting is to sign clients before getting to know them. Clients in a hurry assume trust early, and are more motivated to just give you money to invest. They are also the types of clients who will think nothing about leaving you when someone else intrigues them.

In my opinion, this is a client you do *not* want, no matter how large the check might be.

Consider this example: I'll never forget the morning a gentleman came walking into the office and demanded to visit with my father. Fortunately, there were no appointments scheduled, so we were both able to meet with him in our conference room.

He was an acquaintance of my father's through our local temple, and had recently lost his wife of 40 years in a terrible automobile accident. He had brought along his checkbook, which was recently flush with a million-dollar deposit from life insurance proceeds. He wanted to give us $500,000, and he told us that he was heading down the street to another acquaintance of his who worked for a large brokerage house. His plan was to write a check for $500,000 to that firm as well.

"At the end of one year, we'll see how each of you performed," he proclaimed, "and then I'll decide who I will give the rest of my money to."

He never even asked about the types of investments we might purchase for him. He didn't ask about costs. He didn't care. He wanted one thing—performance. As he pulled out the checkbook he asked, "To whom should I make the check payable?"

I remember my father telling him to slow down. We spent a good 30 minutes trying to learn more about his overall situation and explain our commitment to the financial planning process *first*. He insisted that he wasn't comfortable talking about his personal financial situation until he was certain that the adviser he hired could make him money.

How would you have handled the situation? Would you take this client's challenge and prove to him you could outperform the broker down the street? Or would you do something else?

I suspect that you already know the outcome.

Without hesitation, we told this client that under no circumstances would we accept his money to build an investment portfolio without full disclosure of his entire financial situation. This also meant we would need to be third-party recipients of the investment accounts he would be holding with the other brokerage firm.

For a moment, he considered verbally exposing his financial life to us, but there was no way he would allow us to see how the other broker would manage the other half of the money.

Moments later, we encouraged him to give all $1 million to the broker down the street.

"Am I hearing you right?" he asked with a quizzical, almost astounded look on his face. "You are willing to let $500,000 walk out this door? Haven't you ever heard of competing for business? What kind of investment guys are you?"

Since that day, any client who has ever paid for a financial plan first has never fired us as his or her financial planner. Sure, some clients have moved, died, or had to cash out their accounts, but never have we been fired because someone else was promising a better return on their investment. If you position yourself as a planner who will regularly monitor your clients' goals with the alignment of their personal resources, clients will begin to realize that the growth of their net worth is much more valuable than the performance of a single investment. Never again will you find yourself justifying the investments you selected for your clients over suggestions your client might offer after reading a magazine, watching a pundit, or listening to 30-second sound bites of advice on the radio. You'll spend the majority of your time talking about your client's life and how he or she has been able to accomplish goals and have adventures because you've proved to them that planning first works.

Honestly, it may seem like the greatest compliment you could ever receive when a client pulls out his or her checkbook or asks to sign your contract in the middle of the initial consultation. But the very best planners know that lifelong relationships take time, and you'll earn your clients' absolute respect when you can tell them how flattered you are that they want to work with your firm, but for now, you'd like for them to put the checkbook away. Patience, as hard as it may seem, is a virtue bestowed on the very best financial planners.

Saying "hold on," or "thanks, but let's step back for a moment," is a sign of integrity and commitment to your service standards. It's an expression to the client that their long-term business is much more important than getting started right now. In fact, some planners will diplomatically encourage clients to interview other financial advisers first; they will explain how important it is to interview a cross section of planners in the community. They might also explain that their methodology is more strategic than it is tactical; and maybe someone seeking to rush to judgment is really looking for action rather than advice.

Though it is tempting to take anyone who fogs a mirror, has a pulse, is red-blooded, (fill in your own cliché here), etc., in the end, every prospect you turn away who doesn't mesh with your values affirms your firm's convictions that the right client is more important than any client.

WHAT HAPPENS WHEN A FIRST APPOINTMENT CATCHES YOU BY SURPRISE? THE STORY OF A CLIENT WAKE-UP CALL

Recently, we were contacted by Jim Callum, a senior vice president of human resources for a privately held manufacturing plant. After working for his company for 35 years, Jim was preparing to retire in about 12 months. It happened that he had been a source of referrals to our office for several years. Despite encouraging others to seek the guidance of a financial planner, Jim held a raw skepticism about the financial planning world and had elected to manage the household finances on his own. He was a regular subscriber to investment newsletters, an avid reader of personal finance books, and regular listener to financial talk radio. Yet now, at age 63, Jim was becoming gun-shy. He realized it would be up to him to replace his paycheck upon retirement—and as much as he enjoyed giving advice to others, he wasn't in a position to advise himself in this area.

Jim requested an initial interview with us. At first, I thought it would be a traditional client interview, but something happened that was rather strange—*he* asked all the questions. At the conclusion of our two-hour meeting, I learned more about myself than I ever imagined and, in fact, knew little about this particular prospect's financial situation. For the first time in my 17 years, I was interviewed by a client. Jim had already done research on our firm's background, he had spoken with two retired colleagues who had become clients of our firm, and was well prepared to lead this meeting.

Jim had gathered the traditional interview questions, but prepared ones of his own that I thought were quite impressive. I'd encourage any prospect to use these questions when interviewing a planner.

Here are some of the questions he asked:

1. As a Certified Financial Planner, I know that you are required to obtain 30 hours of continuing education credit. How do you go about obtaining these credits, and do you generally focus on a particular area of specialization?

2. Would you be willing to provide me with confirmations and course descriptions for continuing education credit you've earned within the last 12 months?

3. What are the last few books you've read?

4. Can you explain what each person in your office does?

5. To what extent are you involved in my personal financial plan and subsequent investment accounts, once I become a client of the firm?

6. How might my relationship with you change three to five years from now?

7. I understand that if I choose to implement investment strategies with you, you will earn a fee for the assets I place under your management. Will there be charges for transaction fees, custodial fees, wire transfers, trading costs, etc.?

8. Besides investment management and oversight, what else does my fee buy?

9. I see that you've been active in the financial planning profession and seem to travel quite a bit. How is the office managed when you are away?

10. What services does your firm offer that deal with non-financial issues pertaining to retirement?

As I said, it took us about two hours to get through these questions. I learned that Jim is a skilled interviewer, and he knew when to ask why, when to respond "Tell me more about that," and "Can you think of a time when…?"

Apparently, we answered Jim's questions to his satisfaction, because he scheduled a subsequent initial interview six months later with his wife, and they have now become solid clients in our firm.

It was, however, interesting to sit on the other side of the table. It's so easy to forget what it's like answering the questions rather than asking them. I also noticed how little time Jim spent talking and how effective he was at listening to what we had to say. But more than any question Jim asked, the last one, I thought, was rather unique. Is it our role as financial planners to help clients address the non-financial issues surrounding their lives? And heck, what does "non-financial issues in retirement" even mean? While I was humbled by the question, our firm was inspired by the possibilities.

In Section IV, we will talk about the benefits of incorporating "non-financial issues pertaining to retirement" as part of your client-planner relationship.

SUMMARY

1. Your integrity as a financial planner is your badge of honor.
2. Exploring your clients' emotions reflects your desire to listen more intently and ultimately helps you advise them with more concise strategies.
3. Be willing to lose a client when your integrity could be challenged.
4. Know your values and be true to them, no matter the size of the check.
5. Be prepared. Clients are beginning to interview planners with a list of non-traditional questions that explore your background, values, interests, and services.

8 | *After the Initial Consultation— Why the 30 Minutes that Follow an Initial Meeting Are the Most Important*

OBJECTIVES

1. Convey the importance of capturing your thoughts about the initial consultation in a memo to file while the details are fresh in your mind
2. Explain the importance of following up the meeting with a personalized thank you note
3. Share the characteristics of good contact management software, ideas for its effective use, and the centrality of it to exceptional client service

In the world of personal financial planning, keeping your promises and showing a client you heard what they said builds relationships like no other.

KEEPING YOUR PROMISE

A key distinguishing factor of genuine financial planners is an ability to deliver on their service promises.

During an initial consultation, ideas, feelings, and an array of conversational points are raised. Your first meeting is an opportunity to get to know the client and for them to learn about you—not what products your company offers or which products have been selling effectively. Honestly, they can find that anywhere!

THE MEMO TO FILE

If you meet with your clients by yourself, I strongly encourage you to take notes or request your clients' permission to tape the conversation. After all, you are likely to be distracted by a number of issues when the appointment is over, and how will you ever remember the key issues and unexplored items without a reference point? If possible, you should have another associate in your office join you for the meeting. He or she doesn't need to say anything, but should take notes and capture what both you and your client say. Those notes are an invaluable resource when you begin mentally processing the meeting after the client leaves.

Within one hour following a client meeting, your notes need to be permanently captured. You can only recall the emotions and meaning behind the notes you took during your meeting for a limited time. By translating your notes into a permanent record, you have the ability to add color and texture to your recent conversation and offer depth to your notes that you weren't able to capture while conversing with the client.

Companies like Copy Talk (www.copytalk.com) offer a service whereby you dictate your notes from the meeting to a recording on a toll-free number and they send them back to you in e-mail form within four hours of your phone call.

You can also simply buy a micro-recorder. You dictate the meeting's notes and then ask a staff person to listen to the tape and transcribe it into a client file. If your computer has enough memory, your memos can be saved as mpeg files and stored in your client's record as well.

Below are sample questions you should be able to answer following an initial interview with a prospect.

Initial Memo to File Questions
1. How did these people learn about your firm? Be specific. "They were referred by..., I met them at..., They are related to..."
2. What is the client's and spouse's story? Offer a brief biography of these clients.
   - Age.
   - Employer, occupation, income, etc. How do they feel about their jobs?
   - If retired, from where?
   - Relationship with children.
   - Activities, interests, etc.
3. The reason they sought a relationship with us was ...
4. Their primary long-term goals are (for example):
   - Retirement income planning
   - Wealth accumulation
   - Education funding
   - Estate preservation
5. Their primary short-term goals are:
   - Major purchases
   - Significant expenses
   - Ownership/registration issues
6. How would you describe their financial situation?
   - Make general comment on assets and liabilities
   - Estimate their overall net worth
   - Offer any notable items pertaining to their situation
   - Offer comments on insurance issues

7. What services and/or tasks did you promise to provide them?
    - Financial planning
    - Investment/insurance services
    - Tax planning
    - Insurance analysis
    - Costs for services
    - Deadlines promised
8. What are your next steps?
    - Letters to write
    - Paperwork to process
    - Research to complete
9. How will you next communicate with them?
    - Phone
    - In person
    - E-mail
10. What are the names of clients either related to or associated with them?

Here's a sample memo to file from a first meeting:

Esther and Steven Bartlett are referrals from Maureen L. and have come to our office seeking financial planning advice. Several years ago, they built a relationship with a financial planner at a wirehouse whom they grew to dislike over time because this individual was primarily a stock broker and used the term "financial planning" as a marketing tool. They proceeded to lose hundreds of thousands of dollars in a brokerage account for which Steven holds equal blame in the loss, yet Esther puts primary responsibility on the broker. They chose to liquidate their entire portfolio and place it in cash. They decided to use the vast majority of these assets to purchase an investment property on Plumeria Island, which is currently valued at $1.1 million and carries a $500K mortgage.

Steven is a cardiologist with privileges at Winchendon Hospital, but last year was diagnosed with Parkinson's disease and now collects a disability income of $10K a month after tax. He also receives $84K in compensation from the practice, because he works about 15 to 20 hrs. a week, as needed. He is uncertain about how this disease will affect his ability to work, yet hopes that he'll be able to continue to draw from the practice for a period of time. Esther works for Costello Engineering and has been there for about ten years. She believes she is entitled to a pension and has to travel to Chicago each month. She is about 12 years younger than Steven, and together they have a four-year-old daughter they are considering enrolling at a private school near their home.

Their house is valued at roughly $900K, without a mortgage, in Wenham, MA. Over the past couple of years, they have put several hundred thousand dollars into the property to improve it, yet are considering the possibility of selling the home if they were to send their daughter to a private school 20 miles from home. Esther believes that the 30-minute commute may be a bit onerous, and she is also questioning herself about the necessity for paying private school costs at the kindergarten level.

They've accumulated a variety of assets, primarily in cash, totaling roughly $1 million and primarily held in assorted retirement accounts. They each own individual IRAs at Fidelity, but have never measured the performance of their investments, nor do they have a solid understanding of why they've made such selections.

They are interested in a comprehensive review of their financial affairs and hope that we will offer candid advice on the best use of their resources to support their goals of retirement, as well as potentially funding their child's private high school and college education. They estimate that if they had $100K to spend during retirement, they would more than adequately accommodate their income needs. This, however, does not include the costs that would need to be allocated to education. They are not opposed to selling the investment property in Plumeria Island and believe that this may be a necessity, especially if Steven's ailment requires them to limit their lifestyle. They were further intrigued that we would be willing to review and offer opinions on their auto and home-owners insurance, as well as investment allocations and benefits through their employer. We explained the comprehensive nature of our financial planning work and quoted them a fee of $3K based on 15 hours of our time. Esther was intrigued by our services, yet hoped that we would be enlightening enough that she felt the $3K expense would be worth the money spent. She is clearly looking for some action steps, and I believe that we can provide her with enough resources to empower her to make wise decisions with their money. It is also highly likely that they would transfer their existing investment portfolios to our firm for management. We told them we would provide them with a follow-up letter and fully expect to hear back from them in the near future.

Steven indicated that most of the info we might be looking for was readily accessible at home and that he was an avid Quicken user.

Within 20 minutes following an initial meeting, we dictate our memo to file. Upon receipt of the file via e-mail from Copytalk, we review the memo for errors and cut and paste the memo into the client's contact management record as a completed action to the appointment.

If you've never written memos to file for each of your existing clients, I would encourage you to begin preparing the story of each client you currently serve. It will help you begin to understand how much you really know about your clients. In addition, if anyone were to inquire about purchasing your firm, having memos and stories about your client base would certainly add value and depth to the business you might sell.

The questionnaire below was developed by Greg Zedlar, a financial planner in southern California who has found tremendous success in buying the practices of smaller financial planners and using his firm's economies of scale to offer a wider array of services to serve a greater number of clients. He has graciously allowed me to include it in this book for your use.

Before he buys a planner's book of business, he has a process where the entire staff must meet with the seller so that they can gather a historical understanding of each client. One of the requirements is that the adviser must dictate answers to the following questions in advance of the meeting. Here is his list of questions:

	First Name	Last Name	DOB	SS#	Drivers Lic#	Citizen	Occupation
Client 1						Y / N	
Client 2						Y / N	
Hm Address:			City, State, Zip:				
Hm Phone:	Client 1 Work Phone:			Email:			
Fax:	Client 2 Work Phone:			Email:			

Client Inventory Questions

1. In what year did they become a client?

2. How did they become a client? (AMEX, bank, referral, etc —Name referral source)

3. How easy are they to work with on a scale of one to five? (One is tough, five is easy)

4. How many dependents do they have? Are they clients?

5. Circle: Retired / Working

6. When do they plan to retire?

7. Do they have any accounts outside of LPL (including retirement accounts like 401(k))?

8. What are their major goals?

9. How often do you meet with them? In person or over the phone?

10. Where do you see these clients for appointments?

11. Do they regularly refer clients?

12. Please list all clients who are associated with them (family, friends, referrals, etc.).

13. Do they have a computer? Do they use e-mail?

14. What are the names of their other investment advisers?

15. Who is their CPA? Do you keep a copy of their most recent tax returns?

16. Who is their estate planning attorney? Do you keep a copy of their trust?

17. Do they have any recreational hobbies (golf, skiing, etc.)?

*Printed with Permission from Greg Zedlar, Chairman of California Capital Management, Encino, CA. 2006.

If someone offered to purchase your business, wouldn't any buyer want to know as much as possible about your existing clients? With this data, would your business be more valuable? I believe that maintaining a memo to file and periodically showing a client the historical ledger of all conversations you've ever held validates his or her sense of connection to you and your firm. They see that you really do know them and that your advice is based on both present day knowledge and historical references.

If you do nothing else to improve your practice, begin maintaining detailed memos to file.

THE THANK YOU NOTE

It is critical that, immediately following your dictation of the memo to file, you also dictate or compose a personal thank you note to your client. In a letter, you can express appreciation for their interest in your firm and reiterate the issues they shared with you. In doing so, you show them they were heard. I discourage people from building thank you note templates that are automatically generated following a meeting. In my opinion, this is your first step in distancing your client from your personal services.

Keep your thank you notes *very* personal. Make sure that they recapture many of the items discussed in your meeting and that they highlight the following:

1. Genuinely express your appreciation for having them visit with you. Be sure you specify the date when you met with them.
2. Restate any goals your client discussed. Be sure to reiterate them as specifically as possible; this validates that you were listening during the meeting.
3. Explain what else you may need from them to take the next step in building a relationship with them.
4. Clearly explain any fees you discussed in the meeting.
5. Thank them for the opportunity to be of service.

<<SAMPLE LETTER #1>>
August 14, 2008

Mr. & Mrs. A Pt
101 Easy St.
Canton, MA 02254

Dear C & A:

Many thanks for visiting our office on <date> to discuss your personal finances. We are delighted that you are considering the use of our financial planning services.

During our meeting you indicated that the following items were important to you:

1. *Create a strategy to provide ongoing financial support of $10,000 to each of your two children (ages 24 and 21).*
2. *Determine the feasibility of stopping work in 2009 and creating a retirement income plan that could allow you to spend $80,000 annually, in today's dollars.*
3. *Analyze the collection of assorted investments and insurance policies you've gathered over the years. We understand that we may have to work together to re-build cost basis in some of your accounts.*
4. *Consider the value of long-term care insurance as it relates to your overall financial planning needs and goals.*

As Certified Financial Planner professionals, we have an ethical obligation to place the interests of our clients first. As a result, we believe it is our duty to prepare a comprehensive survey of your financial affairs and offer recommendations based upon your current financial status. Our work begins with the collection of data in an effort to produce a clear net worth statement and cash flow analysis. Once we have agreed that we have accurately captured all of your assets and liabilities, we will then begin our in-depth analysis to touch on areas of investment allocation, risk management, estate planning, as well as retirement, education, and tax planning. Our presentation is delivered interactively in our office, and will provide you with specific action steps to help you better assess your ability to achieve your goals.

We estimate that it will take eight to ten hours of our time (billed at $200 per hour) to complete and present this comprehensive analysis. For

us to begin our work, we would ask that you sign the enclosed contract
and authorization for information forms, and return a retainer check for
$1,000 along with the following pieces of information:

1. Copies of any investment, retirement, and banking statements
2. Three months' copies of checking account statements that reflect
   monthly cash flow
3. Two months' pay stubs from your employer
4. Information pertaining to your stock options and your current
   employee purchase plan
5. Your benefits booklet
6. A statement printed within the last 90 days which details information on Carolyn's 401(k) plan with her previous employer
7. A copy of your current mortgage statement
8. Copies of the endorsement pages for your homeowners, automobile, and umbrella policies
9. Information pertaining to any life insurance contracts you hold
10. Information pertaining to any accounts established on behalf of
    your children
11. Copies of current wills
12. Copy of your 200X tax return
13. Any other information you think may be of help as we prepare a
    financial planning analysis for you

You should expect to receive our personal data review approximately
one week following receipt of your information. This report provides
a net worth statement that categorizes your assets and liabilities
by ownership and type of account. We will likely include additional
questions pertaining to the development of your financial plan. Upon
your approval of the report, we will enter the analysis phase of our
process. We will then plan to contact you within two to three weeks
to present our findings and recommendations on your personal
financial plan.

> *Once again, many thanks for this opportunity to be of service. We look forward to building a long and successful financial planning relationship with you.*
>
> *Sincerely,*
>
> *Marc S. Freedman CFP®, President*

Our contact management system posts a reminder phone call for a planner to follow up with the client one week after the mailing of the letter. During the follow up call, we attempt to learn how they are doing gathering the information for their financial plan and what, if any, questions might remain following our last meeting. Asking them when you might expect receipt of the information you requested provides an indication of their interest in your services. It also gives you a future follow up date to post in your contact management system.

DOCUMENT, DOCUMENT, DOCUMENT

There are multiple contact management systems in the marketplace, and every financial planner should be using one as their primary resource for maintaining every communication, conversation, e-mail, letter, report, spreadsheet, etc., about their clients. It's no surprise that we live in a litigious society, and when it comes to advising people on their money and the emotions attached to it, we all fall prey to clients looking to cash in. By maintaining detailed records, notes of your meetings, and capturing every conversation with your client, you not only lessen your risk for liability, but also increase your connection and historical reference points with your client.

Imagine, for a moment, that an auditor walks in your door. He asks you to produce all communications, both incoming and outgoing, from March 31, 2005 to June 30, 2005, and he wants them in his hand within the next two hours. How quickly could you produce records of conversations, e-mails, letters to clients, notes from meetings, etc.? How about a chronological listing of all incoming e-mails, phone calls, and letters received? If these items can't be produced within 30 minutes, you need to better evaluate the way you maintain your record keeping systems.

I strongly recommend that advisers showcase how they use their contact management systems when meeting with clients during an initial interview. Explain to them that, similar to the way they do at a doctor's office, you believe that it is critically important to maintain a record of all conversations and communications with them. Remember, every time you visit a doctor's office, they keep a record of your personal information, medical history, and changes in your health.

If you proactively share the way in which you use your contact management system, it gives clients a sense of comfort and adds to your credibility. Just imagine how beneficial this historical information might be when unexpected circumstances in your client's life might pressure them to act irrationally or become forgetful. Your experience, knowledge, and an ability to look at your client's historical "big picture" sets you up as a trusted role model and leader in their life.

FOLLOWING IT ALL

I believe that one of the greatest features of contact management software is your ability to assign follow up tasks to your staff, and then produce reports that show what work is outstanding and what loose ends need to be completed. Whether you are a 1-person, 2-person, or a 200-person shop, it serves as a chronological tracking for client transfers, uncompleted paperwork, changes of address, and *so much more.*

What systems do you have in place to address your clients' worries that paperwork in progress won't be completed effectively if one of your key staff people unexpectedly doesn't show up to work for two weeks?

Suffice it to say that contact management software is probably the smartest, most valuable investment for your firm. Just be certain that the product you purchase has personal phone support, an active resource through the Internet, and that your contact management's support team will be there to address periodic hiccups, viruses, human errors, and more. You might also want to talk with other advisers in your circle of trusted colleagues, attend association conferences, and read industry periodicals to find the system that will work best in your office. But in no way should you venture one more day in this business without having an actively running contact management system.

ONE MORE THOUGHT ON CONTACT MANAGEMENT

As e-mail becomes the preferred means of communicating with clients, vendors, and colleagues, be sure to find a contact management system that automatically places incoming e-mails directly into the sender's contact management historical file. Don't use a program that maintains your incoming and outgoing e-mail solely in the inbox. Having to create subfolders and build rules to sort your e-mail is a short-term solution that you're bound to regret as your business grows.

BACK IT UP

Maintaining client data is critically important to strengthening your understanding of your client, but not knowing how to retrieve the data in the event of a virus, data failure, etc., could be devastating to your business.

It goes without saying that you should build a disaster recovery plan for all of your client data, and back up the data daily. But more than anything else, be sure you know how to retrieve the data. Make sure your staff knows how to do it, too. Encourage them to write down procedures to retrieve data that anyone could follow, and be certain that your staff knows where the instructions are kept.

By following these simple items above, you will distinguish yourself from the vast majority of advisers your client is likely to interview. What you may notice is that discussion points for your initial meeting need not focus on your investment skills or addressing mistakes clients have made with previous financial advisers. Your single most important role in the initial meeting is to build trust and a rapport with your clients that will be memorable. Trust should never be built as a smoke screen. Be sincere. Be genuine.

How you conduct your initial consultation and deliver on your "next step" promises to your client are the most important components in showcasing your desire to build a lifelong relationship with them. Challenge yourself to learn more about your clients, and deliver probing questions that open their eyes to the benefits comprehensive financial planning can deliver to them. Your first meeting sets the tone for what future meetings will produce. When your first meeting is spectacular, your clients will expect the same level of dedication during ever other session they have with you. In the next section of this book, you will discover how to deliver a financial plan that validates the services you promised and expands your breadth of advice in areas they had hoped you could help them address.

SUMMARY

1. Memos to file must be captured immediately following every client interaction.
2. Thank you notes should be personal. They should indicate that you've heard your client's goals and objectives and explain the next steps in the relationship.
3. Make your contact management system the central depository for all actions, communication, appointments, and tasks. When an auditor visits your office, you should have a one-stop location to deliver answers to their question "How have you been serving your client?"

Section III:

From Start to Implementation— Crafting a World Class Financial Plan for the Mass Affluent

9 Preparing to Build a Financial Plan for Your Client

OBJECTIVES
1. Review the basic elements needed in every financial plan
2. Revisit the formula for financial planning
3. Instill the importance of planners doing financial planning

Mass affluent individuals need financial planning services more than ever before, and they need it from competent, ethical planners. They need someone who asks questions about their successes. They need help crystallizing their short- and long-term goals, and they appreciate it when you help them uncover their continuing challenges. They need someone dedicated to ensuring that their financial futures are protected through risk management tools and estate planning concepts. They need a planner who remains diligently focused on understanding their *entire* net worth, instead of hyper-focusing on fragments. And more than anything else, they want someone who's willing to offer guidance when it comes to discussions around cash flow.

When your clients know that they can count on you for advice and leadership on *all* of these issues, you have mastered the formula for financial planning and you've delivered financial planning in its most comprehensive form. In the chapters that follow, we will present practical ideas and guidance on how to better deliver financial planning services to your clients.

Do you think you can provide this service to the mass affluent *and* deliver it profitably? You certainly can. But here's the problem— the mass affluent don't know who to trust, and/or where to turn for genuine financial planning services. Remember, as we mentioned in Section 1, this market segment has grown skeptical of planners. They view themselves as being oversold and underserved. Your pitch to them must be authentic, but it must also be one that delivers on its promises and truly embraces the use of financial planning principles as the foundation for present and future client meetings.

Just think about this for a moment. What if the formula for financial planning was recognized as the worldwide template that defined financial planning? Would it help consumers come to grips with the term "financial planning?" Would it create an ah ha moment for consumers? Would the public finally be able to say, "Now I know what to expect from a financial planner. Please, someone, tell me where I can get it!" Could this be the tipping point for the financial planning profession?

WHY FINANCIAL PLANNERS SHOULD DO FINANCIAL PLANNING

The opportunity to craft a financial plan for your clients should be one of the most gratifying components of your job. Financial planning needs to be at the core of your every action, your every advice point, and every conversation you have with your client. Perhaps you are someone who uses the term "financial planner" as a means of describing yourself, but the work you really perform is investment management. So what? What if your real passion is managing money and helping people achieve higher risk adjusted rates of return for their portfolios. What if investment management, constructing portfolios, or thinking about how world economics and social change affect the markets at large is what really fuels your fire? Admit it—it's okay, the investment community needs your passion and intelligence. Yet, if we, as a profession, truly seek to foster the value of financial planning and educate the public of its virtues, we need people who will dedicate themselves to financial planning—not building investment portfolios or noodling over technical research. Planners need to spend the majority of their time addressing individual client issues and introducing their clients to a whole new way of looking at their financial futures.

SEPARATING THE MECHANICS FROM THE MANAGEMENT

As your firm grows, you may find yourself delegating the mechanical components of planning, such as data entry, spreadsheet development, investment analysis, and insurance review to other personnel in your office. Yet you should be responsible for adapting the details into a living, breathing, actionable plan. Do you get excited every time you prepare, develop, and deliver the findings to your client? If not, what excites you about the role you play in your client's life as their financial planner? Could it be that too many of the mechanical functions remain part of *your job*, and you've been unable to spend quality time focusing on the analysis, strategy, and recommendations? If planning is your passion, I believe that you need to be willing to give up the mechanical tasks and allow yourself to concentrate on the stages of financial planning that rely on your wisdom, experience, and practical knowledge.

Be careful, however, that you are delegating the right tasks to others. Recently, you've probably noticed more and more large financial services firms adding financial planning to their menus of client benefits. Many of these firms are encouraging advisers to slide the total development (not just the mechanical elements) of a plan to administrative personnel, interns, and/or outsourced professionals. If financial planning is to truly serve as a profession by its own merits, its comprehensive development should not be handed to just anyone in the office.

Perhaps that strategy works well in firms where financial planning is merely a slice in the investment management pie, but if your firm promotes financial planning as its core benefit, the *planner (the one who builds the personal relationship with the client)* should significantly contribute to the strategic decisions and critical advice components in a financial plan.

As I said earlier, certain elements of the planning process can be systematized and easily taught. But for the most part, these skills occur in the areas of data collection, data entry, basic analysis, and report development. Items such as:

- Data entry into financial planning software
- Running reports, analyses, what-ifs based on specific criteria
- Following up with clients to retrieve missing data
- Building basic spreadsheets
- Packaging a printout of the plan
- Preparing proposals
- Pre-filling necessary paperwork

are all suitable tasks for administrative staff, entry-level planners, and paraplanners. But there is still that breed of planner (myself included) who remains passionate about getting their hands dirty with the details as much as they love the strategizing. These types of planners always believe that there is more to find in the details than what simply appears on the surface.

Nevertheless, when a client hires you to deliver financial planning they surely expect *you* to be responsible for...

- Financial planning intelligence
- Specific recommendations
- Advice and guidance on big picture questions
- Personalized guidance and mentoring

Over the next few chapters, we will highlight a number of concepts, ideas, and presentation strategies that are designed to serve the needs of the mass affluent marketplace. We've been using these concepts in our financial planning practice for decades. We could never capture the thousands of individual approaches that planners use in their day-to-day operations, but I hope that you will find this section to be a resource for ideas as you build plans for your clients.

REVISITING THE FORMULA FOR FINANCIAL PLANNING

You may recall that back in Section 1, we presented the formula for financial planning.

Discovery	(Goals, Challenges, Successes)	+
Capital Protection	(Family, Health, Life, Legacy)	+
Wealth Management	(Net Worth, Net Cash Flow)	+

= Financial Planning

This formula was presented to help you wrap your mind around the high level elements needed when anyone is asked, "How will you know whether your adviser delivered financial planning to you?"

CFP Board's six-step process offers guidance to the public about the financial planning process and can be an effective tool when building a plan. It is important that you dig as deep as possible into each step before moving on to the next one. (from CFP Board's Web site www.cfp.net/learn/knowledgebase.asp?id=2)

The financial planning process consists of the following six steps:

1. **Establishing and defining the client-planner relationship.**
   The financial planner should clearly explain or document the services to be provided to you and define both his and your responsibilities. The planner should explain fully how he will be paid and by whom. You and the planner should agree on how long the professional relationship should last and on how decisions will be made.

2. **Gathering client data, including goals.**
   The financial planner should ask for information about your financial situation. You and the planner should mutually define your personal and financial goals, understand your time frame for results, and discuss, if relevant, how you feel about risk. The financial planner should gather all the necessary documents before giving you the advice you need.

3. **Analyzing and evaluating your financial status.**
   The financial planner should analyze your information to assess your current situation and determine what you must do to meet your goals. Depending on what services you have asked for, this could include analyzing your assets, liabilities and cash flow, current insurance coverage, investments, or tax strategies.

4. **Developing and presenting financial planning recommendations and/or alternatives.**
   The financial planner should offer financial planning recommendations that address your goals, based on the information you provide. The planner should go over the recommendations with you to help you understand them so that you can make informed decisions. The planner should also listen to your concerns and revise the recommendations as appropriate.

5. **Implementing the financial planning recommendations.** You and the planner should agree on how the recommendations will be carried out. The planner may carry out the recommendations or serve as your "coach," coordinating the whole process with you and other professionals such as attorneys or stockbrokers.

6. **Monitoring the financial planning recommendations.** You and the planner should agree on who will monitor your progress towards your goals. If the planner is in charge of the process, she should report to you periodically to review your situation and adjust the recommendations, if needed, as your life changes.

Think back to the last five financial plans you wrote. Was your advice unique for each client? My guess is that you'd probably say yes. But, were there particular threads, steps, and/or analyses that were central to each plan? My guess is you'd probably answer yes here, too.

Is it possible, then, that portions of your financial planning efforts can be systematized? We tend to dismiss the possibility of systematizing financial planning because of its highly personal nature. We convince our peers that systematization is impossible because each client's situation is different, and having a "model" for building a financial plan is impossible. I definitely agree that planners have an obligation to examine the unique characteristics that accompany each client story, but there are many pieces of a plan that can be systematized.

Perhaps if your firm had a standard process (or checklist) to aid you in the development of financial plans for your clients, you could more easily find common threads. I would encourage you to summarize your firm's approach to building a financial plan and begin to outline some of the specifics that fall within each category of the six-step process. Below is an outline we use in our office to keep us focused on serving the client's financial planning needs.

Freedman Financial
Financial Planning Process

Setting Goals and Objectives
1. Hold an initial client meeting
   - In office
   - Spouse must attend
2. Discover goals, successes, challenges
3. Fact review and exploration

Data Gathering
1. Collect data and verify information
   - Investment statements
   - Insurance endorsement pages
   - Tax returns
   - Pay stubs
   - Benefits booklets
   - Estate planning documents
   - Deeds to property
   - Mortgage agreement(s)
   - Liability statements
   - Other
2. Enter data into software
3. Prepare list of unanswered questions to review with client
4. Produce net worth statement and verify with client

Analyze the Data
1. Analyze data within planning software
2. Build set allocation style boxes by ownership
3. Examine pay stubs, tax returns, estate documents, insurance endorsement pages
4. Analyze investment accounts, explore cost basis, fees, expenses, etc.

5. Review debt, confirm payment terms
6. Communicate with related professionals for clarification, if needed
7. Convey unanswered questions to client

Structure Recommendations
1. Begin structuring pieces of executive summary
2. Build what if scenarios
3. Compile analyses that support the strategy
4. Prepare recommendations
5. Write summary letter for client
6. Finalize analyses and produce for booklet
7. Build implementation schedule
8. Prepare agenda for presentation meeting

Implementation
1. Review implementation schedule
2. Offer actual strategies for implementation

Review and Update
1. Determine scheduling for updates to and review of financial plan

In the next few chapters, we will examine each of the above sections in detail. We will start with data collection, because Section 2 talked at length about how to help clients explore their goals and objectives. I discussed the importance of asking questions and seeking as much as you can from the answers. Here are a few reminders from Chapter 7 that we discussed regarding interviewing your clients about their financial planning needs.

1. Find common ground and connections between you and your client

2. Spend more time on qualitative than quantitative data
3. Listen to what prompted them to visit you:
   - Why do they think that *now* is the right time to consult with you?
   - What experiences have they had with other financial professionals?
4. Ask how they have handled money in the past
5. Describe your process and how it is delivered to the client

As you consider how you will begin to construct a financial plan that serves your clients' needs, I'd encourage you to always keep the formula for financial planning handy. Your plan should be a customized creation that honors the components of the formula. If it does, I am certain that your clients will be grateful for your diligence in preparing a plan that serves their personal planning needs.

SUMMARY
1. The mass affluent marketplace needs your help with financial planning.
2. As the firm's financial planner, make sure that your primary role is to oversee financial planning.
3. Leave the mechanics of developing a plan to your staff.
4. Write an outline of your firm's process for preparing financial plans.
5. Incorporate the theory surrounding the formula for financial planning as you develop your plans.

10 Data Collection and Review

Highlight ideas on how advisers can gather the best possible data from their clients to build powerful financial plans.

1. Collect data and verify information
2. Enter data into software
3. Produce and verify net worth statement with client

FREEZE FRAME

Collect Data and Verify Information

Every financial plan, no matter the goal or scope of engagement, must start with a comprehensive look at a client's financial well being. Generally referred to as net worth and cash flow statements, these documents can become the glasses in a world that appears ever so fuzzy to a client. If clients are reluctant to share their entire financial situation with you, I would argue that they are simply not ready for financial planning. In my experience, I have found that mass affluent clients are willing to tell you their whole story. They simply need a patient, sincere individual willing to respect their insecurities about money and deliver a tool to help them organize their thoughts.

As I mentioned earlier, all clients in our office receive our disclosure kit prior to visiting our office. That kit includes our fact-finder, which we strongly encourage clients to complete prior to a meeting. In addition, we ask that they bring copies of supporting documentation with them. The introductory letter "How to pre-pare for a client meeting" that is included in our disclosure kit has offered great clarity to them.

Interested prospects will do what you ask of them—just ask them to do it! When you can convey the processes your office honors for every client you serve, prospects who are interested in working with you (as opposed to those who are just testing the market) will come prepared. In fact, if they've been negligent in totally completing the fact finder, we find that they actually express embarrassment that they haven't arrived fully prepared for a meeting with us. They know that if they aren't willing to expose themselves, they can't receive the best guidance from you.

SHOW ME—DON'T TELL ME

Your planning relationship should never be based solely on what clients tell you, but what they show you and what you can confirm. That's right. If all clients do is recite their net worth to you, or simply jots down a few numbers in your fact finder, beware. Always insist on copies of documentation that support every asset and liability. You owe it to yourself as a planner to build a plan based on facts rather than "I believe." Your client owes it to you if they expect a quality financial planning analysis—after all, garbage in always results in garbage out. For instance, we often find that people have established relationships with a previous investment adviser. While they might tell us that they have $300,000 in a brokerage account, it isn't until we see the statement that we can better understand:

1. Overall asset allocation of the portfolio
2. Which share classes were used to buy the investments
3. What typical trading activity occurs within the account
4. What, if any, fees are being charges to the client
5. Whether the client adds money or writes checks on the account

We often find that clients have a collection of funds in their brokerage portfolio consisting of a mish mash of share classes. A great intuitive question to ask of your client when you notice this is, "It appears that your portfolio consists of a diversified collection of mutual funds. I find it curious that your funds were purchased with different share classes. Can you help me understand why Class A shares were purchased for the XYZ fund, Class C shares were purchased for the OPQ Fund, and M shares were purchased for the FDR Fund?" You will certainly learn more about the relationship your prospect holds with his current investment adviser.

You might also explore the following questions with them.

1. What is your understanding of how your current investment adviser is compensated?
2. How are decisions made concerning investments used in your portfolio?
3. Do you receive any performance reporting on this portfolio?
4. What was the best advice your current investment professional offered to you?

Finally, and I believe this is a critical question to ask during the data collection period, especially when your prospect has reached out to meet with you.

"I'm curious, are you also interviewing your current investment professional for financial planning advice?" Generally the answers that will come from this question will give you a clearer understanding of the services that had been delivered to the client in the past. You now have the opportunity to expand his or her understanding of your services and let them know how the investment advisory component that you can offer them is a piece in the financial planning pie—rather than the pie that offers financial planning services too.

Once a client has agreed to engage your firm as a financial planner, your first quantitative responsibility should be the comprehensive development of a net worth statement and basic cash flow statement. This means gathering copies of current statements (within the last 90 days).

These items would include:

- Bank statements
  - Checking
  - Savings
  - Money market
- Investment statements
  - Personal investments
  - Copies of personally held stock certificates
  - Retirement accounts
  - Employer-sponsored retirement program
  - Etc.
- Insurance endorsement pages
  - Life, disability, long-term care
  - Auto, homeowners, umbrella coverage
- Tax returns
  - The most recently completed one—the past two years is even better
- Pay stubs
  - At least three months

- Employee benefits booklets and current statements
  - You need to understand the benefits offered to your client.
- Deeds to property
  - This will be a confirmation of ownership.
- Mortgage agreement(s)
  - Terms
  - Principal and interest
  - Due date
- Liability statements
  - Terms
  - Principal and interest
  - Due date
- Estate planning documents
  - Wills
  - Trusts
  - Powers of attorney
  - Health care proxies
  - Etc.

During the first stages of building the net worth statement you want to be sure that you pay particular attention to the actual registration on each account. Here are a few hints on things to look for:

- Is your client the only owner on the account? Too often, when clients simply tell you about their accounts rather than show you statements, they inadvertently forget how the actual registration on each account reads. If estate planning is part of your client's objective, accurately indentifying registrations will be a key component of your plan.
- Do any accounts include maiden names? Be sure maiden names, middle initials, and suffixes are indicated on your net worth statement. If your recommendations include combining account registrations, having access to "one in the same" letters and/

or marriage certificates may be a necessary piece of advice to
include in your recommendations.

- Are children listed in custodial accounts now of majority age?
You might make a note about sharing with your client how easily
accessible custodial accounts might be to children of majority
age if they learn that these accounts exist. It will likely lead to an
open conversation about how your client may want to educate
their children about money. Don't be surprised to learn that your
clients of majority age still own assets in custodial accounts that
their parents purchased decades ago. Help them to change the
registrations to their individual name.
- What is the titling on each asset? JTWROS, Tenants-in-common,
SEP IRA, SIMPLE IRA, trust, etc. As you build a net worth
statement, be sure that you categorize each asset by its proper
registration and tax category. Different rules apply to each registration. You want to be certain that your advice contains specific
thoughts for each account, rather than generalizations that may
not apply to each account.

A few other items of note:

- Many financial institutions and brokerage firms are now offering "household statements." As you examine these statements,
be sure that you read beyond the consolidated cover sheets and
dig into each sub-account. Separate each account appropriately
by ownership.
- Clients are generally unsure of cash values on insurance policies, cost basis of investments, and withholdings on their pay
stubs. They are also usually uncertain of company matches and
profit-sharing contributions, available employee-related benefits, and interest rates earned on bank accounts. All of these
pieces of information need to be collected to build an effective
financial snapshot.

We insist that, in addition to a client signing our financial planning contract (see appendix) all clients must also sign an authorization for information form (see appendix). Accompanied with a cover letter, we use this authorization to request data that a client has difficulty obtaining or to gather answers to questions the client simply doesn't know to ask. I've found that human resource offices, accounting firms, and law offices are exceedingly accommodating about providing this information when you have an authorization for information signed and dated by your client. In my experience, the most difficult institutions to gather current data from are insurance companies. Generally, even when we send our authorization, they still insist on sending the data directly to the client and will not speak with us over the phone. We've even gone to great lengths and had clients sign a personal letter to the company insisting that they speak with us, but policy prevents the insurance companies from talking with us. This does slow down the planning process, but it's also nice to know that client privacy and security is honored.

The other industry that's interesting to talk with is the investment world. Many large mutual fund companies require you to pay a fee to obtain cost basis info for clients who purchased funds prior to the mid 1990s. Information is provided at a cost of about $25 per year, per fund, because these firms are willing to obtain the data for you, but they need to dig into their archives and produce year-end statements from microfiche. Gathering cost basis is much easier for clients who purchased investments within the past 15 years, but long-term investors can often bear a costly burden if they neglect to truly capture cost basis. If you find that you will need to research cost basis for your client, be sure that you inform them of the out-of-pocket costs involved and incorporate them into your financial planning fee.

Assisting your client in gathering cost basis for investments is a task that you should take seriously as part of the initial financial planning process. Done correctly, it establishes a layer of confidence in your commitment to effectively serving the needs of your client and it makes your role as a planner easier when it comes to the advice and recommendation phase of your analysis.

Most of the data collection process can be handled by your administrative team, but be careful—employees feeling pressure to complete a task, or those who find it difficult to obtain information can produce uncomfortable results.

FIXING PROBLEMS

In the mid-1990s, we had a client service specialist named Donna. It was her job to prepare paperwork for clients, update their accounts for reviews, and support the planners during the analysis process. One of our new clients, a woman in her late 70s, had a personal portfolio with about 25 individual stocks. She did not know the cost basis for any of the securities, but was certain that she had bought them from the broker many years ago. While it is our normal course of action to send an authorization for information form signed by the client (which we had) to the registered representative, Donna chose to take a different path. Instead, with Social Security number and date of birth in hand, Donna spoke with the broker's assistant to request the information and impersonated our client. While the assistant readily provided Donna with the information she needed, we later learned of Donna's inappropriate (let alone illegal) activity.

It just so happened that the broker on the account had been one of our largest client's next-door neighbors when they were both kids. Mrs. Carter was this client's mother—who of course had met this (soon to be) broker several times while her kids were growing up. It seems that after the boys graduated college and headed into their own careers, our client's mother elected to hire the nice young boy from the old neighborhood and use him as her stockbroker. Upon hearing from his assistant that Mrs. Carter had called the office, the broker found it strange that she hadn't called to speak with him directly. In fact, Mrs. Carter hadn't called in about five years, but they still had a cordial relationship and periodically saw one another over the holidays.

Later that week, we received a call from Mrs. Carter's son. He was furious about what had happened and questioned the integrity of our firm. Needless to say, Donna was fired on the spot. We were fortunate this time, because our relationship with the Carter family has blossomed to one that now includes four generations of families, but, nevertheless, it was a mistake that will never be made again. No matter how hard we try to do what's best for our clients, sometimes it seems easier to skirt the straight, and sadly, more time-consuming approach. As deadlines approach or the end of the day nears, we sometimes feel pressure to find a quick response. Yet deadlines and pressure are the best tests of your firm's integrity— never let them convince you to break the rules.

Produce and Verify Net Worth Statement with Client

Once you have entered all of the client's data into your financial planning software, spreadsheet, or yellow pad, it is important that you produce a user-friendly, easy to read, net worth statement. This document (no more than two pages), should list all of your client's accounts *by ownership*. It should also separate each account by sub-categories, such as investment assets, retirement assets, personal assets, long-term debt, etc.

Before you begin crunching the numbers, we recommend sharing the net worth statement with your client to be sure that you've captured all of their information accurately. In fact, insist that they sign off on the document. This gives you added assurance that the planning analysis is based on data that the client agrees is true and accurate. In addition, it provides him or her with a clear life snapshot, and the opportunity to provide you with any feedback, changes, and/or omissions before you begin the analysis. You need not provide all of the sub-securities data for each account at this

point. All you want to show your client is that you've captured an
overview of net worth, not the details that support it. You'll get to
the details in the analysis phase of the plan.

Data collection is an exceptionally important first step in any
financial plan. By having accurate information in an easy to read
format, you can now begin the analysis phase of your planning.

SUMMARY:

1. Every financial plan must begin with the creation of a net
   worth and cash flow statement.
2. You should rely on actual statements and not a client's rec-
   ollection when preparing financial statements.
3. Capture as much detail as possible when gathering the data.
4. Produce a financial statement for your client's review before
   advancing to the analysis phase.

11 | *Analysis Like No Other*

OBJECTIVES

1. Provide steps needed to properly analyze a client's financial situation
2. Offer practical ideas and examples
3. Discuss the importance of digging deep into the data

HOW YOU CAN HELP THE MASS AFFLUENT TRULY APPRECIATE THE VALUE OF FINANCIAL PLANNING

There are multitudes of financial planning tools, as well as spreadsheets, yellow pads, and specialized software to help crunch numbers. Whether you choose to rely on one system or integrate a multitude of systems into your practice is up to you. What's most important is that you never rely on results until you've used your own eyes to examine the details. Asking someone else to write a plan for you may meet the efficiencies of your office, but neglecting to scrutinize the findings and the data prior to presenting it to a client is a costly error that could cost you a long-term client. We are all fallible. Neglecting to enter an inflation assumption correctly or forgetting to stop a stream of cash flow when you know it has a specific maturity date can severely misrepresent your planning outcomes. Finally, you should always have audited supporting data, if needed. Most clients would prefer that you get to the point rather than bury them in analysis, but they need to know you have access to the data that support your findings.

PREPARING TO ANALYZE YOUR CLIENT'S FINANCIAL SITUATION

You should always start your analysis with a fresh recap of your initial meeting notes and memos. It is likely that more than a couple of weeks have passed since your first meeting and your client will recall much more of the first conversation than you will. Try to break your analysis down into the following groups:

1. Re-examine and add definition to the goals
2. Establish assumption parameters
3. Examine cash flow and tax implications
4. Determine whether resources align with a particular goal
5. Create asset allocation snapshots for each account
6. Separate qualified accounts from non-qualified accounts
7. Gather cost basis for all taxable accounts
8. Develop a snapshot for each insurance policy
9. Craft insurance and risk management scenarios
10. Review and comment on estate planning documents
11. Identify miscellaneous findings
12. List points of vulnerability
13. Begin writing the outline for your financial plan

Of course, there are several points of sub-analysis that are unique to each client's situation. We'll briefly comment on each area, but remember that every client's situation is unique and should be addressed with emphasis on areas of importance in their lives.

1. Re-examine and add definition to the goals.

By the time you reach the analysis phase, you should have a strong sense for your client's hopes and dreams. In most cases, your client shared goals such as retirement, paying for their children's educations, funding a wedding, buying a boat, or purchasing a second home. Make sure that you have crystallized the details of these goals as clearly as possible during your initial meetings with a client and that you have notes that support these details.

If at any time you feel as though you don't have enough information regarding their goals, stop your analysis immediately. Never assume (or guess about) the specifics surrounding a client's goal. Take a few minutes to pick up the phone, drop an e-mail, or schedule a subsequent meeting, if needed. You'll be so glad that you clarified the issue, and your client will be impressed that you cared enough to ask more questions. No matter where you are in your relationship with a client, continue asking why or making the statement "Tell me more about…"

You'll be surprised that your clients have some preconceived visions of their goals—certainly the single-expense items. If the goal is a single expense such as a boat, car, wedding, etc., try gathering answers to the following questions:

- Tell me more about your dream boat. What color is it? What size? How many people would it seat? Where would you go? Where would you dock it?
- In thinking about paying for a wedding, what are some of the "gotta haves" versus "wish I could haves?" Have you given any thought what it would cost to fund either of these?
- Have you already earmarked money to begin funding this purchase?
- How would you anticipate paying for this item? Cash, financing, etc.?

When it comes to funding retirement (or lifestyle issues), you'll want to gather answers to questions such as:

- What does your ideal vision of retirement look like?
- What would need to happen for you to say "We've made it"?
- In today's dollars, how much money each month would you anticipate spending to cover fixed expenses?
- How much would you need each month for discretionary expenses such as vacations, recreation, entertainment, and other leisure and social activities?
- Have you envisioned a certain amount of money you'd need to ensure your retirement goal is secured? (Often, people have a magic number in mind, and it's important that you understand this.) As a financial planner, seek wisdom from the answers to this question and focus on the macro issues that will better align their resources with their goals.
- What are three "gotta do's" in retirement, no matter the cost? How much would it cost to do them?
- In what year(s) might you and your spouse retire?
- What does it mean to retire? Could you describe a picture of what you hope your retirement might look like?
- How much of your income during retirement might come from employment? For how many years do you anticipate working?
- Are there any significant expenses that are likely to escalate or disappear in the years ahead?
- How would you describe your desire to be on track to fulfill your retirement goals relative to meeting your previously stated one-time large expense goals?
- How often do you purchase vehicles? How much do you usually pay? What pattern should be projected in our analysis?

This is far from an exhaustive list. Hopefully these questions have sparked your thinking about additional questions to ask of your client.

While they are fresh in your mind, go ahead and jot down three more questions.

1. _____

2. _____

3. _____

You run a great risk if you agree to build a retirement income plan for a client who provides cursory data, such as "I want to retire at 65. You tell me how much I need and whether I've put enough money away."

Let me share a story that stresses the importance of continuing to understand a client's goals.

Client Story—Mr. Atlantic
When we met with Mr. Atlantic in 1994, he clearly expressed that he had one goal for his $600,000 investment portfolio. "I want to have $1 million by the time I am 60 years old." He was 52. On November 16, 1999, on the heels of a strong bull market, I happily called him to let him know that his financial goal had been achieved *three years earlier than anticipated.*

"Mr. Atlantic, I wanted to be the first to let you know that your collective accounts with our office have reached $1 million."

Mr. Atlantic's response shouldn't have surprised me because I soon realized that I hadn't checked in with him in awhile, to see if it was still his goal. I suspect the "good times" mentality of the bull market periodically distracted planners from revisiting goals. "Since you were able to reach $1 million by 1999, what do you say we go for $2 million over the next five years?" asked Mr. Atlantic.

Because I neglected to revisit his goals and align them with his money, he saw the growth of his portfolio as a game and not something he needed to preserve. When I asked him why having $2 million was so important to him, his response to me was "Why not? Can you ever have enough money?"

The financial plan we had crafted for him suggested that, with modest growth, his retirement years could easily be financed through his investments and his other sources of income. We assumed that, now that he had achieved his numeric goal, we could limit the volatility in the portfolio, rather than risk further market gyrations. He didn't see it that way, and he soon moved his account to a stockbroker who expressed an interest in helping him achieve his goal.

Fast forward to 2003. As we approached the tail end of a painful bear market, our phone rang, and once again, Mr. Atlantic was on the other end of the line. He started our conversation with a calm and even tone. But as he began to tell us the story about why he was calling, he grew more agitated and erratic over the phone. We learned that he had been through two minor heart attacks and had moved his account to three different stockbrokers, and each one of them had helped lose money in his accounts. In fact, he was planning on taking two of them to arbitration.

So why was he calling us today? He had a new goal in mind. He wanted to have $1 million in his portfolio before he turned 65. We judiciously decided to pass on his request. Instead we encouraged him to revisit our office for a financial planning discussion. He declined. He said he was looking for someone to help him grow his money back to where it once stood. He didn't want to talk about financial planning goals; he wanted a magic elixir that would make everything better, and the only possibility to do that, in his mind, was rebuilding his portfolio to $1 million.

Mr. Atlantic is a great example of how important it is not only to dig deeper into a client's goals initially, but remain diligent about revisiting what's most important in your client's life each time you meet with them. As we all know, life changes, and so do the expectations of our clients.

2. Establish assumption parameters.

Your office should maintain a list of assumption parameters that serve as the global default for every plan you build. When you select your defaults, I strongly encourage you to err on the side of being conservative. Assumptions on inflation, portfolio growth rates, cost of education, and capital gain tax rates should all start from the same baseline. If you feel it's necessary to tweak the assumptions, be certain that you maintain clear notes about which assumptions you changed and why. If you don't, you'll forget why you made them. When you look back at a financial plan from a few years ago, you'll want an understanding of the framework you built when constructing the plan.

Academics and engineer-types enjoy researching, projecting, and hypothesizing over variables and statistics. They find success when they can mathematically justify the rationale and baselines for constructing research and generally rely on finite theories that support their answers. Unfortunately, the world of financial planning can't effectively operate when "exactness" is the outcome required to solve a problem. The profession of financial planning needs to pay equal attention to both the scientific and artistic components of our clients' lives. Overestimating returns on investments and/or underestimating inflation, taxes, and medical costs have the potential to create even more unrealistic outcomes. As planners we need to be *very* comfortable with the fact that almost all long-term projections and forecasts we build for client plans will be virtually useless when real life is built into the equation. Life happens. Expenses rise and fall, and no matter how hard we try to predict changes in clients' lives, surprises will always occur. You, as a financial planner, must keep this reality top-of-mind with your clients. Honestly, engineers, academics, and statisticians hate this reality of planning. In their world, everything is an exact science, and if they err in their recommendations they risk compromising the integrity of their work, and possibly losing their jobs. Never let your client believe that financial planning is an exact science. It is a fluid process that requires continual change and review through the journey toward your client's goal. It is absolutely imperative that your client hears you state this reality and that you don't bury this fact in an investment policy statement or a financial planning contract.

If your client is asking for a projection that extends longer than 20 years, be very, very cautious. While Monte Carlo scenarios and regression analysis will propose an array of possibilities for investment portfolios, the likelihood of your client's spending and/or savings pattern remaining the same is highly unlikely. Remember to always err on the side of conservative assumptions; after all, you can always change them if needed.

3. Examine cash flow and tax implications.

If there is one skill that I think financial planners need to hone more than any other, it is their understanding of how cash flow and tax planning advice can cement a relationship with their client. Below, I'd like to discuss several ideas that mass affluent clients find remarkably revealing. Your advice in this area, alone, is generally worth the financial planning fee they pay you. We have found that, in most mass affluent cases, we can find savings or offer ideas that more than cover the cost they paid for the plan. Clients will understand how financial planning services are different from investment advice when you commit yourself to spend time analyzing your client's cash flow and tax planning issues. Honestly, they can't wait to hear about the mysteries in their financial lives that you will help them uncover.

Reviewing bank statements
Take the time to examine your client's use of money. Dig hard and be curious. In the end, your client will appreciate you for taking the extra step. In my opinion, this is one area where many planners miss a golden opportunity to connect with their clients and give them some advice they will value forever.

Too many clients come to our office asking, "Please, help me get my financial house in order." This doesn't mean that they are buried in debt; more often it is an indication that your clients simply don't know where money is going and what money they have. Often, the best thing we can do is provide tools that will help them examine how money is spent. I'm not talking about examining whether they buy Green Giant green beans or the local supermarket brand, but that, to help our clients to begin building a perspective around fulfilling their goals, we need to enlighten them to their spending habits and history.

One of the best ways to assess a client's spending pattern is to ask how many bank accounts he or she uses to pay expenses. In most cases, you will find that either one or two accounts pay most, if not all of the household and personal bills. In addition, ATM card spending is generally captured in these statements. At our firm, we insist that our clients provide us with at least six months of bank statements that we can review during the analysis phase of our plan. Even if clients don't save their statements, they are now readily accessible online. Furthermore, if needed, this can be a wonderful way to introduce your clients to account access over the Internet, by simply showing them how to establish a username and password through the bank's site.

With bank statements in hand, you need not analyze every detail of each statement. Instead, build a simple spreadsheet that lists "total deposits" and "total withdrawals" from the front page of each monthly statement.

In most cases, this will give you a clear picture of your client's average monthly spending need. It will also raise your client's awareness of how much money moves in and out of his or her household each month.

All Checking Accts.	Total Deposits	Total Withdrawals	Net Cash Flow
June			
July			
August			
September			
October			
November			
Totals			

THE EVER-PRESENT LARGE PURCHASE

We all know that there are times in our lives when large purchases, unexpected expenses, periodic bonuses, and surprise windfalls of money come into our lives. When you see those numbers, bring them to your clients' attention, but remind them that there will always be unexpected expenses each year. Try to identify which ones are truly unique and others that are likely to recur. We have found that, by using the bank statement assessment test, we can help clients smooth out the hills and valleys of cash flow and help them better predict their normal spending patterns.

MARGINAL TAX RATES VS. AVERAGE TAX RATES

A fact finder is an important tool that helps clients begin to organize their thoughts. Usually they include questions like, "If you were to retire today, how much monthly income, in today's dollars, would you need to provide for the lifestyle you want?" In most cases, clients don't have an answer to this incredibly important question, and it's not worth guessing, using a rule of thumb, or asking leading questions that might settle them into a monthly number that's not nearly accurate.

However, when clients take the time to really explore their living expenses and examine how much money they might need for retirement, they typically provide you with a gross, and not a net, spending number. The gross spending number probably includes a formula that adds an assumed tax rate to their annual spending amount. They probably overestimated the amount of money they allocated towards paying income taxes. Rarely do consumers understand marginal rates, or the effect that deductions from Schedule A, personal exemptions, and others have on the actual average tax rate they pay each year. They generally determine their tax brackets by adding up their combined salaried income and looking to a tax chart that posts the highest marginal tax rate that's required to be paid on their earnings. From our experience, most mass affluent clients (especially those in the retirement phase of their lives) pay an average combined federal and state tax rate between 13 and 23 percent on their adjusted gross income, but if you ask them, they think they are in the 28 or 31 percent bracket (and usually they are just referring to their federal tax). Clients will truly appreciate education about the difference between marginal tax rates and average tax rates.

ANALYZING THE PAYCHECK

During my first years in the business, one of the most valuable skills I learned was how to understand withholding and exemptions when calculating tax withholdings on a pay stub. In my opinion, this is one of the great mysteries to the average consumer, and an area where planners can provide guidance and leadership.

How many times have you been told by a client that the number of exemptions selected on the W-4 form (www.irs.gov/pub/irs-pdf/fw4.pdf?portlet=3) is directly correlated to the number of children they have? How about the misunderstanding that married couples can only select "married" on the W-4? Do you have clients who insist that proper tax management means receiving a sizable refund in April?

Publication 15 (www.irs.gov/pub/irs-pdf/p15.pdf) should be available to every financial planner as a means of helping a client understand the effect tax withholdings have on their earnings. Easily accessible online, this publication is a tool every planner should have in their arsenal to help a client maximize his or her take-home pay and balance taxes due with their other sources of income.

REVIEWING THE TAX RETURN. FINDING OUT WHAT'S MISSED.

There is so much to learn from a tax return. In my opinion, a proper financial plan can only be crafted after the planner has developed a historical perspective by reviewing a client's past few tax returns. Many mutual fund companies have prepared transparent overlay sheets that can help planners identify opportunities buried in a client's return. AIM Investments offers an overlay sheet that you can wrap around a client's tax return. It introduces a collection of questions and tips that help you discover areas of possible deficiencies in your client's tax planning.

There are numerous parts of a tax return that reveal secrets about a client. Here are just a few that you should be looking for each time you complete an analysis for a client.

The Social Security Number. Here's a simple one: did you know that Social Security numbers indicate the location in the country where someone either obtained their number or was born? Generally, if someone has a Social Security number beginning with a 0, you can assume that they were likely born or spent their childhood in the New England states. The lower the first three digits, the further east they were likely born. If a Social Security number starts with a 5, you're likely from the middle of the country and a 9 suggests you're from the West Coast.

Taxable Interest. Some clients will be surprised to learn that taxes are due on the reinvested interest they maintain in bank accounts. With interest on bank deposits hovering around the lowest rates in decades, the tax due on the interest may be negligible, but it's worth reviewing anyhow. However, many states offer favorable state tax treatment when dollars are deposited in their local banks. While some clients might favor dot-com certificates of deposit, they may be unaware that the tax liability on this investment could be greater than had they invested in a financial institution based in their state of residence. Share this with your clients.

Qualified Dividends vs. Ordinary Dividends. Under current tax law, qualified dividends are taxed at lower rates than ordinary dividends. We find that clients, especially ones who choose to prepare taxes on their own, misread the 1099s sent from financial institutions and double count the qualified dividends. Periodically, we see the qualified dividends included on the line reserved for ordinary dividends and then restated on the line reserved for qualified dividends.

Alimony Payments. Alimony payments from an ex-spouse are taxable to the recipient, child support payments are not. If dollars are listed in the alimony section line, consider this an opportunity to ask about previous marriages as well as what, if any, qualifiers could affect how your client might receive alimony in the future. Perhaps the amount of money is based on a percentage of the ex-spouse's earnings. If the ex-spouse sells real estate, for instance, it is likely that his or her income has fluctuated. How might that affect alimony payments? Also, what happens if the ex-spouse dies or becomes disabled? Are there protection mechanisms in place, such as insurance, to offer continued support to your client and/or the children?

Schedule A—Itemized Deductions. You can learn a tremendous amount about a client from Schedule A of their return. Here are a few things to look for:

1. Medical deductions—Medical costs are only deductible if they exceed 7.5 percent of a client's adjusted gross income; however, if medical costs are significant to your client, they are likely reported even if the deduction isn't used. This may be an opportunity to ask about your client's medical history. It may help you understand what, if any, challenges may lie ahead if you had considered a life, disability, or long-term

care insurance proposal for their consideration. It may also help you understand why premiums on existing insurance policies may be higher than normal.

2. Mortgage interest—The number one deduction a client will always mention is their mortgage interest deduction. If they have owned a home for many years though, the interest payments on their mortgage may not be as great as your client thinks. In fact, if their collective Schedule A deductions are less than the standard deduction (currently $10,900 for those who are married filing jointly), they may not be able to use the deductibility of their mortgage interest. You'd be surprised by how many people still believe their interest payments are deductible when they are not.

3. Charitable contributions—I have always found it interesting to see how clients elect to be charitably inclined. Generally, there is a statement near the back of their tax returns that details how much money they contributed to various charitable entities. It may also list "in kind" donations, such as a car, computer, or refrigerator they gave to a local nonprofit. Consider what questions you could ask during your next client meeting regarding their charitable interests and future plans in this area. As I mentioned in Section 1, we find that mass affluent clients see themselves as being more charitable to their children than they are toward not-for-profits. They do provide token contributions to an array of community non-profits, but they are generally not interested in significant charitable planning because they don't believe they have the financial resources to do so.

4. Unreimbursed business expenses—If clients receive professional services, such as tax, legal, and even financial planning advice, they may be able to aggregate these expenses and list them as unreimbursed business expenses on Schedule A. If these expenses collectively exceed 2 percent of their adjusted

gross income, the amount over 2 percent is a potential additional deduction they can use. Interestingly, investment advisory fees may also be included in the calculation if they are paid by the client. Commissions are not eligible to report as unreimbursed business expenses. In fact, mass affluent clients can often be in a position where the asset management fee they pay for advisory services allows them to use Schedule A, instead of relying on the standard deduction. For instance, assume your client has an adjusted gross income of $100,000. The following are eligible for itemization on Schedule A. However, the total itemized expenses are less than the standard deduction of $10,900.

State and Local Taxes	$1,500
Real Estate Taxes	$2,500
Mortgage Interest	$5,200
Charitable Contributions	$500
Unreimbursed Expenses—Tax preparation - $275 Financial planning service - $1,500 -multiply total by 2% then subtract from adjusted gross income	$0
Total Itemized Deductions	$9,700
Standard Deduction Allowed	$10,900 *(client uses standard deduction)*

Now let's assume that the following year, your client agrees to pay you 1.5 percent on advisory accounts he or she has placed under your management totaling $300,000. The estimated annual fee is $4,500.

State and Local Taxes	$1,500
Real Estate Taxes	$2,500
Mortgage Interest	$5,200
Charitable Contributions	$500
Unreimbursed Expenses—Tax preparation - $275 Investment advisory fee - $4,500 -multiply total by 2% then subtract from adjusted gross income	$2,775
Total Itemized Deductions	$12,475 *(Client uses itemized deductions)*
Standard Deduction Allowed	$11,000—est'd for 2009

By incorporating your fees as part of the unreimbursed business expense line, your client was able to take advantage of Schedule A. In addition, the 1.5 percent fee you charged your client actually cost him or her less, based on the ability to deduct a portion of the fee.

We find that more than 50 percent of our mass affluent clients use this section of Schedule A, and view it as a reduction on their asset management fee.

Schedule B—Interest and Dividends. This is a great schedule that will help you uncover assets that may have been inadvertently overlooked when you asked your clients to provide you with details pertaining to all of their investments. We find that many clients (especially those over 70) continue to hold securities in their safe deposit boxes or even in their underwear drawers. Yes, it is "old school," but it has become part of their lifestyle and it's important that you tread carefully when you explain why this may not be the safest way to hold onto stock certificates.

In addition, when a company issues a stock split, decides to merge with another company, or simply has a name change, clients often dismiss the large intimidating envelopes that appear in their mail and are often unaware that shares of stock have been deposited on their behalf with a transfer agent. All too often, we find that clients have both certificated shares as well as shares of stock where dividends are being reinvested at the transfer agent. Schedule B should give you an indication for whether there are interest- and dividend-paying securities and/or cash accounts that have not yet been disclosed to you.

Schedule D—Capital Gains. Always check Schedule D (Gains/Losses on Sales) to determine which parts of your client's reportable capital gains are a function of short- or long-term gains, as well as what percentage of the gains are reported due to capital gain distributions. We frequently see accountants advising clients to make quarterly estimated tax payments based on the tax liability they owed from last year. While that would make good sense, consider whether the advice to make larger estimated payments was possibly due to a one-time event. We all know that there are certain years when capital gain distributions play a more significant role in our client's tax liability than others.

There are so many little nuances that tell so much about clients through their tax returns. I'd encourage every financial planner to regularly polish up on their tax knowledge. You need not prepare taxes, but knowing how to uncover part of your client's story using this government document is a skill worth keeping current.

4. Determine whether resources align with a particular goal.
It's always important to understand whether a client has mentally assigned portions of money to a particular goal.
Client Story
I remember meeting with a couple in their 40s who, among other assets, held a $267,000 joint brokerage account. Over the course of the initial interview, we asked them, "Could you tell us how you were able to accumulate money in this account?"

We learned that this portfolio wasn't all theirs. They explained that a few years ago, the wife's mother gave her $85,000 to hold for her. In addition, three years ago, their 11-year-old son received a $60,000 inheritance. Rather than placing the money in a custodial plan or 529 college savings vehicle, they elected to keep the money bundled in their names so "they'd have a better chance to apply for financial aid."

While the clients had lumped all of the money into one joint account, they didn't have any way to measure and monitor the change in value of this portfolio and allocate it to the various "buckets" they had mentally designated.

In this case, we began our analysis by creating a simple spreadsheet that initially designated percentages of deposits to the total portfolio. This way, as money was drawn from the account or if growth enabled the account to increase over time, there would be a fair allocation to each of the buckets. Be certain that, as you review each asset, you determine whether each investment was specifically attached to one of the designated depositor's accounts. Your client may be mentally allocating the money differently from what you might assume.

Some would argue, "Why not simply set up three joint accounts and add a descriptor title to each one?" In many cases, that idea would work just fine, but in this instance, the client didn't want to separate the money. Instead, they wanted simplicity, efficiency, and as little mail as possible. However, the simple spreadsheet we developed more than adequately met their needs. When you, as a financial planner, can give a client the peace of mind and confidence that you will alleviate a burden by taking on the responsibility to organize and manage the "sub-accounts" on their behalf, you've earned a lifelong client.

PRIORITIZING THE GOAL

Earlier in the book we talked about the Greens. This couple came to our office after their planner died suddenly. While they were initially seeking someone to simply take over their accounts, they were excited about taking a more comprehensive approach with their overall finances. You may recall that one of the lessons we learned from them was that Patty's goals were significantly different from Paul's. In their case, it was clear that Paul's number one goal was to insure that there were adequate funds available for them to spend in retirement according to their pre-retirement habits. However, Patty's priority was to insure that her two children had the resources necessary to maintain a full life regardless of whether either earned a substantial living, married well, or elected to remain single forever. In fact, she admitted, much to Paul's dismay, that she would be willing to sacrifice her own lifestyle in retirement if it meant providing for her grown children.

So before you assume that you understand your clients' priorities on financial goals, it is important to get a clear picture from your clients and allow them to articulate their feelings as openly as possible. In many cases, if you ask the right questions, you will uncover secret priorities for the clients that they've been unwilling to explore on their own.

5. Create asset allocation snapshots for each account

There are hundreds of ways to show clients a snapshot of their investments. Vendors continue to try to upstage one another on who has the prettiest, most graphical, most technical report on the market. In the end, though, I think it all comes down to helping a client understand the positions they hold and how they relate to one another. After all, your initial analysis in financial planning is to help clients get a clear picture of their current financial position and identify any points of vulnerability that exist. This is not about creating a sales opportunity, it is about education and showcasing your firm's understanding of a client's overall risk exposure as it relates to fulfilling his or her financial plans.

Morningstar, Inc., continues to be a leading vendor in the world of mutual fund research and their style box has become a staple in each of their reports because it is an easy (yet not perfect) way to identify a mutual fund manager's investment style and get a general sense for the overall securities within the portfolio. At the same time, the use of "overlay" software has become more prevalent in the market. These programs help advisers identify what, if any, securities are held in more than one of the funds owned by a client. Years ago, clients sought mutual funds that exclusively held the elusive five star Morningstar rating. However, when clients used the star system as their benchmark for building portfolios, they found themselves diversified yet poorly allocated in the traditional sense of asset allocation theory. In many cases, clients would have all of their money in one corner of the style box.

Recognizing this dilemma, we attempted to build a one-page visual piece for our clients that showcased their current investment allocation. Below is an example from one such client:

Current Combined Retirement Portfolio Value $375,000 (approx.)							
STOCK & STOCK FUNDS 85%					BOND FUNDS & CASH 15%		
	VALUE	**BLEND**	**GROWTH**		**SHORT**	**INTERMED.**	**LONG**
LARGE CAP	Dodge and Cox Stock 15% TD Bank North 22% Fidelity Growth & Income 15%	Vanguard Inst. Index 500 12% Fidelity Spartan 500 Index 10% Fidelity Balanced Fund 11%		**HIGH**	Federated Capital Preservation 10%		Pimco Total Return Inst. 5%
MID-CAP				**MED**			
SMALL-CAP				**LOW**			

By simply showing clients how their portfolios are positioned inside style boxes, we can open their eyes to the extreme overlap within their portfolios. It creates an opening for dialogue surrounding risks and opportunities. The second style box report offers an asset allocation recommendation that highlights a possible growth with income model. Notice that investment names do not appear in the analysis. This allows the clients to implement a recommendation wherever they see fit, but have a resource to turn to if they want to invest on their own, or with a broker with whom they really don't want to reveal much about their financial life.

There are a great number of portfolio management programs that provide more detail, substance, and analysis, but for our mass affluent clients, we find that they appreciate pictures, stories, and simple graphics instead of complex analysis, audited reports, details, details, and more details. If you try to explain beta, alpha, efficient frontiers, and standard deviations to the mass affluent clients, they are likely to excuse themselves from the meeting to take calls on their non-ringing cell phones.

6. Separate Qualified Accounts from Non-Qualified Accounts

This may seem rather obvious, but too often, clients don't quite differentiate the rules governing taxable accounts vs. qualified accounts. Clients need to understand that Mary's IRA can't be merged with her husband Stuart's IRA, and that Roth IRAs must be kept separate from rollover IRAs. While we may take this information as given, quite often clients wonder about these issues, and it's your job to raise their awareness rather than let it fester for them.

It's also important to consider the tax implications involved with selecting securities within qualified and non-qualified accounts. Because much of our financial planning training is focused on just this topic, I won't spend much time on this issue except to remind you to consider asset dedication issues as well as asset allocation issues, when analyzing a client's portfolio. If you'd like to learn more on this subject, authors Stephen J. Huxley and J. Brent Burns wrote a white paper worth reading entitled "Asset Dedication: The Next Step in Asset Allocation?"[1]

7. Gather cost basis for all taxable accounts

Earlier in this book, we discussed the importance of gathering cost basis to help clients better understand the tax liability in the event they sold securities. Too often, advisers are quick to take over accounts and make portfolio decisions before understanding the tax liability of the positions held. I hear too many people in our business telling clients that cost basis is the clients' responsibility and that they should seek guidance from their accountant. If financial planning is to be a profession of relevance, we need to recognize that getting our hands dirty is equally valuable as providing advice. Sometimes, it will take effort to determine cost basis, and sometimes it's as simple as typing a date of a security into Big Charts (www.bigcharts.com.) Nevertheless, it's imprudent for us to deliver advice on our clients' investment portfolios without understanding what they paid for securities and/or explaining the implications for not including it on their statements.

BEATING THE COST BASIS SYSTEM—ILLEGALLY

A few years ago, I was surprised to learn about a strategy that was being used to solicit older clients into an adviser's practice. While the concept horrified me, clients were convinced it was a way to "beat the system," and from what I can tell, only one's conscience would trigger a red flag. Here's the story.

So often, we find that people, typically those born before 1940, insist on gathering stock certificates and holding them in a safe deposit box. For years, they continue to receive dividends to their mailbox, or simply know that the securities they hold have accumulated to such a great value that selling them would be too costly. Thus, many people elect to die with the stock and simply pass it on to the next generation. What if, however, you could suggest to clients that they could deposit the certificated shares of stock into a brokerage account and that they could sell the stock for little to no gain? Illegal? Yes. Common? Unfortunately, also yes. You see, when securities are bought, collected, and deposited into a brokerage account, the cost basis that appears on the statement is generally "N/A" (not applicable). It's the shareholders' responsibility to maintain cost basis information. But what if they never bothered to keep their records in order? It is my understanding that prior to 1980 (and probably later than that) the IRS didn't have a well maintained electronic gathering and reporting system for cost basis information. Thus, it was up to the shareholder to determine the cost. As companies have changed names, merged, split up, and reconvened, the cost basis on these securities has become virtually impossible to gather. Have you ever tried to recreate cost basis for a client who owned AT&T shares and all of the subsequent baby Bell stocks?

Fortunately, most brokerage offices now allow for the adviser to input share lots and basis cost into their software systems so that records can be maintained and accessible. But here's where the illegal activity occurs. Imagine for a moment that your client tells you that her father purchased shares of American Safety Razor for her in the early 1950s. This stock is now Phillip Morris (which has been changed again to Altria Group). Your client doesn't have cost basis, because the father has since passed away, and your client has always insisted on receiving certificated shares of any splits and mergers because, as she says, "that's the way my father taught me." Now all of her certificates are held in the safe deposit box. Even with this cursory information, most planners could take an educated approach to recreate cost basis for a client. However, with the opportunity to manually enter cost basis onto a client's brokerage statement, we witness advisers posting cost basis on shares that would suggest they purchased the securities just more than a year ago. Thus, when the securities are sold, the client pays a minimal capital gains tax. The adviser now has proceeds for alternative purchases. The client is happy and together they have (illegally) beaten the system. The adviser looks like a hero and has created an opportunity to make money.

As I said, I'm not proud this strategy exists in our business, but I assure you that it's part of what you compete against each day. Do whatever you can to build the proper cost basis for your client. I believe that the IRS will look favorably on you if you can show a best effort and a reasonable justification for the basis you developed. Be sure you put your work in writing, and that it is easily accessible in the event you need to provide it. But more than anything else, keep your integrity intact and explain to the client why you've taken the best approach you could, versus one that could potentially slide under the radar screen.

8. Develop a snapshot for each insurance policy

We find that very few clients understand what insurance coverage they currently hold and whether the coverage they have is even appropriate. An insurance analysis should start with an assessment of each policy. You should ask your clients to provide the endorsement page for all of their coverage; however, in most cases, all the relevant data aren't easily accessible. Typically, you will need to send a letter to each of the insurance companies along with an authorization for information (see appendix) requesting the following pieces of information.

Letter signed by client to request additional information on insurance policy

---

< Date >

Re: Policy No.(s): < Insert Policy Number(s) >

Dear < Insurance Company Name >

I am currently reviewing my life insurance coverage and I am requesting the following information on policy number(s) < Insert Policy Number(s) > as of < Date >
- Current owners/insureds
- Current beneficiaries
- Policy cost basis

- Current policy summary including cash surrender values
- Death benefit
- Taxable gain to date

I am also requesting an in-force policy ledger for policy number(s) _____, showing all years to age 100, on both a present and guaranteed assumption basis. Please assume current interest rates, as well as mortality and expense rates in the future. In addition, you may assume current premium payments for the life of the policy.

Please accept my signature as authorization to provide the requested information. The attached Authorization for Information Form expresses my wishes that you provide any additional details needed on the above referenced policies to my financial adviser, _____. You may forward illustration to the financial adviser listed below:

Send to: Name: _____

Address: _____

_____

Fax:

E-mail:

Thank you for your prompt attention to this request.

Sincerely,

<Policy Holder Name>

Use this information to build a spreadsheet that helps clients clearly see the coverage they hold, who it protects, and what it is costing them.

One other thought on insurance. So often, we neglect to talk about automobile, homeowners, and personal liability coverage with our clients. To do comprehensive financial planning, it is important that these components are reviewed and addressed in your analysis. If you are uncomfortable offering advice on this coverage, seek a relationship with an independent agent in your area and ask them about what they believe are appropriate limits, deductibles, and features for clients who fall into certain demographic parameters. They will not only be happy to help you, but it's likely that you'll learn about an important segment of financial planning that you probably forgot after you took your insurance licensing exam.

9. Craft insurance and risk management scenarios

Many software programs allow you to produce capital needs analyses for clients; however, it is important that you talk with your clients about what would happen if they died today. Help couples to formalize their wishes in the event one of them died suddenly or they both died in a common accident. It is imperative that you control the assumptions that are built in any capital needs analysis. Computer models make too many assumptions. They simply establish defaults for costs of probate, burial costs, paying off the mortgage, funding education costs, and income replacement. Ask your client in advance so that your analysis is more meaningful and relevant to the conversations you've held with your client.

I've heard of stories where an adviser will ask a spouse to step out of the room during a discovery meeting, and once that spouse is outside, the adviser says, "Imagine what would happen if Roger (who just left the room), died. What would you do?" This, can lead to a wonderful dialogue and guide the client down a path of personal exploration they may have never pursued. You've just given them a launching point. They may not have an answer today, but it's fair to bet that the question will be the topic of conversation with them in the days to come.

10. Review and comment on estate planning documents

In general, financial planners are not attorneys, they are not qualified to prepare legal documents. But in your lifetime, you will likely read more wills and trusts than any of your clients. More importantly, you'll also observe the tremendous diversity and variety among the documents, because each attorney takes his or her own approach to crafting them. Many wills and trusts start as templates but are then customized to meet the needs of a client. I like to find attorneys who will prepare an executive summary of their work as a preface to the documents, because it's quite likely that clients will simply nod their heads when signing and initialing the encyclopedia-sized estate plan.

It is imperative that you request a copy of all of your clients' estate planning documents prior to building their financial plans. In many cases, you will learn about the wishes and desires that they simply didn't have time to share with you during a recent visit, but more importantly, you can find items they would never have identified. After all, how many times have you read your will after it was drafted?

Client Story—Dan and Elaine
After years of managing money on their own, primarily through the 403(b) program at the hospital where Dan had worked, Dan and Elaine thought it was time to establish a financial planning relationship, with the intent of having someone manage his $700,000 403(b) account and helping him determine whether they could sell their home and move to Florida full time. Dan was excited that we asked them to look at the big picture of their financial life first, which included our requirement to prepare a financial planning analysis. Dan felt that one of the things he had done right over the

past several years was meeting with an estate planning attorney in 2001 to establish wills for the two of them. After all, he said, with the health scares they've had recently, it offered peace of mind to know that their wishes had been captured.

As always, we completed a financial planning analysis and scheduled time for our presentation. A day or two before the meeting, we glanced again at the information they provided us to be sure that we had covered everything they requested.

The next day, Elaine and Dan arrived at our office for their financial planning presentation. Dan could tell from the look on my face that something was wrong. During our review of his will, we found something that sickened us because we knew the medical challenges they had faced over the past few years. We elected to start our meeting with a discussion of this topic, and once it was revealed, Dan grew so distraught that we couldn't proceed with our presentation and agreed to meet later next week.

During our review of Elaine's will, we noted that all of the typical wishes of a married couple with two grown children were noted. I think we assumed that Dan's will would hold the same wishes, and probably didn't review his documents until the day or two before our meeting.

The will was essentially blank. The template used by the attorney was never filled in; it simply had empty spaces for where the client's name, beneficiaries, etc. would appear. Yet, the client initialed each page and the attorney notarized the final page. After going through bouts of illness and family challenges, the one document Dan had ultimate confidence in just failed him. Their tears turned to anger, and clearly their heads weren't prepared for the continuation of our plan. Upon adjournment from our shortened meeting, Dan promptly headed to the attorney's office to remedy the situation. Needless to say, Dan is a client for life, and every day is grateful for the analysis work we included as part of his financial plan. He is also a great referral source to our office.

11. Identify miscellaneous findings

I think this part is the most fun in analyzing a client's situation. I'd encourage you to find three items that your client would view as "Geez, I never knew this." We've already talked about how you can analyze a pay stub, review a legal document, or identify overlap in a client's portfolio. Here are a few other items that your clients would surely appreciate:

- Check for beneficiary designations on all accounts
  - It is very common to see clients still listing their parents, ex-spouses, friends, etc., as beneficiaries. In many cases, clients may still have small insurance policies that were purchased by their parents years ago, or are held with a current employer. You'll be amazed at how few people remember to change these beneficiary designations.
  - Be sure to obtain beneficiary designations on all old retirement plans that a client has elected to leave with the previous employer. How would your client's second wife like to find out that her husband's old 401(k) plan still listed his first wife as primary beneficiary?
- Identify opportunities to discuss the value of transfer on death as a means of avoiding probate. So often clients ask about placing assets in trust to avoid probate. Use this as an opportunity to explain how the probate process works and that simply including TOD (transfer on death) to their personal investments may be all that's needed— rather than having to pay an attorney for a revocable trust.
- Review your client's benefits booklet from work and identify a program or opportunity available to them. Many health insurance programs offer a rebate for individuals who hold gymnasium memberships. Would your client like "free money?" Clients may also have the opportunity to purchase additional life insurance coverage at a rate that is significantly less than what's available on a retail basis. If your client has health concerns and

is likely to be rated, check to see if his current employer offers a group life and/or disability benefit that allows a guaranteed insurability enrollment period. Of course, you'll want to check on the portability of this coverage in the event your client is either laid off or seeks employment elsewhere.

12. Use software analysis functions

In addition to all of the unique analyses you will prepare for a client, the financial planning software systems that contain much of your client's data can produce fabulous graphical and statistical analysis on:

- Funding strategies
- Spending strategies
- Wealth accumulation projections
- Monte Carlo analyses
- And more

As I've said earlier, never present an analysis to a client unless you've audited the numbers that support it. Remember, often, projections are misrepresented because we were accidently negligent in adjusting an assumption, changing a time period, misrepresenting an investment rate of return, or a number of other variables. As a planner, talk through your analyses to yourself first, before you present them to clients for the first time. You don't want to get caught making a presentation that could misrepresent the client's goals and objectives.

13. Begin writing the outline for your financial plan

At long last, the initial analysis portion of your work is primarily complete and it's time to put it all together. The work you've done on behalf of your client is valuable and worthy of your time. In fact, after reviewing the analysis items, can you imagine that anyone would ever suggest that it should be offered for free?

While your work as a planner will be unique for each client, were you able to identify a series or thread that you could touch upon no matter the client's situation? Yes, there are a number of analysis elements that could be incorporated into a financial plan that haven't been included above. In fact, you'll notice that I purposely refrained from spending much time on how best to analyze investment portfolios. There are enough opinions on how to handle this area of analysis that one more person's ideas would be overkill.

I hope that you will use these tips and techniques as a foundation that helps you get started. Your analysis should be reflective of your skill sets and the needs of your clients. In the end, what matters most is that you create an analysis your client will understand and that you are proud to deliver as a member of the financial planning profession.

So take a breather. Reflect for a moment on what you've retained, because in the next chapter we're about to take all of the qualitative information you've gathered from your client and weave this into the data collection and analysis work you've done. It's time, finally, to write the financial plan.

SUMMARY

1. Pay close attention to the specific details of a client's data—assume nothing.
2. Hone your tax planning and cash flow skills. Your clients will be most appreciative.
3. Attempt to find hidden elements and surprise your clients with your findings.
4. Review all analyses in detail before including them in the presentation for your client.

ENDNOTE

[1] Available at www.assetdedication.com/Asset%20Dedication%20art%20one%20col%205_55_03.pdf

12 | *Writing Your Client's Financial Plan*

OBJECTIVES

OBJECTIVES
1. Discover elements needed to prepare an effective financial plan.
2. Discuss the importance of writing a plan vs. relying on artificial intelligence.
3. Offer ideas to consider when delivering a plan to a client.

If you've spent any reasonable amount of time in this business, you've undoubtedly come across one of those beautiful, leatherette-bound financial plans. These encyclopedia-sized reports generally include colorful charts, enticing graphs, and a masterful use of font-types and character spacing. Yet rarely is the document ever opened beyond the day on which it was delivered. The large financial institutions known for producing these impressive reports seek to out-colorize and more vividly present flowcharts, worksheets, rules of thumb, and

artificial intelligence (otherwise known as boilerplate). My father
often referred to this as "planning by the pound."

If I've learned anything in this business, it's that when it comes
time to share thoughts about financial planning, clients want you to:

1. Get to the point
2. Let them know what you've identified
3. Give them ideas about how to fix problems

The last thing clients want is too much information. That's right,
size doesn't matter. When there is too much to digest, it leads to
paralysis—the inability to make changes in one's financial life
because the planner has identified too many things that need
changing, and that's simply too complicated.

CREATING A PERSONAL FINANCIAL PLAN

Whenever you discuss financial planning or begin writing a plan, be
sure that you always state that financial planning is a fluid process
and it *will* require change throughout your clients' lives.

One thing about financial planning is certain—the minute you
place financial analysis in writing, the projections are almost guaranteed to miss the targets. Too many events change in our lives for
us to think that any projection beyond a couple of years will be realistic. Just think about what you were doing 10, 15, or 20 years ago.
Could you have ever predicted that your financial situation would
look like it does today? So, if you believe in the above statements,
why do we put analysis in writing for our clients? We do it because
our clients need a roadmap.

A financial plan serves as a guide to a path with frequent detours
along the way. As your client's planner, it is *your* job to keep that plan
alive and make sure that it is regularly reviewed. If it sits in the garage
collecting dust, the likelihood of achieving goals is the same as winning the lottery. This is why I find it incomprehensible that anyone

would consider building a retirement planning analysis for a 30- or 40-year-old that expresses how much money they will have accumulated over their lifetime. Isn't it fair to assume that any assumptions regarding savings, spending, earnings rates, inflation, and family status are bound to see changes over time? Shouldn't it be your job to help a client understand what it means to simply save for the future, rather than presenting a 20–40 year plan that's not likely to reflect the surprises that will occur in the next phases of his or her life?

When it is time to write a plan, remember to offer commentary that reflects your client's current financial situation. Prophesying on "what could be" places you in a risky position that could lead to unfounded conclusions. We live in a very litigious society. Thus, as you begin to offer advice in writing, be very careful about the words you choose. Be sure that your advice is clear, but be careful not to make guarantees. Use softer verbs like "may," "could," and "consider," rather than stronger verbs like "should," "will," and "commit," that express a level of certainty. As planners, we know that all too many things change in our clients' course of life. Your writing should reflect an understanding of this reality.

We have found that the best way to write a financial plan is to prepare an executive summary letter that is about three to six pages long. You should always consider "appreciative inquiry" as part of your writing style. Do your very best to avoid using negative language such as "can't" and "won't," and attempt to deliver statements with a positive perspective. For instance, let's assume a client is not saving enough money to fund his daughter's education cost. Which phraseology would sound better to you?

1. "It appears that you are currently under-funding your daughter's 529 plan. The monthly contributions of $200 are less than half of the monthly amount needed to fully fund this goal. Our attached analysis suggests that you won't be able to adequately fund your daughter's education costs.

Neglecting to increase your contributions will result in a funding shortfall and your daughter won't likely be able to attend the private university she had hoped."

-OR-

2. "During our last meeting, you indicated that providing the full cost of your daughter's education was important to you. You were smart to establish a 529 savings plan, since money deposited into this account will grow and be withdrawn tax-free, as long as it is used for qualified education costs. Automatically having money deposited each month into the 529 plan is a strategy that expresses your commitment to building an account for the future. We would recommend that you seek to increase your monthly contribution by at least 30 percent. The attached analysis shows how increasing your contributions will bring you closer to achieving your education funding goal. We believe your cash flow should be able to handle the increase."

Clearly, these are two different ways to present the same concept, and of course, there are a number of other possibilities.

When you start writing your plan, you should begin with a review of your client's stated goals and objectives. Try to use simple, easy-to-understand descriptors and be sure you explain your concepts concisely. Clients are not looking for "read between the lines" recommendations. They have hired you for honest, genuine advice, and it's your responsibility to place that advice, guidance, and continuing conversation points in written words they can understand.

We believe that the best way to write a plan is to keep it simple and concise. A summary letter often best suits your client's needs. We find that it is easiest to craft when it is written in letter form and covers a wide array of financial planning topics. This is your opportunity as a planner to place your findings in writing and create a snapshot of your client's current financial status with a glimpse of what changes are needed to fulfill his or her goals.

Your executive summary should include the following items:

1. A recap of your client's goals, and an indication that you are prepared to comment on them
2. A disclaimer-type reference to state that financial planning is a fluid process and requires continued monitoring to be effective
3. Commentary on the client's current financial snapshot
4. High-level comments on asset allocation and current investment portfolios
5. An introduction to funding and/or spending analyses which includes a listing of assumptions you've used in the analysis and a statement regarding your findings
6. Thoughts on existing personal insurance, such as homeowners, auto, umbrella, etc.
7. Comments as needed on life, disability, and long-term care needs
8. A brief review of existing estate planning documents and items to consider
9. A section addressing miscellaneous items that appeared during your analysis
10. A closing paragraph

Below are two summary letters for your review.

SAMPLE FINANCIAL PLANNING LETTERS

Mr. & Mrs. Peter Plan
5 NeedIt Street
Bymemore, MA 99099

Dear Patty & Peter,

It is our pleasure to have this opportunity today to present our initial findings regarding your financial plan.

During our initial consultation, we spent time identifying both your short- and long-term financial goals, and you stated that the following three goals were of primary importance to you:

- *Peter wishes to retire from full-time work at age 60*
- *Patty wishes to fully fund Michelle's education for at least five years of college*
- *Patty wishes to purchase an investment property in the greater Boston area that will eventually be passed to Michelle so that she will have a place to live upon graduating from college.*

During our meeting today we will:

1. *Continue a conversation on prioritizing your goals*
2. *Present scenarios and strategies that better align your resources with fulfilling your goals*
3. *Discuss both past and current cash flow so that we can better understand your use of money to support expenses both now and in the future*
4. *Offer perspective, analysis, and recommendations pertaining to your existing investments, annuity, and insurance portfolios*
5. *Provide you with actionable ideas*

Please remember that financial planning is a fluid process. Changes in spending habits, lifestyle, market conditions, inflation, and a number of other factors will likely affect ideas we will offer today. Unlike the science and precision of engineering, we believe that blending mathematics with emotions creates a more realistic model for our clients. With that in mind, we are pleased to present our initial findings.

Cash Flow Analysis
We have reviewed your tax return from 200X as well as your pay stubs from

200Y. We generally perform this exercise to craft an estimate of the cash flow coming into your household and available for spending and saving. In 200Y, it appears that Peter took home a net annual income of $126,870, after withdrawing taxes, Social Security, and the maximum $20,000 deferral into his 401(k). Other than the $50 monthly deposit into Patty's MFS account, it appears that the bulk of this money went to expenses.

In reviewing your W-2 from 200X, you showed a gross income of $127,000 after deferrals into the 401(k) plan along with federal taxes of $17,000 and state taxes of $8,000 for a net income of approximately $102,000. Thus, in 200Y, it appears that you had more than $2,000 per month in additional take-home pay beyond what was available in 200X.

During our last meeting, Peter indicated that a reduction in overtime wages will likely create a reduction in annual income from 200Y. Since we were unable to account for how your excess income from last year was used, we are concerned that you may need to dip into your savings to cover expenses in 200Z, or you may simply need to reduce your out-of-pocket costs.

Also, you indicated during our initial meeting that you expect to spend $75,000 after tax annually during retirement. This is significantly less than what you appear to be spending now. Although your daughter should no longer be dependent on you, there will still be mortgage payments of $11,456 annually for the first 19 years of retirement, and likely continued payments for an automobile, since one of your cars is leased. You may wish to further consider whether a $75,000 annual spending plan adequately addresses your needs for the retirement lifestyle you desire.

Planning for Emergencies

We recommend that you keep three to six months' living expenses in a highly liquid bank account as an emergency fund. Assuming a spending level today of $100,000 annually or $8,000 per month, you would want to bring your bank savings level up to at least $25,000 from the current $18,000. During our analysis we noticed that your Bank of America CD (which you've earmarked as emergency money) has been reduced to $18,000 from an initial reporting of $25,000. Have you pulled money *from this account to meet certain expenses? Do you have intentions of rebuilding this emergency fund in the near future?*

Retirement Income Analysis

One of your goals was to better understand your current status relating to your ability to fund your retirement needs. The following basic assumptions have been used for our projections:

- *Peter would retire from full-time employment at age 60 in 2013.*
- *Patty would retire in 2013 at age 59.*
- *Your anticipated annual after-tax spending needs would be $75,000 in today's dollars.*
- *Inflation would increase at 2.5 percent annually.*
- *Peter would continue to defer 10 percent of his salary to his 401(k) plan until age 60.*
- *You would begin collecting Social Security benefits at your respective age 62. Based on the benefits statements you provided, it appears that Peter's estimated benefit would be about $1,660 per month, and Patty's would likely be close to half of Peter's benefit (about $800).*
- *We are projecting an average annualized rate of return on all current investments at 6 percent.*
- *Our current planning horizon continues until Peter reaches age 92 and Patty reaches age 95.*
- *For the three years that Patty would be on her own, we anticipate that her spending needs would be equal to 80 percent of the joint need or $60,000 per year.*

Given the above assumptions, our analysis indicates that you may have difficulty achieving your stated retirement goal if it remains your objective to place equal priority on funding all three of the goals listed on page one.

If, however, we prioritize your goals and list retirement as the number one priority, our analysis suggests that you should achieve the retire-

ment spending goal, but it would be at the expense of being able to fully fund five years of education for Michelle and not having any ability to purchase the income property for your daughter. This suggests that now, more than ever, you need to understand how aligning resources towards certain goals will affect your ability to support other goals.

Of course, there are a variety of alternatives to consider that could help you improve the results above. Here are just a few:

1. **Remain in the full-time workforce longer.** *A major issue that you would face by retiring at age 60 would be obtaining adequate health care benefits for the family at a reasonable cost. This could significantly affect your ability to maintain your current lifestyle on $75,000 per year spending. Peter would have six years before Medicare would be available and Patty would have six and one half years.*
2. **Work part-time.** *Peter indicated that he would anticipate working part-time for five years after age 60. This would significantly improve your ability to meet your retirement spending goals.*
3. **Save more prior to retirement.** *The larger the amount that you have available prior to retirement, the longer it would last during your non-working years.*
4. **Reduce your desired spending level during retirement.** *Here again, you could stretch your funds over a longer period of time.*
5. **Obtain a higher rate of return on investments.** *We have used an estimate of 6 percent in our analysis. Of course a higher rate of return would improve your ability to meet your goals, but always remain aware of the additional risks inherent with assuming higher rates of return.*

Investments

Your investment portfolio contains a total of about $575,000 in mutual funds assets. The collection of investments breaks down in the following ownership (as reflected on your net worth statement):

$250,000 — Jointly owned
$25,000 — Patty's IRAs
$175,000 — Peter's IRAs
$125,000 — Peter's 401(k) plan

In total, you hold more than 50 individual mutual funds with MFS, AIM, Oppenheimer, Putnam, and American Funds. Your 401(k) plan assets are held in a single lifestyle fund managed by John Hancock, which has an asset allocation of 80 percent stock funds, 20 percent bond funds.

Apart from the relative merits of any one of these funds, owning more than 50 individual funds makes it extremely difficult to monitor the progress and annual returns, especially when you are collecting individual statements from each of the fund companies as your sole means of reviewing your portfolio.

From a big picture perspective, we would encourage you to review the style box illustrations that we've prepared for you (see attached). We have also included a recommended asset allocation for a growth portfolio along with the asset allocation of your current portfolio.

Overall, it appears that the volatility inherent in your portfolio is greater than the recommended allocation given your heavier weighting to stock funds and specifically to foreign markets. We have also included an in-depth analysis of your mutual funds which we are prepared to discuss if you so desire. It would, however, be our recommendation that we first focus on making sure that your personal goals are clear, and then we identify which resources to align with them, before worrying about which specific changes should be made to your investment portfolios.

Insurance—Life
We have prepared an insurance needs analysis in the event of your premature death (see attached). Since Peter is the primary earner, you have

expressed a priority for him to carry sufficient protection that provides an income stream to Patty for her lifetime in the case of his premature death. Our analysis indicates that Peter's current coverage of $800,000, along with the assets Patty would inherit, would provide an income stream equal to 80 percent of your current revenue to Patty throughout her lifetime. Since Patty is not bringing employment income into the household at this time, and there are no dependents remaining at home, our analysis suggests that there is no significant need for Patty to maintain life insurance.

Peter currently holds a $200,000 policy through his employer as well as a $500,000, 20-year level term life policy which is in its fifth year. These policies should be maintained, but be aware that when Peter chooses to retire, his company-owned policy for $200,000 would not be portable, and thus you may wish to consider whether Peter's term policy would provide the protection Patty needs. Our attached analysis features a variety of "what-if scenarios" that highlight the affect on your cash flow if Peter were to prematurely die in 2, 5, 10, and 15 years.

Disability
Peter has a long-term disability policy which is paid for through his employer. In the event that he became disabled, he would receive 60 percent of his salary up to a maximum benefit $5,000 per month, which would be subject to taxes. There is an initial 180-day elimination period, and the policy would pay until age 65 if he were not able to perform any occupation. At Peter's current age, we believe that this policy is adequate, and that no further changes should be made at this time. Your current resources would provide the supplemental income you might need in the event of his disability.

Homeowners/Auto/Umbrella
Your current homeowners coverage includes a value on your dwelling of $272,000, not including the value of the land. According to www.zillow.com, your home's total estimated value is about $500,000. You should contact your insurance agent to discuss whether your current

dwelling protection is adequate, particularly in light of the fluctuation in home values over the past few years.

We have reviewed both your $2 million umbrella policy and your individual auto insurance liability coverage. They appear adequate at the present time, however, you may consider contacting your insurance agent to discuss whether your insurance rates are competitively priced. It is our understanding that the state of Massachusetts is now allowing additional insurance companies to compete for your business. In the past, auto insurance was state mandated, and the costs were the same from all carriers.

Estate Planning

You have provided us with copies of your wills, health care proxies, and powers of attorney, and we have reviewed them. These documents were executed in 200X and are very straightforward. You should certainly review them periodically, especially if your situation changes and updates are needed.

Under current federal law, in 200X, each individual is allowed to pass on $2 million to their heirs free of federal estate tax. This amount is scheduled to increase through 2010. These laws have been in flux and it is an area that we are carefully monitoring for our clients. At the current time, your estate would not be subject to federal estate tax.

The above and attached represent our initial findings and recommendations relating to the information you have provided. As we indicated above, financial planning is not a science—rather, it is a fluid activity that requires adjustment throughout one's financial life. Changes in market conditions, interest rates, spending habits, and lifestyle will affect the recommendations we will offer today. With that in mind, we look forward to establishing a long and successful financial planning relationship with you.

Sincerely,

Marion B. Gilman CFP®   Marc S. Freedman CFP®

Below is another summary letter prepared for a client. You will notice many similarities in the flow of the letter, but the content is clearly customized to this particular client:

Dear Elaine & Dan,

We are delighted to have this opportunity to present your financial plan.
During our initial consultation, you shared several financial and life planning goals. They are:

1. *To secure a comfortable retirement lifestyle for the two of you.*
   - *Elaine would anticipate retiring at the end of May 200X.*
   - *Dan would potentially scale back to part-time employment in 200X.*
   - *You would sell your Summer Street home to your daughter.*
   - *You would anticipate spending $80K for a residence in Florida.*
   - *You would split time living between the Florida residence and your Wells, Maine property.*
   - *Anticipated after-tax spending (in today's dollars) would be $72,000 per year.*
2. *To address concerns regarding the allocation of investments in your 403(b) account(s) as you approach the retirement phase of your life.*

We will address these issues in our analysis today, along with commentary on cash flow issues, insurance needs, estate planning concerns, and tax planning considerations. Since financial planning is a fluid process, we will discuss our findings in an interactive format.

Cash Flow
You have anticipated after-tax spending needs of $6,000 per month, or $72,000 annually, in retirement. This figure appears to be in line with

---

*your current spending level. Upon review of your 200X tax return, we
noted earned income, excluding interest, dividends and capital gains,
of approximately $116,000. After withholding federal taxes of $17,000,
$6,400 in state taxes, and an additional $6,800 in Social Security
tax, you netted $85,800. You have indicated that you plan to sell your
home to your daughter in the near future. By selling the property, you
will eliminate your monthly mortgage payments, thus justifying your
$72,000 per year spending plan.*

*It is our understanding that Dan will be eligible to collect a pension
benefit from the Salem Hospital retirement plan beginning as early as
November 1, 20XX. The projected monthly benefit would be $2,170.27, if
Dan elects to take the income stream over his life only. There are several
survivor options available that would protect Elaine in the event of Dan's
premature death, and we would strongly recommend that you review all
of the possible options no later than September 1, 200X. As the date draws
closer, let's schedule time to contact Provident Life together. We could then
confirm all the numbers and consider all of the available options.*

Emergency Fund
*We believe that a prudent way to manage against emergency expenses
is to keep three to six months' living expenses in a highly liquid cash-
based fund. Currently, you have approximately $118,000 in various bank
accounts, and of that money, you anticipate spending approximately
$80,000 on a property in Florida. We believe that the remaining money
could sufficiently serve as your emergency fund.*

Retirement Income Analysis
*During our initial meeting you indicated that your primary goal was to gather
an understanding about your ability to achieve a retirement strategy that
reflects your current spending lifestyle. To create our projections of your potential retirement income stream, we used the following initial assumptions:*

* *Elaine will begin retirement at the end of May 200X.*

- Dan will retire from full-time employment in 200X.
- When you are both retired, you will need $6,000 after tax in today's dollars for your monthly spending needs ($72,000 annually).
- Dan will be eligible to collect Social Security benefits of $2,035 per month at his full retirement age.
- Elaine will be eligible to collect Social Security benefits of approximately $850 monthly, when she stops working this year.
- Dan will continue to collect $14,000 annually for the next 15 years in rent from the medical office building, in which he owns a 6 percent share. He anticipates the building will be sold for $5 million in 20XX.
- Dan will be eligible to collect a pension from Salem Hospital of approximately $2,000 per month at age 65.
- Elaine will continue to collect her payment of inherited lottery winnings of $1,000 per month until October 20XX.
- We have projected your retirement years to last until 2035, when Elaine would turn 93.
- Inflation will average 2.5 percent per year throughout your time horizon.
- The average annual rate of return on investments will be 6 percent.

Given the assumptions stated above, our analysis indicates that you would be able to achieve your retirement spending goals throughout your lifetime with a high degree of confidence (see enclosed).

Investments

At the current time, your joint assets of approximately $118,000 are held in CDs and bank accounts. Since you anticipate purchasing a property in Florida with much of this money in the near future, it is appropriate to keep this money in a highly liquid account.

Dan's retirement assets are in three different plans through the Medical Group: TSSMC 401(a), TSSMC 403(b), and Salem Hospital. We have created a style box reflecting the current investment allocation (see enclosed). As you can see, 100 percent of your fund selections are focused on large company stocks, with a heavier weighting toward growth stocks. Also, given these specific funds, there is considerable overlap among the stocks represented in each portfolio (see the attached overlap report). During our meeting you indicated that you viewed your-selves as "conservative investors." We believe that your current collective retirement portfolio lends itself to a fairly aggressive strategy based on your current financial situation.

With such a heavily focused weighting in large cap stocks (see the overlap report), your portfolio is exposed to significant volatility in the event the broad U.S.-based markets stumble. We would strongly encourage you to realign your portfolio to reflect more of a 60/40 stocks to bonds/cash portfolio.

We have included a style box depicting a recommended growth with income portfolio investment allocation. We would recommend diversifying into mid-cap, small-cap, international, and bond funds in conjunction with your current large cap exposure.

Tax Planning

Given your sources of revenue in retirement, it appears that you will continue to have significant taxable income throughout your retirement years. In addition to your pension and Social Security income streams, your supplemental funds will come primarily from Dan's retirement account, which will be taxed at ordinary income tax rates. Given that more than 85 percent of your investment assets are in retirement accounts it would be advisable to manage the distributions from the retirement account as evenly as possible throughout your retirement years—rather than waiting until the IRS imposed age 70½ to begin drawing your minimum distribution.

With the exception of your emergency fund, your retirement plans remain the only other liquid investments you hold—that is, until you receive the sales proceeds from the office building in about 15 years. As large, one-time expenses occur, such as the purchase of a new car, you may be forced to draw upon your retirement account. Remember that every dollar drawn from these assets is taxable. Thus, if you needed $30,000 for a car, you might need to draw as much as $40,000 from your IRA to accommodate the taxable nature of the distribution. It is very important that we continue to monitor your cash flow and encourage you to build money in non-retirement accounts to ensure that you have adequate on-hand financial resources when you need them. Beginning to take distributions from your IRA prior to age 70½, and depositing the proceeds into a non-retirement account may be a strategy worthy of consideration.

Education Funding
You currently have small personal accounts set up to benefit your grandchildren at the local bank. If these funds are anticipated to be used for college education, a tax-advantaged method of saving for college is through 529 plans. These plans allow for funds to grow tax-free if used for qualified higher education expenses. This would be particularly advantageous for the younger children. You can continue to remain owner of the accounts and, as such, by holding the lion's share of assets designed to help pay for your grandchildren's education costs, you address your objective of helping your children to qualify for financial aid. We have prepared some information on 529 plans for your review.

Risk Management

Life and Disability Insurance
Dan has a life insurance policy through his employer equal to one times his salary. In addition, you personally own a $20,000 paid up life policy through Boston Mutual. Given your current asset base, your stated income needs, and assuming Dan provides for a continued income stream to Elaine through his pension options, there is no need for additional life insurance.

Dan also has short- and long-term disability insurance through his employer to a maximum benefit of $1,000 per month. This will serve to protect his income stream for two and a half years now, declining to one year should a disability occur at age 69.

Long-Term Care

At this point, another type of insurance to consider is long-term care insurance. Should one of you become incapacitated and need assistance in daily living activities, it could result in a significant drain on your financial resources—leaving the well spouse without adequate funds for income. We understand that you have had some health issues in the past, and as a result, you may not be eligible for long-term care coverage, but we do believe that it is worth submitting an informal inquiry to determine whether this type of coverage could be extended to you. If long-term care insurance is unavailable to you, this should further heighten a need to manage your financial resources.

Estate Planning

You have provided and we have reviewed copies of your wills, health care proxies, and powers of attorney. It appears that they were recently revised in 200X by the law offices of Valerie Wexler. Upon reviewing the original documents, it appears that Dan's last will and testament is incomplete, yet it was notarized, witnessed, and signed on February 15, 2005. It is imperative that you have Ms. Wexler update Dan's will to reflect his wishes immediately. It does appear that Elaine's will and all other estate planning documents are in good order.

As always, it is important to review these documents periodically to be certain they remain up-to-date.

Under federal law, each individual is allowed to pass on $2 million in 20XX to heirs free of estate taxes. Your net worth currently falls under this limit, avoiding federal taxes. However, the laws are in flux, as are your asset values, so this is an area that we are continually monitoring for our clients.

The above and attached represent our initial findings and recommendations relating to the information you have provided. Please understand that financial planning is not a science—rather it is a fluid activity that requires adjustment throughout one's financial life. Changes in market conditions, interest rates, spending habits, and lifestyle will *affect the recommendations we will offer today. With that in mind, we look forward to establishing a long and successful financial planning relationship with you.*

Sincerely,

Marion B. Gilman CFP®   *Marc S. Freedman CFP®*

As you can see from the two letters, each contains information that is specific to the client, but they follow similar formatting and tone. Try to find a writing voice that works for you, and then craft a basic outline that could be used in every plan you write.

ADDITIONAL THOUGHTS ON WRITING A PLAN

Reviewing style boxes and asset allocation models, analyzing tax returns, and examining cash flow may be daily activities and part of the normal conversation in your office, but they are probably new concepts to your clients. What may seem the most obvious perspective to you is often seen as a fresh new angle, and it's important that your client has the opportunity to hear these thoughts from you, as simple as you may think they are.

More often than not, planners seek to use technical analyses, spreadsheets, Monte Carlo projections, and a series of other quantitative programs. While these number-crunched analyses are wonderful resources to justify *your* findings, remember that the best financial planners know how to integrate an emotional component that is difficult to solve for in a computer program.

Whether you choose to include reports, historical charts, a series of what-if scenarios, an appendix, or links to dozens of Web sites in your plan, try to remind yourself that all of your data processing will likely need to be "tweaked" over time. When preparing an initial plan for a client, keep it as simple as possible. You should always have backup data to help a client answer the question, "Where did this number come from?" But beyond that, your presentable analysis should be simple. Simply ask yourself, "Will my client leave today's meeting with a greater sense of peace of mind than he had on the first day we met?" Just because someone is paying you a fee for your advice, it shouldn't translate into the sense that you need to overwhelm them with every chart, research piece, and editorial story you can find. Again, keep it simple!

Find the trigger points that address the most pressing issues in their lives and make sure that you keep them aligned with the goals they have stated. If they've changed without your knowledge, then the plan you wrote may be as worthless as the paper it's printed on. I can't stress enough how important it is to discover and re-discover your clients' goals each and every time you meet with them. Neglecting to do so and offering advice under the assumptions that everything in your client's life is the same could lead you down a dangerous path.

Finally, it's important to include a disclaimer as part of your write-up, to reflect the reality that the best financial plans are never complete. You'll probably remember the following paragraph from each of the above letters.

> *The above and attached represent our initial findings and recommendations relating to the information you have provided. Please understand that financial planning is not a science—rather, it is a fluid activity that requires adjustment throughout one's financial life. Changes in market conditions, interest rates, spending habits, and lifestyle will affect the recommendations we will offer today. With that in mind, we look forward to establishing a long and successful financial planning relationship with you.*

Remember that your client's financial plan is only an *initial* attempt at aligning your client's goals and objectives with the resources that exist in his or her life. To deliver financial planning successfully, your client must understand that plans are fluid documents and periodic reviews of all the elements in your client's life are essential to ensure that her plan continues to remain on the track she wants.

As you become more skilled at writing plans, you'll find that you can delegate many components of plan development to staff, but never present a plan to a client without carefully reading the plan first, and aligning your words to the analysis that supports your presentation. Try your best to listen to your plan through the ears and eyes of a client. Imagine what questions they may be pondering in their heads. Wonder where they may just tune you out completely. And finally, think of ways to fully engage them with your presentation.

One final thought. Always remember that your financial plan should be written in a manner that allows it to stand on its own. Your client should be able to take this document and implement it anywhere he sees fit. Writing about how your firm could assist with the implementation of your findings within the context of the financial planning letter is a conflict of interest, especially when your client is paying you for an objective review of his or her financial affairs. Be patient. A well written plan, and a genuine presentation of your findings will ultimately lead to your client wanting to work with you and using your services to help them implement strategies as well as continue to monitor financial planning projections. Just be patient and professional.

When you can present complex concepts in a manner that people find easy to understand, your client will feel safe asking you more questions and truly listening to your responses. It's a way that people naturally build trust with one another. In the next chapter, we will discuss presentation techniques that lead to building that trusting relationship the mass affluent are seeking from a financial planner.

SUMMARY

1. Personally written financial planning summaries allow for you to personalize your recommendations, and better connect with the client's needs.
2. Use words like "may," "could," and "consider" as you convey ideas and concepts through your plan.
3. Understand the responsibility that a client has entrusted in you. Financial plans are road maps that help people envision a course for their financial life. How you write the financial plan could be the spark that focuses your client on achieving his or her life's goals.

13 | *Presenting the Plan— My Favorite Days of the Year*

OBJECTIVES

1. Guidance on preparing for the financial planning presentation
2. Offer ideas that convey concepts and findings to your client
3. Managing the meeting
4. Wrapping up with confidence

PRESENTING THE PLAN—MY FAVORITE DAYS OF THE YEAR

Now that you've written your financial plan, it's time to actually present it to a client. I love presentation day in our office—and you should, too. It's your day to perform. It's also the day that will likely determine whether this client meeting will be the start of a lifelong relationship, or the conclusion of just another project. For me, I view presentation day as "showtime." I prepare myself with the same seriousness and intensity as I would have when I played the leading role of

Harold Hill in my high school's fall production of *The Music Man*. All eyes are on you, and you are standing on the grand stage. I don't say this to intimidate you—but to stress the importance of the moment. It is your job to hold the attention of your clients who have paid to see you "perform." They are expecting a quality experience and it's your job to ensure that they feel like they got their money's worth.

Remember, your plan presentation meeting is an opportunity to reconnect with your client face to face. It's your chance to check in with their emotions, their fears, and their points of confidence. But more than anything else, it's your opportunity to show them you truly listened to them, and that you are prepared to deliver your findings (both good and bad) in clear, straightforward language. They are relying on your presentation today to serve as a launching point to a better future. That's right: your leadership skills are on display on presentation day, and your clients are counting on you to deliver.

Are you ready?

GUIDANCE ON PREPARING FOR THE PRESENTATION

What excites you about financial planning presentation meetings? Do you view them as an opportunity to change your clients' lives, or are they meetings that finally allow you to gather the assets you've been hoping to manage? I'd like to think that your answer is the first one. Gathering assets, implementing ideas, and selling product should be on the back burner today. You'll have plenty of opportunities to implement strategies at a later date. If you present your plan with integrity and sincerity, your clients will be eager for the opportunity to work with you going forward. For now, your clients have hired you to straighten out their financial house and they are looking for advice and leadership—not sales ideas and applications to complete. Do your very best today to ensure that the meeting is *all* about them and their financial planning issues.

As we mentioned in earlier chapters, you should review your protocol regarding impressions with your staff. Your clients are likely to be a bit nervous when they arrive, and they may be uneasy about what you've discovered and the recommendations you'll make. Make sure that when they walk in the door, their initial impressions are pleasant and welcoming.

Generally in our office, the conference room is pre-set as follows:

1. Any analyses and financial planning software projections are already pre-loaded (but minimized) on the computer screen.
2. The client's executive summary is printed on stationery and copies are made for all attending.
3. Your paraplanner has prepared an agenda that highlights particular items from the summary letter.
4. A half-inch, three-ring binder is prepared with the client's name inserted behind the clear-view cover on the front.
5. Labeled tabs with topics such as net worth, cash flow, investments, income planning, etc. are inserted in the binder.
6. Snapshot reports, such as a client net worth statement, client investment style boxes, and current cash flow reports, are printed and placed under the related tab in the binder. There are still other analyses that may need client confirmation and will be presented interactively on the presentation screen in the conference room.
7. We generally wait until the conclusion of our meeting to print all "what if" scenarios for our clients. Generally, we find that clients enjoy participating and watching how changes that they propose for their plan could affect the results. Once we have agreed on the "what if" scenario(s) that feel best to them, we will send these analyses to the printer, three-hole punch them, and insert them in the binder along with the other reports and findings.

AN INTRODUCTION TO DELIVERING A FINANCIAL PLAN

Before you ever begin a planning presentation, it is important to ask a client whether any events have changed in their lives since you last met. Often, it can be four to eight weeks from the time you first met with them until the time you present the plan. You'd be surprised how often things change. Perhaps a client has purchased a car, they've received a promotion at work, an inheritance is in the works, or they are ready to announce that they're pregnant with another child. Never be surprised when the data and assumptions you've been working with have changed. Life happens—be prepared. This is exactly why we refrain from printing reports that offer projections in advance of a meeting. Always confirm and reprint any changes to the assumptions and data before handing your client their financial plan. After all, if you expect your client to review the plan at home, it should be reflective of the most current issues you discussed—not what you printed in advance.

As you begin your presentation, be sure to deliver an overview of what they should expect and about how long you anticipate the meeting will take.

I generally like to highlight the following items:

1. Mention that you're prepared to offer initial ideas and strategies that may lead toward helping your clients achieve their financial goals. (I always say *initially* because we need to express to our clients that financial planning is fluid.)
2. Present them with the three-ring binder and cover letter. Explain that today, you will refer to the summary letter and periodically review the analyses in the binder.
3. Remind them that many of the analyses are not yet in the binder because you hope to tighten them up today with their input. The binder will be made current before they leave.
4. Let them know that today's meeting will run about 90 minutes. Tell them you will cover a tremendous amount of material and

that you do not expect them to make any decisions regarding recommendations today.

5. Point their attention to the action plan at the back of the binder. This schedule provides them with the tools they'll need to implement strategies you have recommended. This is your opportunity to mention that many of these strategies can be implemented through your firm or elsewhere. *Remember:* Financial plans should be written in a generic enough manner that your client can implement strategies anywhere they see fit. Today, they are paying you for independent, objective financial advice—not sales ideas.

6. If it's a couple, request that, at the conclusion of today's meeting, they take home your plan and review it both independently and together.

7. Encourage them to prepare questions and decide whether further analysis and/or "what if" scenarios are needed.

8. Let them know you will follow up with them in about one week to see if any questions remain.

If you present your financial plan correctly, most clients will not wait for your call. Generally, their next call to you will be to see how they can implement strategies with your firm. We find that, as much as clients might suggest they want independent, objective advice, they also want a trusted resource to turn to for implementation. If you present your plan with objectivity and authenticity, you won't need to ask them to implement with you; they will be salivating at the opportunity to build a life long relationship with you. Not only will they want to place money under your management or purchase an insurance product, they will want you to maintain the same commitment to detail on their collective financial planning needs as you did in the initial plan presentation. Over the years, we have learned that close to 100 percent of clients who have us *first* prepare a financial plan choose to implement strategies through our firm. I suspect you will find the same success in your practice.

Oversold and Underserved: A Financial Planner's Guidebook to Effectively Serving the Mass Affluent

AN ICE-BREAKER IDEA

It's finally time to get on with the presentation. We have found that a great ice-breaker when presenting a financial plan is to introduce a SWOT analysis.

The SWOT Analysis

When you are hired as your client's financial planner, they expect that you'll share both the good and the bad news. Delivering an honest assessment in a balanced presentation can be challenging for some, because many advisers seek to find what's wrong with a client's situation and how they can be the champion who delivers better results. Weaving a conversation that celebrates a client's successes but alerts them to potential dangers is a skill that takes time to develop.

One way to help you capture a representation of your client's financial outlook is to create a SWOT chart. SWOT charts (Strengths, Weaknesses, Opportunities, and Threats), are a business management tool used in most MBA programs in America. By building a simple four-quadrant box, you can show your client's current prospects for achieving their goals by simply filling in the boxes with ideas and expressions. This tool should be interactive and presented in a manner that encourages their feedback and your openness to listen to their thoughts.

Bob & Maureen Wilcox *S.W.O.T. Analysis* **April 6**	
Strengths	**Weaknesses**
• Available cash for investment • Pending incentive grants • Minimum debt level • Earnings capacity • Guaranteed pension stream	• Impulsive spending • Heavy real estate concentration • Too much mutual fund diversification/ too little asset allocation
Opportunities	**Threats**
• Potential employer pension • Possible future grants • Consulting income • Equity in real estate	• Under-protected survivor lifestyle needs • Lifestyle change at retirement • Uncertainty of tenure at place of employment

What discussions might stem from the presentation of a SWOT analysis?

Generally we have our SWOT analysis prepared on a flip chart in the office. We run through each of the quadrants and ask the clients to comment on whether they agree with our findings. More often than not, they not only agree, they are delighted to see that there are as many positive perspectives in their SWOT analysis as there are negatives. When preparing a SWOT analysis, do your very best to deliver a balanced presentation. If you find that there are more negatives than positives, consider whether a SWOT analysis works best for these clients. You want your clients to feel good at the end of a meeting, not sick to their stomachs.

COMMUNICATION SKILLS AND THE PRESENTATION OF THE PLAN

The financial plan you've written needs to be a major highlight of your planning presentation. Whether you choose to read it aloud or simply highlight segments from your write-up, it is important that your clients remain participants in the presentation.

You should:

1. Ensure that the goals you've identified remain current for your client.
2. Encourage your client to take notes along the way. Make sure pads of paper and pens are readily accessible.
3. Tell them to stop you immediately if something you say doesn't make sense or they disagree.

Each time you refer to a section in your write-up that discusses an analysis you've prepared, you should ask your client whether they'd like to review the analysis now or wait until you've read through the letter. You can also preface your presentation by letting them know your preference.

CHECKING IN

Periodically, you should stop reading your letter and ask what, if any, questions they might have. You can ask whether the assumptions you've used make sense to them, and whether you've accurately captured elements within each subset of the plan, such as investment planning, estate planning, education funding, etc.

Once you've completed your letter, remind them again that you know there is a lot of information to review and you hope that they will take time to review the letter and subsequent analysis at home.

DIGGING INTO THE ANALYSIS

When it's time to present your analyses interactively, be sure that you are adept at using the software. Be prepared to make changes to your software on the fly, and have a strong working knowledge of where the numbers came from prior to presenting them to your client. Each time your client catches an abnormality in the plan and you need to fix or address the outcomes, remember that it could have a multiplier effect on recommendations you've made in your plan. Running a mock presentation with a co-worker is an excellent precursor to a client presentation. Be sure you are prepared to answer your client's questions about your plan. After all, whether or not you actually prepared the analysis, your client fully expects that you support the conclusions and that you have audited the numbers.

One skill that clients love is an ability to play "what if." When you have a large projection screen, a wireless mouse, and keyboard, you can simply hand the controls over to the client and suggest that they point to, and/or play around with, some of the possibilities. In fact, if your financial planning software is Internet accessible, you can often create a copy of your plan and give your client access to play with it further at home. They love this.

Another thing clients love to see is their tax return or estate planning documents up on the screen as a PDF. Many financial planning software programs, such as eMoney Advisor, allow for a client's private documents to be uploaded and stored in a virtual vault that is attached to their private Web site.

INTRODUCING AH-HA MOMENTS

Any opportunity to create ah-ha moments during a financial planning presentation enhances the likelihood that your clients will look forward to building a long and successful financial planning relationship with you. In fact, this is your opportunity to show them tricks and tips that can save them more money than the fee they paid you to prepare the plan. Here are just a few:

1. **Review the cost to prepare their tax return.** Many mass affluent clients feel that because they earn an income in excess of $100K, they require the services of a CPA firm to prepare their return. Generally, mass affluent clients have relatively simple tax returns to prepare, which include only Schedules A and B. We've seen clients paying as much as $1,200 annually when they could have their returns prepared for less than $400 elsewhere.

2. **Highlighting the dangers of living without an umbrella policy.** Most mass affluent clients don't carry an umbrella policy. Bringing to light the risks of someone slipping and falling on their front walk or injuring themselves at their swimming pool over the summer enlightens your client about the possible legal action that could be taken against them. Explaining how an umbrella policy can provide coverage in excess of their homeowners and/or auto insurance is a welcome discussion. What's even more interesting is when you explain that the cost is only a few hundred dollars a year for a million or more dollars' worth of coverage. In addition, most insurance companies offer discounts on umbrella policies if you maintain your auto and homeowners coverage with the same company.

3. **Educate them on their "real" tax rate.** Too often clients have preconceived beliefs that they are in a particular tax bracket. In fact, they often believe that they need to add,

for example, 28 percent to their expected spending needs in retirement to cover the tax liability. It is very rare that mass affluent clients will find themselves with an average federal tax rate on their adjusted gross income in excess of 17 percent. Showing clients how personal exemptions and itemized deductions affect their tax rate can be enlightening for some. Many clients don't believe that their Social Security income can be taxed differently based on the way they choose to draw money from accounts to support their income needs. Clients truly appreciate your help exploring the multiple ways they can draw money from their assets to meet their lifestyles. Here's an example: Imagine your client calls and asks for $20,000 to purchase a used vehicle. Their choices are either to take the money from their IRA or their joint savings account. While drawing money from their bank account is non-taxable as opposed to the IRA being a taxable distribution, you might be able to further justify your recommendation to take money from the bank if you can show your client that their Social Security income won't get hit with an additional tax due to an increase in their income cause by a taxable distribution from their IRA. (Not to mention they'd have to probably take $25K +/− from their IRA to net $20,000). Thomson Financial's "UltraTax-Planner" is one tool that can help you analyze multiple tax vs. cash flow scenarios for your client.

4. **Explain why tax-free bonds are oversold to the mass affluent.** If most mass affluent clients pay average tax rates between 12 and 17 percent, why do so many insist on holding tax-free bonds? It's because they've been solicited by individuals who have probably bought lists of names of high net worth people or individuals with incomes in excess of X amount. A mass affluent client's net worth and/or annual earnings should have little indication of

the tax rate they pay to the IRS. It is rare that a cold-call salesperson is aware of your client's deduction and exemptions allowed on their tax return. Generally, the key term that sells consumers on the need to purchase tax-free bonds is the term "tax effective yield." For instance: "Mr. Client, we can offer you a tax-free bond with a tax effective yield of 6.15 percent." What did the client hear? They heard the broker say they could earn 6.15 percent on a tax-free bond. Does it matter that the broker's tax effective yield example was based on the assumption that the client was in the highest marginal tax bracket? In this case, the tax-free bond had a coupon of 4 percent, due in 20 years, and selling at a par. If you divide 4 percent by the inverse of the marginal tax rate of 35 percent [$.04/(1 - .35)$], the result is a 6.15 percent tax effective yield. But what if the client pays an average tax rate of 15 percent? That same (4 percent) bond has an effective tax rate of 4.7 percent. Cold-callers tend to suggest that your clients are earning a higher tax effective yield through tax-free bonds by assuming they are in a higher tax bracket—which, in many cases, is false. Take a look at your client's tax return and see whether tax-free bonds are really the proper investment for them. You'll likely learn that taxable bonds might actually deliver a better return.

5. **Read estate planning documents.** Planners are generally not qualified to write legal documentation; however, *planners all know how to read.* Like we mentioned in an earlier chapter, sometimes simple things such as noticing that a will was signed and notarized without having the details of the client's specific needs entered into the template document are life-saving details that your client will never forget. In addition, it's important that you remind clients of the trustees, beneficiaries, and powers of attorney they have assigned in their

legal documents. It has probably been a while since clients have reviewed these documents and their wishes may have changed since the documents were prepared.

6. **Review beneficiary designations.** It is important that you confirm the beneficiary designations on life insurance, retirement plans, and other accounts that carry named beneficiaries. Too often, we find that clients who have been working with their companies for a great number of years have named their parents or first spouses as the primary beneficiary. Bringing the current beneficiary designation to your client's attention will earn you significant credibility, especially if it's someone that he or she has no intention of bequeathing money to at his or her death. And if the new spouse is in the room during the planning presentation, it could open a whole new conversation that may need further exploration.

7. **The value of transfer on death (TOD).** Mass affluent clients are generally unlikely to pay estate taxes under current laws. Yet all too often, they want to avoid probate costs and they believe a revocable trust is the only way to accomplish this goal. Rather than establishing a trust for the sole purpose of avoiding probate, introduce your clients to the term "transfer on death" (TOD). Simply adding this designation on personally owned accounts eliminates the probate issue without having to endure the costs to establish a revocable trust. (This isn't to say that trusts don't hold value for clients, but if the primary reason for establishing a trust is to avoid probate, you have an obligation to show your client that there are easier, less expensive ways to fulfill this goal).

8. **Explain that IRA accounts can be something more than bank accounts.** Too many clients still believe that IRAs can only be held in bank money markets or certificates of deposit. It is important to check in with your client and

make sure they understand that IRAs can be held in multitudes of vehicles.

9. **Discuss the importance of maintaining cost basis.** I find that too many people instruct clients that maintaining cost basis is the client's responsibility. When you help a client by managing cost basis for them, you have offered a tremendous service and probably saved your clients money in the process. Imagine how appreciative they will be when you recommend selling a mutual fund in advance of a pending capital gain distribution because it would be smarter to sell their fund for a tax loss than have to pay tax on a distribution that never benefited the timing on their particular investment. Had you not been aware of their actual cost basis, could you proactively make proper tax-based recommendations?

10. **Encourage them to spend their money**. Too many clients approach planners with the improper assumption that they will run out of money early in life. In many cases, this assumption is due to the belief that one should only spend the interest earned on investments and leave the principal intact. As planners, you know this adage prevents many people from living life to its fullest. In fact, with proper planning and guidance, you can encourage your clients to spend *more* money in retirement than they ever thought was possible. You can help them fulfill dreams they only imagined and help them manage a legacy to their children that doesn't sacrifice your clients' ability to live well.

There are so many more little things you can do that enhance the value of the planning relationship you build with your clients. I bet you could come up with dozens of other ideas. Think about it. What tips have you offered to clients that validated your wisdom and experience in their eyes? Write three concepts you've delivered that have solidified your planning value:

1. _____

2. _____

3. _____

THE ACTION PLAN

Earlier in this chapter, I mentioned the action plan. This document serves as a next set of steps for your client. It should be generically written in a manner that allows them to implement ideas on their own (or with you). Following are two sample action plans:

Action Item	Explanation
Cash Flow	• Keep three to six months' living expenses in a highly liquid money market fund
Retirement Investments	• Review your current asset allocation within each portfolio relative to the recommended models • Consider the use of a fee-based asset management account to consolidate investments and provide flexibility and ease of management • Position your assets appropriately in anticipation of drawing funds throughout your retirement years
Grandchildren's Funds	• Review the benefits of using 529 plans for your grandchildren's savings as this money is designed to assist with college expenses
X Pension	• Contact X life insurance company by X date to get the exact figures for the various pension options • Determine most advantageous method to receive benefits
Estate Documents	• Revisit with your estate planning attorney immediately to modify the omissions in current will • Review all documents annually or if any changes occur
Financial Plan	• Monitor your progress toward goals at least annually with our office

Action Item	Explanation
Retirement Investment Strategy	• Maintain your current allocation and contributions to 401(k) • Consider the use of a fee-based advisory account for the consolidation and management of your eligible IRA assets • Review our proposed allocation changes to reduce exposure to small growth, international, and large blend • Move forward with reallocation and diversification of portfolio
Joint Investment Strategy	• Consolidate all joint assets for ease of investment and management • Establish a fee-based advisory account to help you better manage your collective accounts • Determine price targets for sale of X stock • Review overall asset allocation annually
Long-Term Care Insurance	• Review details pertaining to long-term care insurance • Apply for coverage with a licensed agent
Homeowners, Auto, Umbrella Insurance	• Schedule appointment with your insurance agent to review homeowners coverage • Consider the purchase of an umbrella policy for additional liability coverage
Estate Documents	• Set up a meeting with an attorney at your earliest convenience to execute wills, health care proxies, and powers of attorney • Review all documents annually or if any changes occur
Financial Plan	• Monitor progress toward goals at least annually with our office

Notice how each of the action plans offers generic recommendations that allow your client to implement ideas wherever they see fit. Don't be surprised to hear your clients ask how you can help them implement certain strategies as you review the action plan with them. In fact, view this vote of confidence as a successful affirmation of your planning presentation. But resist the temptation to begin opening accounts for them. Allow your clients to appreciate the financial planning advice and analysis you've built on their behalf. Allow them to further examine the plan you've prepared and encourage them to develop more questions and scenarios for consideration. While some might call this approach teasing the client, I view it as an expression of your professionalism and integrity.

CLOSING THE PLANNING PRESENTATION

Finally, as your financial planning presentation comes to a conclusion, know that your client is likely to be mentally exhausted. As easy as it was for you to present concepts to them, it is likely that they are overwhelmed with all of the information. Remember, you should never expect them to implement any strategies, nor should you ever be proposing the idea during your presentation. This is best left for a subsequent meeting, after they have had a chance to review the information you've prepared.

What's most important is that you promise to follow up with a letter to them that highlights items from the meeting and addresses issues they would like you to respond to following the meeting. In addition, craft a memo to file so that you remember what you talked about with this client. Below are a sample letter to a client and a sample memo to file.

SAMPLE LETTER TO CLIENT FOLLOWING PLANNING PRESENTATION

Dear Elaine & Dan:

Many thanks for visiting our office on Tuesday, March XX, 200X to participate in the presentation of your financial planning analysis.

We are delighted to hear that you found the analysis insightful and we hope it also provided you with assurance that a spending lifestyle of $72,000 per year is very achievable. As your financial planners, we would like to help you continue identifying various strategies that encourage you to spend more of your resources to achieve goals today. You seemed very surprised that over $2,500,000 could be remaining in your estate (exclusive of your home) if you continued to spend at your present level and our modest assumptions remained intact.

You also mentioned that you'd like to see both your children and grandchildren receive periodic gifts from you with hopes that they would

---

put this money to good use and recognize that you were the benefactors of these gifts. During our next meeting we would be delighted to discuss strategies that help you fulfill this goal.

We were also pleased to learn that you would like to establish an investment advisory relationship with our firm. We should schedule a subsequent meeting with you to establish IRA rollover accounts for both of you. Enclosed you will find paperwork requiring your signatures so that we can open accounts for you.

You will need to contact Fidelity directly to request the paperwork to establish Dan's IRA rollover. Since we understand you've had some difficulty getting the answers you want from Fidelity, we would be happy to schedule a conference call with you so you can ensure that the correct questions are being asked and that the appropriate paperwork is being sent to you.

Regarding Elaine's IRA, we can open this account by transferring her Fidelity account directly to LPL Financial. Upon Elaine's retirement, her 401(k) balance could also be added to this retirement portfolio. Elaine, please send us an up-to-date copy of your Fidelity IRA statement. In addition, please send us a copy of your driver's licenses. The USA PATRIOT Act requires that we hold his information in our files. Dan, we hope you've had a chance to contact your attorney to confirm that your will addresses the omission in your current estate planning documentation.

We would also encourage you to speak with your mortgage broker about changing your adjustable-rate mortgage to a 15-year fixed rate at 5.75 percent.

Once again, many thanks for this opportunity to be of service. If you have any further questions regarding our financial planning analysis, please don't hesitate to contact our office. We look forward to building a long and successful financial planning relationship with you.

Sincerely,

Marc S. Freedman CFP®, President

Memo to File—Elaine and Dan

Marion and Marc met with Dan and Elaine to present their financial plan today. The meeting lasted about 90 minutes and provided them with insights regarding their current financial situation. They admitted being very impressed with the overall presentation. We needed to cut our last presentation meeting with them short after Dan learned of the error in his will and he left our office to visit with his attorney. Today's meeting was very cordial and they expressed their deepest appreciation for our diligence in reviewing all of their data completely.

Most of today's conversation was spent giving them confidence that their income and resources could more than adequately fund their retirement spending goal of $72,000 per year. Dan wondered why he worried so much over the past decade that he hadn't accumulated enough wealth to support his needs. He had never really thought about the income streams available to him during retirement and the minimal draw he would need to pull from his investments to support their lifestyle.

Dan and Elaine agreed that consolidation of their retirement accounts was an important next step for them. They expressed a desire to schedule a subsequent meeting where they could explore our firm's investment advisory services.

During our review of their life insurance, it occurred to Elaine that Dan held an additional $250,000 term life insurance policy through MetLife. We didn't seem to capture it on our financial plan and he believes he may have forgotten to give us that information. He's going to look into this further.

They're heading down the Florida next week to look at some more property. They have plans to sell their current home to their daughter and use part of the sales proceeds to purchase a double wide trailer in Florida. During the summer months they would live at their home in Maine.

<End of memo>

Four weeks later, Dan and Elaine scheduled an implementation meeting with the firm. Below is the memo to file. But more importantly, notice how quickly events changed in their lives regarding their Maine property.

Follow-up Meeting Memo to File—Elaine and Dan

Dan and Elaine came in to go through the packet of paperwork we prepared to help them transfer their assets to our office. Dan reiterated his thanks to us in reviewing his will. He has corrected the omission with his attorney. In addition, he and Elaine expressed pleasure over the professionalism, preparation, and communications that they have experienced with our staff. I suspect that they will be very satisfied, lifelong clients.

They signed all the paperwork to set up an advisory account for Elaine and an advisory IRA for Dan. We called Fidelity while they were in the conference room with us to request the appropriate paperwork to move his two 401(a) and 403(b) plans, and requested a check from the hospital, which was being managed by Fidelity as well. In addition, we asked them to liquidate the mutual funds in each of their respective IRAs so that they could be transferred into their accounts here as cash.

We were surprised to learn that they had sold their property in Maine for cash in three weeks and now have to move out this weekend. They were very surprised that this happened so quickly. After some further reflection, they decided that they didn't want to maintain two homes. Instead, they are looking to purchase something a little bit larger in Florida and plan on renting the in-law suite of their current home after they sell the house to their daughter. They felt badly that living in Maine and Florida would prevent them from spending quality time with their grandchildren in Massachusetts.

Cathy will process the new account paperwork and will look for the checks from Fidelity.
<End of Memo>

IN CLOSING

The financial planning presentation is your opportunity to combine your experiences, knowledge, and leadership in a manner that changes people's lives. Your clients are counting on you to deliver this information to them, and it's your obligation not only to serve them well, but to seek out points of vulnerability that they may never have considered before. My passion for delivering a financial plan overshadows everything else I do in my practice, and I can only hope that some of my enthusiasm has rubbed off on you throughout this section. Financial planning is so much more than investment or wealth management, especially in the eyes of the mass affluent client. They appreciate your guidance on tax planning, employee benefits, and cash flow management as much as (if not more than) guidance on investment and insurance issues.

In the next chapter we'll stress the importance of maintaining your financial planning services during each subsequent visit you have with a client. Your client review meeting should be as exceptional as your initial financial planning presentation. The next chapter will explore how to keep your review meetings as fresh as the first presentation you ever delivered to a client.

SUMMARY

1. Prepare your mind, your office, and your work in advance of your financial planning presentation.
2. Recognize that life happens. It is possible that the analysis you prepared today may need tweaking due to changes in your clients' lives.
3. Give your clients an overview of what to expect during the meeting. After all, you're prepared to present a lot of information; they need to be prepared for what's in store for them.
4. Use graphics and easy-to-follow illustrations that help them understand their financial situation.

5. Take time to check in with your clients throughout the presentation.
6. Prepare ah-ha moments for your clients.
7. Craft an action plan.
8. Draft a memo to file.
9. Send a follow-up letter.

14 The Extraordinarily Outrageous Client Review

OBJECTIVES

1. Highlight the importance of making each client review compelling and valuable
2. Present a process for preparing for a client review
3. Introduce tools and questions that create interactive review meetings

The success of a great financial planning relationship hinges on your ability to keep your client's eyes focused on his or her goals and away from the minutia. Too often, we hear of clients visiting planners' offices for review meetings with clippings from magazines, newsletters, and Web sites that offer advice on why they should be reallocating their money into a hot sector, a newfangled investment product, or wondering why their current adviser doesn't hold the newest set of initials after his or her name. The issues that these clients are focusing on are micro in scope, and it's your job to keep them focused on the big prize—the successful achievement of their life's goals and objectives.

THE ROCKS

I am reminded of a story that might help to drive home this message. One day at a local university, a professor of philosophy started his class with a demonstration. He stood behind a skirted table and reached down to grab a five-gallon glass container. He lifted the empty jar high into air and then proceeded to place it in the center of the table.

He turned to his class and asked them (by show of hands) to let him know when they thought the large jar was full. He then reached under the table again and struggled to lift a plastic milk crate containing a large number of fist-sized rocks onto the table. One at a time, he delicately placed rocks into the glass jar until there was no longer room to fit any more. Once it was clear that there wasn't any more room for rocks in the jar, hands began to appear in the air.

"Is this jar full?" asked the philosophy professor. Some students nodded their heads, while others wondered if this was a trick question.

The professor bent down again and lifted a medium-sized bowl filled with pebbles and stones that had been hidden under the table. He grabbed handfuls of pebbles and sprinkled them carefully over the large jar holding the fist-sized stones. Slowly, each pebble navigated its way through cracks and crevices into the jar until there was no longer any room for the stones.

"Is this jar full?" asked the philosophy professor. By now, more and more of the students sensed they knew where the professor was going with the story, and many shook their heads no.

The professor smiled at the class and then, once again, reached under the table and produced a pail of playground sand. Using a small plastic shovel, he sifted the sand into jar, filling each and every air pocket available. Eventually, there was no longer room for any more sand and the residual granules overflowed from the jar.

"Is this jar full?" asked the philosophy professor. A few students suggested that water could be added to the jar, and then it would certainly be full.

"You are right," remarked the professor. "But instead of adding water to the jar, I have this simple question for you. What lesson can be learned from this demonstration?"

There was a brief silence. Then someone yelled, "There's always room for more."

"An interesting response," said the professor, "but not quite the right answer. For the demonstration to work, the big rocks need to go into the jar first. If I filled the jar with sand first, pebbles second, and rocks third, it would be impossible to fit all of the larger stones into the jar. In the simplest of terms, the lesson is that you need to take care of the big rocks first, before handling the smaller ones."

The reason I tell you this story, is that your job as financial planners is to manage the priority in which "rocks" are addressed in your client's life. Think of the fist-sized rocks as the things that matter most in your client's life. It's the big stuff:

1. Retiring with peace of mind
2. Developing a legacy plan
3. Providing the best for their children
4. Remaining challenged and valued in a career that brings meaning to their lives
5. Living with values, love, and integrity
6. Protecting their families and their lives

And so much more…

Think of the pebbles as the tools that will help your client fulfill what matters most. This might be:

1. A well constructed investment portfolio
2. The use of a 529 education plan, a 401(k), or long-term care coverage

3. The establishment of wills and trusts
4. Coordinating a family vacation
5. Proper tax planning
6. More...

The grains of sand, of course, are the details. Yet, more often than not, these tiny little granules become what a client wants to talk about more than anything else. Those details might be:

1. A Treasury bond you bought on your client's behalf has dropped in value, and she thought they couldn't lose money.
2. A national news show has presented a negative story on annuities and your client is wondering why you sold him one.
3. The market has surged 10 percent over the past quarter and your client thinks his portfolio is too conservative.
4. Your client's employer has decided to change the retirement plan provider and she doesn't want to get rid of the funds she owns.
5. A surprise tax bill in April, when in previous years they got a refund.
6. Increased gasoline prices are worrying your client—but you know that they've owned the same car for the past ten years and it only has 30,000 miles on it.

When you can help your clients refocus their energies around the big rocks, you have mastered the most important role a planner serves in changing the lives of clients you serve. Generally, the tool that keeps clients focused on the big rocks is the client review.

THE CLIENT REVIEW
Each time you visit with a client, it is an opportunity to revisit the elements contained within the formula for financial planning:

Discovery	(Goals, Challenges, Successes)	+
Capital Protection	(Family, Health, Life, Legacy)	+
Wealth Management	(Net Worth, Net Cash Flow)	+

= Financial Planning

Each component of the formula should be an integral discussion during your review. We have a rule in our office that if more than 25 percent of the meeting revolves around discussing a client's investment accounts with our firm, we have violated the formula and have not delivered genuine financial planning to our client. Honestly, it's really not that hard to do it. But it's very easy to allow yourself to get wrapped up in justifying performance numbers and digging into the minutia.

We view the client review as an opportunity to "polish the big rocks, reinforce the pebbles, and sift through the sand for unnecessary debris." Our office's policy is to let clients know that they can visit with us for review meetings as often as they want. Typically, we conduct one to two client review meetings a day, and generally we meet with our clients once a year. As a means of maintaining checks and balances, we produce a monthly report through our contact management system that lists which clients need scheduling for an annual review. This system ensures that each client is contacted proactively by our firm for a meeting. On a very rare occasion though, a client may not respond to calls. We follow up our calls with a letter.

LETTER TO NON RESPONSIVE CLIENT FOR ANNUAL MEETING

<Today's Date>

<Client Name>
<Street Name>
<City, State & Zip>

Dear <Client:>

It has been our pleasure managing your financial planning needs over the past several years. Recently, we have made several attempts to contact you for a review of your financial planning and unfortunately have not heard back from you.

Silence can often be considered an expression of approval, yet we want to be certain that your financial planning needs are being met.

While we do our very best to create strategies that align with your personal financial planning goals, it is important that we meet with you face-to-face to ensure that these goals remain consistent.

We believe it is essential that we coordinate a time to schedule a meeting in the very near future so that you might bring us up to date on events going on in your life.

We know that your schedule keeps you busy, but it is essential that the strategies you've built with our firm continue to remain in line with your personal goals and objectives.

If nothing else, please call and let us know what's going on in your life. We'd welcome the opportunity to visit with you again.

Sincerely,

Marc S. Freedman CFP®, President

By sending this letter as a follow up after a few reminder calls, you are doing your duty as a financial planner to proactively contact your client and offer your continuing service. If a client chooses to not respond to the letter, you will have a written record and you should be sure that you store it in your client's folder. When a client is non-responsive to our letter, we typically post a follow-up call three months later, and begin calling them again for a review.

I know that many planners enjoy meeting with clients quarterly, but we have found that once a year is usually adequate. However, in the first year or two of establishing a relationship with a client, it is more likely that we would schedule meetings more often. If your practice is designed to schedule review meetings quarterly, perhaps your conversations are focused more on investment performance and economic issues rather than bigger picture financial planning items. If your clients are truly hiring you for financial planning advice, once they've built a trusting relationship with you, is it really necessary to meet quarterly?

One of the reasons I enjoy working with the mass affluent marketplace is that once you've defined your role as their financial planner, they are more than happy to defer with the details to your discretion. They really don't care why you've chosen to rebalance a portfolio, change an investment, or tweak the overall asset allocation. In fact, they are prone to saying, "that's what I pay *you* for," when we, as planners, can't help but share some of the granular issues with them. What your clients *really* want is a sincere conversation with you. They want you to ask provocative questions. They want to be reminded of the valuable *financial planning* service you continue to offer them. In essence, all they want is the same degree of peace of mind you delivered during your initial financial planning presentation.

BUILDING SYSTEMS THAT WORK

A few years ago, I attended a session at an FPA Retreat that introduced me to mind-mapping. This software allows you to turn projects and tasks into pictures and graphs quite easily. In fact, I have used mind-mapping to help write this book and to plan FPA's 2008 national conference in Boston. The software we use can be found at www.mindjet.com. As a means of translating a mind map into reality, we decided to map our client review process. As a staff, we agreed that the client review was one of the most consistently followed processes in our office. Of course, there would always be unique nuances to each client's review preparation, but when we stepped back and looked at our process, it was actually easy to identify steps and build our mind map.

The graphic below is a high-level view of the nine steps we follow when preparing for a review.

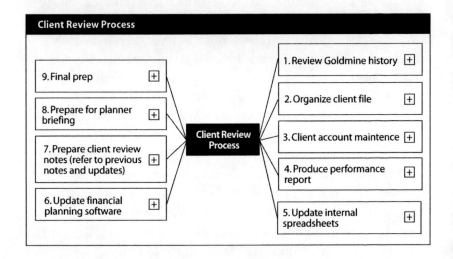

If you read the mind map in a clockwise direction, you can see the steps we take when reviews are prepared. You should note that after each step, for example, *Step 3: Client account maintenance*, there is a plus sign. If you click on the plus, the map will open to a series of sub-steps and instructions. (See following)

OUR CLIENT REVIEW PROCESS

Over the next few pages, we will walk you through the steps used for completing the client review process. Ultimately, a paraplanner can be assigned to perform steps one through seven on their own. We have found that it generally takes between 30 and 90 minutes to put all of the necessary details together prior to the planner briefing (Step 8). Throughout this chapter, we will dig deeper into some of the steps and simply highlight some of the others. You will be introduced to some specific tools we use for client reviews in our own office, and in other parts you will be presented with some ideas that should serve

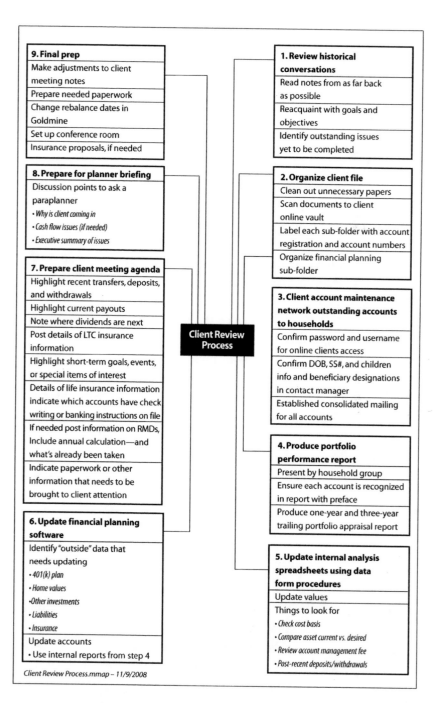

9. Final prep

Make adjustments to client meeting notes

Prepare needed paperwork

Change rebalance dates in Goldmine

Set up conference room

Insurance proposals, if needed

8. Prepare for planner briefing

Discussion points to ask a paraplanner

- *Why is client coming in*
- *Cash flow issues (if needed)*
- *Executive summary of issues*

7. Prepare client meeting agenda

Highlight recent transfers, deposits, and withdrawals

Highlight current payouts

Note where dividends are next

Post details of LTC insurance information

Highlight short-term goals, events, or special items of interest

Details of life insurance information indicate which accounts have check writing or banking instructions on file

If needed post information on RMDs, Include annual calculation—and what's already been taken

Indicate paperwork or other information that needs to be brought to client attention

6. Update financial planning software

Identify "outside" data that needs updating

- *401(k) plan*
- *Home values*
- *Other investments*
- *Liabilities*
- *Insurance*

Update accounts

- Use internal reports from step 4

Client Review Process.mmap – 11/9/2008

Client Review Process

1. Review historical conversations

Read notes from as far back as possible

Reacquaint with goals and objectives

Identify outstanding issues yet to be completed

2. Organize client file

Clean out unnecessary papers

Scan documents to client online vault

Label each sub-folder with account registration and account numbers

Organize financial planning sub-folder

3. Client account maintenance network outstanding accounts to households

Confirm password and username for online clients access

Confirm DOB, SS#, and children info and beneficiary designations in contact manager

Established consolidated mailing for all accounts

4. Produce portfolio performance report

Present by household group

Ensure each account is recognized in report with preface

Produce one-year and three-year trailing portfolio appraisal report

5. Update internal analysis spreadsheets using data form procedures

Update values

Things to look for

- *Check cost basis*
- *Compare asset current vs. desired*
- *Review account management fee*
- *Post-recent deposits/withdrawals*

as a baseline process. More than likely, you will want to draw upon the unique tools and programs that are germane to your particular business's operation. My intent is to offer proof that when you have a system for preparing a client review, it can be outrageously effective and as fresh as the first time you presented your client's first financial plan.

I'd encourage you to think about how you have prepared for client meetings in the past. Ask yourself what elements you could add to your process that could freshen up your current approach to review meetings.

So here we go. Let's jump in and take a look at a client review process. Our nine steps in preparing for a client review are:

1. **Review Goldmine (contact management) history**—This is probably *the most important* step, because it forces you to review past conversations, meetings, and uncompleted activities pertaining to your client. Whether you use Goldmine or some other contact management system, you should always allow your historical notes to serve as the foundation for the preparation of every client review. Here are a few things we typically look for when reviewing notes:
   - Read notes from as far back as possible.
     - Focus on memos, e-mails, and other communications
   - Search for the big rocks, what's important to the client. Is it...
     - Replacement of income
     - Wealth accumulation
     - Meeting unique client goals
     - Providing for children
     - Etc.
   - Identify outstanding issues not yet (or expected to be) completed.
     - Long-term care proposal
     - Life and/or disability proposal

- 529 info to set up accounts for grandchildren
- Possible need to change income needs
- A potential rollover due to employment change
- Certificates of deposit coming due
- Funds held elsewhere now beyond surrender charges
- Upcoming events that need attention
- Etc.

2. **Organize the client file**—Whether you've managed to build an electronic file for your client or you still maintain copies in file folders, this should be the prime opportunity to clean up old statements, ensure that the folders are in good working order, and make sure that there aren't any unneeded documents floating around. Believe it or not, you may even come across a piece of paper that has been misfiled. Here are a few items we look to address during our review process:
   - Clean out unnecessary papers, statements, and old documents.
   - If you come across any handwritten notes that aren't recorded in Goldmine, enter them as completed actions on the date the notes were captured.
   - Ensure that labels on subfolders are in good order. We use a color-coded system that separates each type of account and client registration. For example,
      - Purple main folder—this houses all subfolders and holds all information pertaining to planning details
      - Red folder for individual advisory account
      - Blue subfolder for retirement advisory accounts
   - Ensure that copy of client's drivers license/passport is current.

- Ensure that all accounts have been placed into a single household record for our account management software system.
- Ensure that all accounts are included as part of our household combined mailing service.

3. **Client account maintenance**—Use this opportunity to ensure that the clients' details, pertaining to both their financial life and financial accounts, are appropriately captured in your CRM, planning, or broker-dealer software. If accounts need to be linked or added to a consolidated mailing, this is your chance to do it. Perhaps your client has added a child to the family, purchased a summer cottage, or been through a name change due to marriage or divorce. This is your chance to:

   - Convert client notes you come across on scraps of paper and post them to the history section of your client's contact management record. Once you enter them here, they are more easily accessible for the next client review and potential audits.
   - Update data fields in your contact management system. Recently we've added fields in our CRM software that allow us to insert beneficiary designations, update trust information, insurance premium details, etc.
   - Make updates to any Web sites or online vaults you maintain for your clients. Make certain that their personal documents are current and accessible.
   - Ensure that your client's usernames and passwords that provide access to client sites are current and active.

4. **Produce performance reports**—Yes, you do need to let clients know how they are doing. Generally, we prefer to produce performance numbers for our clients on rolling one-, three-, and five-year timeframes. However, if a client has been dollar cost averaging (DCA) into an account, we recommend refraining from presenting performance numbers until

at least one year after all of the money has been invested. Presenting performance figures while a DCA is in progress gives a questionable impression of a portfolio's performance and could deliver an improper message to the client. When preparing additional information concerning investments your clients hold, I would encourage delivering fact sheets rather than statistical analyses. We find that most clients prefer to scan a graph, analyst commentary, or style box. They aren't as interested in technical indicators such as alpha, beta, correlation variances, and regression analyses. My experience suggests that your client is paying you to understand the details, all they want is high-level information.

Another report worth producing is an updated net worth statement. This document will show your clients the true growth and/or reduction in their total financial worth. Be sure that your net worth statement includes columns for ownership as well as categories for different types of assets and liabilities. A sample net worth statement is on page 246.

5. **Update internal spreadsheets**—I find that some of the best ways to convey your commitment to delivering customized advice and investment management is through the use and maintenance of spreadsheets and graphics you've developed internally. Of course, financial planning software does a nice job presenting projections and information, but it is difficult to capture just the right details in prepackaged software. Frankly, it is the reason why we built a spreadsheet in 1991 that still serves as the core worksheet and presentation tool when we talk with our clients about their investment accounts. I am delighted to share a description of this worksheet with you in this book. Let me preface by saying that current technology could likely automate many of the processes I'll present below. While our clients continue to rave about the data we provide in this Excel sheet,

Oversold and Underserved: A Financial Planner's Guidebook to Effectively Serving the Mass Affluent

Sample Net Worth Statement / *Prepared for <Client Name>*				
ASSETS:	**Client**	**Spouse**	**Joint**	**Total**
NON-QUALIFIED ASSETS:				
Cash Equivalents:				
Bank of America checking	--	--	$14,674	$14,674
Bank of America savings	$13,480	--	--	$13,480
Bank of America savings	$28,871	--	--	$28,871
Nuveen money market	$1,559	--	--	$1,559
National Grand passbook	$21,634	--	--	$21,634
National Grand Bank CD (due 1/13/09)	--	--	$26,491	$26,491
National Grand Bank CD (due 1/13/09)	--	--	$15,895	$15,895
National Grand Bank CD (due 5/23/10)	$10,215	--	--	$10,215
National Grand Bank CD (due 5/23/10)	$52,982	--	--	$52,982
Zephyr Bank checking	--	$4,484	--	$4,484
Taxable Investments:				
AXA Annuity	$18,308	--	--	$18,308
Morgan Stanley Brkg	$24,354	--	--	$24,354
Morgan Stanley Brkg	--	$1,475	--	$1,475
Total: Non-Qualified Assets	**$171,403**	**$5,959**	**$57,060**	**$234,422**
RETIREMENT ASSETS:				
Qualified Retirement:				
Children's Hospital Retirement Plan	$981,333	--	--	$981,333
Putnam SEP-IRA	$12,643	--	--	$12,643
Equitable Annuity IRA	--	$146,297	--	$146,297
Morgan Stanley IRA	--	$47,749	--	$47,749
Red Sox 401(k)	--	$94,814	--	$94,814
Total: Retirement Assets	**$993,976**	**$288,860**	**$0**	**$1,282,836**
TOTAL LIQUID ASSETS	**$1,165,379**	**$294,819**	**$57,060**	**$1,517,258**
REAL ESTATE ASSETS:				
177 Champion's Way	--	--	$700,000	$700,000
Total: Real Estate Assets	**$0**	**$0**	**$700,000**	**$700,000**
TOTAL ASSETS	**$1,165,379**	**$294,819**	**$757,060**	**$2,217,258**
TOTAL NET WORTH: $2,217,258				
LIABILITIES:	**Client**	**Spouse**	**Joint**	**Total**
TOTAL LIABILITIES	**$0**	**$0**	**$0**	**$0**
NET WORTH	**$1,165,379**	**$294,819**	**$757,060**	**$2,217,258**
LIABILITIES + NET WORTH	**$1,165,379**	**$294,819**	**$757,060**	**$2,217,258**

I'd welcome the opportunity to build another report that reflects today's technology. Anyone up for the challenge?

PRESENTATION OF THE FREEDMAN FINANCIAL SPREADSHEET

When I joined our firm in 1990, I found it disconcerting that most investment companies made it difficult for clients to know the value of the securities in their accounts. In fact, most mutual fund companies were famous for providing a monthly statement that simply told the clients how many shares they owned of a fund. It was up to them to go to the newspaper (the Internet was a relatively unknown concept in the early 1990s) and look up their share prices. If your clients were like most, they were investing in commission-based mutual funds that listed two share prices for their funds: the "POP" price (what you paid per share), and the "NAV" price (what you could sell it for). The difference (the spread) between POP and NAV was generally the commission to purchase the fund.

As I mentioned earlier in the book, 1991 was when we began to introduce fee-based advisory accounts to our clients, and honestly, these statements weren't all that much better. As a result, we decided to construct a spreadsheet that would always answer four questions for our clients:

1. How much money did I give you?
2. How much money have I withdrawn from my account?
3. How much money do I have in my account?
4. How do you manage my account relative to its asset allocation model?

Our goal was to produce a viewer-friendly, one-page document that could answer all four of these questions. We constructed a spreadsheet for this purpose in 1991 and it is the same one we use in 2008.

The formulas were constructed with help from the tech-support desk in Washington state by an emerging company called

Oversold and Underserved: A Financial Planner's Guidebook to Effectively Serving the Mass Affluent

SAM Worksheet *(For Internal Use Only)*				
Date:				
Client Name				
Account #				
Invest. Object.				
Acct. Type:				

Trans/Sold Securities

Date	Description	#/Shares	Value	
				STOCKS
				BONDS
				CASH
				TOTAL
		Totals		

	Net $s Invested				**Current Value**
	This is a retirement account			*Est. Cost as of*	
Style	Fund Name	# of Shares	NAV	without a R/D	Value on
	Total Current Values:				

		Systematic Payout-Monthly	
Acct Opened:		Start Date:	
Last Rebalance:		SPO Yield to Current Value -->	
Mgt. Fee		Current Portfolio. Yield	
Phone #		Estimated Income	

Dollars In			*Dollars Out*		
Date	Deposits	Source	Date	Withdrawl	Purpose
			SPO Totals		
Totals					

% Gain or Loss	Estimated Gain/Loss	Current Allocation	Desired Allocation	For Perfect Balance	Current Yield	Current Income	Rebalnc'd Income

Microsoft. Believe it or not, if you were willing to pay the toll call, their techies would stay on the phone with you for hours, helping you to construct a formula that met your needs.

How Much Money Did I Give You?
The upper left-hand section (TRANS/SOLD SECURITIES) allows us to list items that have transferred into the client's account. The upper middle section (DOLLARS IN) allows us to post deposits received. We've also included a source column that answers the question, "Where did the money come from?"

How Much Money Have I Withdrawn from My Account?
In the DOLLARS OUT section, we itemize where money has been withdrawn over time. Our Systematic Payout area shows the monthly amount drawn from the account, and then the cumulative amount of money the client has withdrawn appears at the bottom of the DOLLARS OUT section. It can be quite enlightening to show a client how much money he or she has cumulatively withdrawn from an account.

How Much Money Do I Have in My Account?
In the middle of the spreadsheet we list:

Net Dollars Invested—This number is calculated by adding ("TRANSFERS IN" + "DOLLARS IN") and subtracting "DOLLARS OUT."

Current Value—Located in the heart of the spreadsheet, this value is derived from the total current value of the portfolio and is captured by copying the value from the bottom middle of the spreadsheet.

How Are You Managing My Account Relative to Its Asset Allocation?
The bottom half of our spreadsheet is designed to itemize each of the investments, as well as its asset class. We use a look-up table from an Excel source document that automatically inserts:

1. A description of the investment
2. The current asset allocation style
3. The current 30-day yield, if any

Our paraplanner needs only to manually insert

1. Number of shares
2. NAV price per share
3. Estimated cost basis

Each of these items is readily accessible from our broker-dealer's Internet portal. The remainder of the spreadsheet generally calculates itself.

The Current Allocation and *Desired Allocation* columns are where the financial planner does any rebalancing that may be necessary. This is the only task necessary for our financial planners—all other tasks relating to the upkeep of the spreadsheet are handled by our paraplanner.

During our client review meeting we would discuss our rationale for making portfolio rebalancing decisions. Some of the reasons that might lead to a change are:

1. Basic rebalancing
2. A manager change
3. Underperformance of a fund to its benchmark
4. Asset allocation tweaking
5. Changes in internal cost structure

MANAGING TAXES

IMPORTANT NOTE: When we are using our spreadsheet for retirement accounts, we *do not* update cost basis. Instead, the cost basis column houses the actual dollars invested in the fund. In this instance, the client can visualize changes in each investment without the distraction of reinvested dividends being added back into the cost basis.

We *never* allow our clients to take this sheet home with them. We tell them that this is our proprietary worksheet that we maintain especially for them. While we're happy to share it and discuss it during a review, we prefer to keep the details pertaining to the way in which we manage their accounts under our supervision. Our compliance department has also suggested that we keep this as an internal document because the numbers on the spreadsheet have not officially been audited. We certainly wouldn't want to upset the people who are paid to protect us.

…and now back to our mind map listing of our client review process.

6. **Update financial planning software**—Take time to update any manually entered details pertaining to your client's financial life into your software. This might include:
    - Refinancing your client might have done since your last visit.
        - Changes in interest rates, monthly payments, and terms of new debt could affect the cash flow management components of your software
    - Updates to accounts held outside your management. This might include:
        - Employee retirement accounts
        - Bank accounts
        - Outside brokerage accounts
        - Stock certificates held personally
        - Collectibles, hard assets, and real estate
        - Insurance policies
        - Other miscellaneous items

We have elected to use eMoney for our clients who maintain an ongoing financial planning/advisory relationship with our firm. In doing so, many of our clients' assets and liabilities are aggregated daily into the software.

Many planners elect to contact clients at least a few days in advance of the review meeting to obtain details that may have changed since their last visit. In my opinion, one of the biggest wastes of time during a client review is when you have to update your financial planning software while the client sits in your office with you. Do your very best to proactively prepare for a client meeting.

7. **Prepare client review meeting notes**—This becomes an opportunity for you or your paraplanner to prepare notes, findings, and checklist items that need to be discussed during the meeting. Below are some of the items we ask our paraplanner to capture in "Meeting Notes" in advance of the planner briefing:

    - Detail any transfers, deposits, and withdrawals that have occurred in non-advisory accounts. We only maintain our spreadsheet for advisory investment accounts.
    - Detail any systematic payouts (SPOs).
    - Detail any automatic investments.
    - Identify if any DCA programs are in process. If they've recently ended, when did they stop?
    - Identify any current withdrawal yields from investment accounts.
    - Indicate where any non-reinvested dividends and other payouts are being sent.
    - Detail pertinent information on long-term care policies.
        - Premium (mode of payment)—Source of funds to pay premium
        - Daily benefit
        - Elimination period

- – Benefit period
- – Etc.
- Identify pertinent info such as
  - – ID expired
  - – Missing e-mail address
  - – Not registered for account view
- Detail life insurance information
  - – Premium (mode of payment) – How paid
  - – Death benefit, type, term
- Are there check writing or banking instructions on account?
- Does client need to take RMD? (include calculation)
  - – Is paperwork attached?

8. **Prepare and conduct a planner briefing**—This is your opportunity to review all of the data that have been prepared and have an in-depth conversation regarding your client. It may also be a time when it's necessary to:
   - Gather paperwork to open a new account
   - Prepare applications for insurance
   - Gather forms for changing beneficiaries
   - Add transfers on death to an account

   It is also a great opportunity to mentor a younger planner in your office and discuss your thought process in mentally preparing for a meeting. Try thinking back to the first time you presented their financial plan. How did your clients react? Could there be some reports or analyses you prepared years ago that might be worthy of a comparative analysis? Clients can find humor and insight in old data forms and notes that:
   - Identify their old salaries
   - Show them how much money they *thought* they'd need to spend in retirement

- Capture the balances of their investment accounts and bring to light the time value of money
- List the estimated value on their homes from years past
- Explore how they've reduced their debt over the years
- Remind them about their fears and worries that are long gone

Yes. Looking back at the work you've done for a client can be self-serving too. But more than anything else, it reminds you and them about the true *financial planning* value you've delivered to them over the years.

9. **Final prep**—As you prepare for the final step I'd encourage you to do the following:
   - Pull out your formula for financial planning, and ensure that your final agenda includes discussion points on discovery, capital protection, and wealth management. If it doesn't, ask yourself why not. Perhaps there is something you've missed in preparing for the review.
   - Consider whether a new SWOT analysis may be of value to your client. It may be interesting to see whether anything has changed since your last visit.
   - Think about the value these clients have brought into your life, your practice, and the lives of people you work with. Could there be a story that a staff person shared about them that brought a smile to your face, or a referral they sent your way? Lightening the atmosphere and turning your client review into a conversation makes for an exceptionally enjoyable 60 minutes.
   - Of course, make sure your conference room is neat and that the presentation of your office would exceed a client's expectations. Take a few moments

> to look back at Section II, Chapter 6, "Impressions that Matter Most."

Think about it. How different should a review meeting be from the first time you met your client? If you could impart that same level of enthusiasm, the same feeling of warmth, and of course, your personable charm and wit during every client encounter, what impressions might your client make about you? Imagine how outrageously different and proud your clients would feel about your commitment to helping them truly achieve their life's goals.

That's it. That's the client review process.

If you can create an experience where your client can remain centered more on the big rocks than those pesky grains of sand, you have become an exceptional financial planner. When you hit that milestone, your clients will sing your praises not because you helped them earn a certain return on their investments, but because you delivered them peace of mind through genuine financial planning. And that's why they hired you in the first place.

I hope that this section has opened your eyes to some of the various methods and approaches you can implement when delivering financial planning. This list of tools and techniques is far from exhaustive, but it should add ideas to your quiver when your goal is to build a financial planning-based relationship with your client. If you've read this far through the book, I would suspect that you are serious about being a genuine financial planner and advancing the profession of financial planning. Never be ashamed of getting paid for your wisdom, advice, and planning skills. Give your clients confidence and peace of mind and they will be loyal to you.

The final section of this book is titled, "From Simple to Spectacular—Marketing and Practice Management Ideas that Retain the Mass Affluent Client." While finding new clients should be a continual goal of your firm, you should be paying equal attention to identifying your target market and working to retain existing clients who provide the foundational value for those you wish to serve in the future. The section will begin with an in-depth exploration of how we reduced our client base by 25 percent and became instantly more profitable. In doing so, we were able to better indentify our core values, as well as the clients who best represented our target market. Our goal is to provide you with the tools to help you consider turning a "knowing" in your practice into a "doing." In the end, you'll be amazed how empowering it becomes.

In addition, we will introduce you to a series of practice management and service techniques, as well as present a special section, written by my father and the founder of Freedman Financial, Barry M. Freedman, CFP®, on seminar marketing techniques. This is a collection of practical ideas that come in all shapes and sizes and costs, from as little as pennies to thousands of dollars. No matter your budget, I am certain that you will find value in Section IV.

SUMMARY

1. Keep your clients focused on the big rocks.
2. Design a template that creates a memorable client review experience.
3. Never be ashamed of charging for financial planning services.

Section IV:

From Simple to Spectacular— Marketing and Practice Management Techniques that Retain the Mass Affluent Client

15 | *Market Segmentation— The Story of a Practice Transformed*

OBJECTIVES
- Strategies to help you identify your target market
- Ideas for how to implement these strategies
- How to begin to view your client base from a business perspective

How we did it: (Our stories)
- How we identified our target market
- How we initiated our practice transformation
- The results of our efforts

How has your client base been developed? Perhaps you've relied upon seminars, direct marketing campaigns, word or mouth, or cold calls. In doing so, how does your client base today look like the client base you had imagined when you first started in this business?

Over the years, was it possible that the characteristics of your client base weren't as important as having people willing to buy your products and services? If you're like most planners, intuitively you know that your current client mix isn't ideal, but the thought of examining it might be as scary as it is valuable.

The practice of financial planning has been a part of my family's life since 1968. Though it has survived different styles, techniques, and philosophies, the focus on holistic financial planning has always been paramount in the relationships we've formed with clients. Today, though, after 40 years in business, our community-based, independently owned financial planning practice now has purpose and vision. The goal of this chapter is to help you begin thinking about your strengths as a planner, and to begin aligning these values with the clients you could serve best.

When I joined my father's practice in the early 1990s, our firm was nothing more than a convenience store for those who sought financial services. We hadn't consciously focused on a particular type of client because our natural presence as active citizens in our local community led to our building a client base made up of local people with varying needs for services.

ANALYZING YOUR CLIENTS

More than anything else, I believe we want to work with people we like. But for many of us, our client base consists of anyone who expresses a desire to engage our services.

You know intuitively that refining your client base should lead to efficiencies. But have you ever considered how focusing your business could result in the emergence of a practice that reflects your values and beliefs?

If you've been a reader of financial planning publications or have attended association meetings, you've surely heard stories and presentations about "taking your practice to the next level." I've attended more of these sessions than I can remember, and each time I leave the room, I'm motivated for an hour or two and then find myself heading back to the same old routine, because the thought of analyzing my client base and confronting significant unprofitable pockets is a scary proposition that's better left unknown.

As I mentioned, we essentially enrolled anyone as a client. In fact, we viewed our practice as profitable and successful, because as much as we enjoyed helping our clients improve their quality of life, we were able to do it, too.

Then, one day, a virtual anvil fell on me and I was sickened by the reality that our business was not profitable, and it was, at best, adequately managed.

According to the 2002 FPA Financial Performance Study designed by Moss Adams, my firm, Freedman Financial, was classified as an elite ensemble. Comprising three CFP practitioners and four support staff, our firm had been serving the financial planning needs of a segment of Massachusetts called the North Shore. The center point of our radius was about 12 miles north of Boston. In fact, 90 percent of the 450 households we served lived within 15 miles of our office. It was common to see our clients in the supermarket, at school assemblies with our children, in line at Dunkin Donuts, and at cultural events around town.

In mid-2002, with the help of Moss Adams' templates, we learned that our profitability per client was $41—a dismal number by any standards. On a referral from Bob Barry, former FPA Chairman, we hired Kevin Poland in July of 2002 to help us better understand the purpose of our practice and determine a way to retool it so that it reflected our core values and helped us become more profitable. It was something we had never done in the 34 years of our firm's existence. We thought about it a lot but had never before turned our thinking into doing.

To say that it was brain-stretching and time consuming would be an understatement, but the end result led us to reduce our client base by 25 percent and become more efficient and more profitable almost overnight. On the pages that follow, you will read how we accomplished our goal. Rather than just provide you with a checklist and a series of questions to contemplate, I'd prefer to also show you what we did, what questions we asked, and what tools we used, all with the hope that you'll be inspired to transform your practice as well. If you're willing to dedicate the time and commit the resources needed to run your firm like a business, the results will not only be rewarding for your clients, but you will be charged with a new sense of purpose and you'll hold a vision that can easily be shared with whomever you meet.

You do have the ability to make dramatic changes to your practice!

THE STORY OF A PRACTICE TRANSFORMED

If "mammals," is your answer to the question, "Who is your target market?" you should find this story of great value.

To help us find our target market, Kevin had us try to organize our existing client base into a few categories. Each category was designed to highlight the types of overarching services and products we offered to each group. After much slicing and dicing, we identified a few high-level parameters that would help create these segments of clients. Based on the 450 households we served, we agreed that the following groupings best represented our existing client base:

SEGMENT #1—Assets Under Management (AUM) Clients (50 percent.) These households had established a relationship with our firm by first paying an up-front financial planning fee ($1,000–$4,500), for a customized analysis, written recommendations, and strategies. An action plan was written so that clients were empowered to implement any of our recommendations with anyone of their choosing. While they were under no obligation to implement any strategies with our firm, AUM clients did choose to establish fee-based advisory relationships with our firm by moving their available investment assets under our management. We continued to provide ongoing updates to their financial plans as

well as delivering overall management of their wealth. They paid
for these ongoing services through our fee-based advisory program,
where annual fees range from 0.6 to 1.75 percent of the assets they
placed under our management. Generally, these clients had placed
between $100K and $2 million with us, and in 2002, the average household maintained assets under management of $315,000.
Today our average household has almost $500,000 in average assets
under management with our firm.

SEGMENT #2—Related Clients (22 percent.) These clients were
essentially family members of AUM clients. While they may not
have had sizable financial resources, they viewed their financial
planning needs as significant, and we believed their relationships
with us were as important as the ones we maintained with their
AUM parents. In many cases, we charged them a small financial
planning fee and then used commission-based funds to help them
implement investment strategies. Typically, they had investable
assets of less than $75K. In most cases, they were in the early stages
of building investment portfolios. They were excellent candidates
for term insurance and disability protection. They needed tax planning advice and usually a referral to an estate planning attorney for
a simple will. But more than anything else, as relatives of our AUM
clients, we viewed them as an important segment of our practice—
just one that might need a different level of attention and services.

SEGMENT #3—Other Clients (28 percent.) This type of client
usually hired our firm with a particular implementation need. Typically, they were referred to us to handle IRA rollovers from previous
employers or they wanted to begin building investment accounts. In
most cases, the solution resulted in the sale of a commission-based
product. We agreed to do light modular planning at no cost because
we felt an obligation to deliver it to our clients. They typically had
no real desire to explore their financial plans. At a bare minimum,

we always prepared a simple net worth assessment before implementing any strategy.

What became apparent was that no matter what relationship we had established with "other clients," we always felt committed to deliver some element of planning before agreeing to any implementation strategy. Unfortunately, we had never set a standard that required clients to pay for it prior to implementing strategies.

DIGGING DEEPER

We agreed that we needed to better understand our AUM clients as they were clearly the largest segment and likely produced the largest revenue stream for our office. Kevin asked us to identify key adjectives that would describe our very best clients who had been allocated into this category. He reminded us to search for adjectives that described our existing clients—*not clients we hoped to serve in the future.* They are listed below for your review.

Key Characteristics of Core Clients	Key Characteristics of Core Clients
At Freedman Financial	*Your Firm (List below)*
Loyal	
Seek friendships and caring	
Optimists (view the world positively)	
Genuinely happy	
Sociable	
Generous (to family)	
Trusting	
Proud	

We then used these adjectives to build a profile paragraph for them.

OUR BEST CLIENTS

Our best clients want to know that their business is appreciated. They expect quality, professionalism, integrity, and responsiveness. They want to know that we care as much about their families as we do about them.

*They want to lead fulfilling lives, but have a strong desire to protect
a legacy for their children. They have a growing interest in including
other family members (children especially) in their financial affairs, but
are careful not to be too overbearing. As a result, these clients become
responsible for their own well-being by protecting themselves, yet are
sure to share with their children that they have a relationship with a
financial planner whom they trust, and in many cases they have introduced their children to our firm.*

With a written profile of our very best clients, we agreed to look
more carefully at the characteristics of our AUM clients and further
categorize them by their needs and services they seek from our
firm. Certainly not everyone hires you for the same reason. Each
client has their own set of unique characteristics—but could there
be similarities as well? Ultimately, three segments emerged among
our AUM clients, and as a result, we were about to identify three
targetable markets within this category. We called them family
stewards, accumulators, and survivors.

We called our dominant segment "family stewards." This segment
represented about 60 percent of our client base and we classified this
group as our *primary target market*. Common traits included:

- Over age 50
- Married to their first spouse
- Lived in the same home for 20 years or more
- Expressed a strong set of family values
- Stated a desire to stay active and visible in the local community
- Generally held middle and upper middle management positions
- Active participants in company retirement plans
- Kept liabilities to a minimum
- Viewed themselves as having multiple financial planning issues

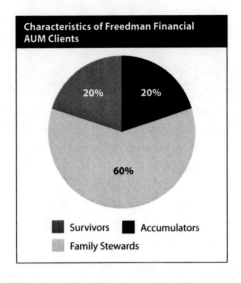

We further learned that many sought to find a snowbird location during retirement where they would likely *rent* for a month or two in the south, but not buy. Collectively, their household income was between $75K and $175K, and they found ways to save at least 10 percent of their earnings each year. They maintained traditional family values and rejoiced over grandparenthood. Their lifestyle suggested that $4K–7K per month would cover their overall spending needs. Generally, they had investable assets between $300K and $1 million. They were *not* charitably inclined and they had strong feelings about whether they wanted to leave an estate to their children or spend their last dollar before they died.

In addition, they appreciated conversation more than numbers and would much prefer the big picture to the details. They sought advice and not analytics and they valued our ability to re-state previous conversations and remind them of their goals and objectives. They looked to us as their "trusted advisers" and had often remarked that previous advisers had never proactively raised financial planning ideas beyond investment strategies. They found our approach refreshing. These clients welcomed the opportunity to include their children in client meetings and appreciated our offers to host family meetings. They encouraged their kids to hire us as planners and we always said yes, regardless of their financial situation.

The other two groups that emerged out of our AUM clients were the accumulators and the survivors.

Accumulators—20 percent of our client base. More than 50 percent of these clients were related to a family steward client. A few prominent traits included:

- Prospering family
- Excess cash flow
- Strong desire to fund long-term goals
- Time pressured
- High willingness to delegate

These clients were often the children of our family steward clients, but another prominent referral source for these clients came (believe it or not) from mutual fund wholesalers, financial services company executives, and accountants. Generally, they had incomes between $200K and $500K. They were very busy, but desperately wanted to spend more time with their spouses and children. They looked to hire professionals for everything they did and appreciated it when we showcased our ability to proactively orchestrate financial issues. They encouraged us to build relationships with their accountants, attorneys, human resources contacts, insurance agents, and more. They appreciated access to their accounts over the Internet, but honestly, they infrequently looked at the numbers. These clients operated more on impulse and often had short tempers that were easily defused when facts could support their questions.

This group's needs were definitely different from the family steward group, but there was enough of a foundation of clients that we considered them an important secondary target market. The other secondary market was the survivors.

Survivors—20 percent of the client base. More than 50 percent of these clients were the surviving spouses of family stewards. Other survivors included divorcees and sudden money clients. Common traits of this group:

- Overwhelmed
- Feel great pressure from outsiders to make decisions
- Thirst for trusted advice
- Uncertain of the future
- Income needs
- Desire simplicity

These clients were generally over the age of 60 and were widows of our family steward clients. In many cases, they had never written a check or had any involvement in personal financial matters. They sought our services to accompany them to an auto dealership, help them book a family vacation, or be their right-hand person in family, legal, financial, and planning matters. They generally never considered remarriage, but found great strength from their children and circle of friends. Interestingly, they had become one of our strongest sources for referrals.

If you could take the time to identify target markets in your existing client base, do you think you could better evaluate your service and value proposition? Could you begin to focus on your strengths? What are some of the steps you might take to get started?

A REALITY CHECK FOLLOWING OUR ANALYSIS

I'll admit that, after identifying these three target markets, I felt a bit uncomfortable. It was rare that we were serving minorities, single parents, same-sex couples, or people involved in second or third marriages. I wondered if we had been discriminating against people, and I began to feel queasy. After all, it wasn't intentional. It was then that Kevin reminded me that business owners naturally serve people who they relate to best, and their clients find comfort when people just like them are served, as well.

Soon, an ah-ha moment occurred. Remarkably, my entire staff shared many of these same values. In fact, when I shared our findings with clients, they smiled—it's almost as if they knew it. I think they were more surprised it took us so long to figure it out.

Planner Exercise: *Take a look at your client base. If you placed them in one giant room, who might they eventually gravitate toward? Think about this. When you went to college and had to select where you would sit at lunch time, where did you find yourself most comfortable? Was it with different people each day, or was it with people with whom you hoped to build relationships? If you were to ask a client for a referral to a contractor or a plumber, don't you think they'd send you to someone with whom they felt comfortable? Therefore if you were to build a client base from scratch, wouldn't it make sense to find people with interests and styles that could ultimately lead them to referring you to more prospects who were just like them?*

THE DIGGING CONTINUES

Now that we had three target markets (family stewards, accumulators, and survivors), we decided to apply the characteristics of each group to all 450 households. This meant that we would apply the same standards to our AUM clients, our Related clients, and our Other clients. The results that came from this analysis were fascinating. As we began the next phase of our exercise, I found myself gravitating toward a theme. It was that I believed that financial planning services needed to not only serve as the core function we delivered to our clients, but our clients also needed to know that it was our primary core belief. It was just as important to me that clients could articulate our role in their lives as that they understood how committed we were to delivering it to them.

Also, if ongoing financial planning services were going to be an important part of our business model, could one-time commission-based strategies provide enough of a predictable revenue stream from each client to offset the time we wanted to spend serving their needs and building lifelong relationships?

With that question in mind, we decided to analyze the revenue that each of the three groups produced in *year two* of the relationship with our firm. What we learned was that our AUM clients produced 83 percent of second-year revenue, Related clients produced 16 percent, and Other clients produced 1 percent.

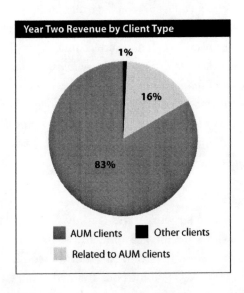

Frankly, this wasn't too surprising, since second-year revenue from Other clients primarily stemmed from 12b-1 fees. Yet, 1 percent in revenues translated to $10,000 to the office (or about $10 million in assets held in commission-based funds). In all fairness, we looked back to year one and learned that Other clients produced 7 percent of first-year revenues (about $70,000).

Related clients justified the 16 percent allocation because many of them were adding money each month to a commission-based investment account.

It's important to note that many AUM clients also purchased commission-based items, such as insurance products or alternative investments. We believed that if there was a product that could serve them well and address a particular point of vulnerability in their life, the compensation we earned on the product wasn't nearly as much of a deciding factor as knowing the clients' interests were well served.

The next statistic was the most alarming. We asked our staff to measure the time they spent, either on the phone or in person, with each group of clients. Each time a client called the office, we asked staff to identify which category they would fall under and how much time serving their needs took.

Time Management Spreadsheet			
Client Name	**AUM, Related, Client**	**Time Spent (minutes)**	**Issue**
Smith, John	AUM	15	Question on refinancing
Adams, Sylvia	Client	20	Didn't receive monthly check
Drower, Bill	Client	20	Review 401(k) options and answer question about his mother's finances.
Fields, Ben	AUM	5	Called to schedule appointment

When we saw the results, I felt we pinpointed our firm's ailment. The time spent with each segment was as follows:

> AUM clients—60 percent
> Related clients—10 percent
> Other clients—30 percent

That's right; *we had been spending 30 percent of our staff's time serving clients who generated 1 percent of the annual revenue to the office.*

Other clients represented 125 households (almost 25 percent of our client base). A few of these clients dated back to when my father started the firm in 1968. Today, many were taking systematic payouts from their investments or had simply made a

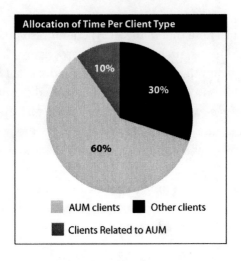

single investment (years ago) with little prospect for additional contributions. Yet, each year, we would proactively contact them for an annual review of their total financial situation. We would continue to send them our quarterly newsletter. We would invite them to client events and support their charitable endeavors. They'd inquire, as needed, about whether to finance, lease, or pay cash for a car. They'd ask about refinancing strategies. They'd call for updates on the value of their accounts. They'd want allocation suggestions for their 401(k) plan and they'd want to introduce us to their friends, neighbors, and relatives who had similar needs—and of course, we'd welcome them into our practice.

We knew that they were just like all our other clients—they simply wanted a trusting relationship. In truth, we cared deeply for each of them and treated each as our most important client. Yet, they were costing our firm money. To be fair, I think we knew it—we just didn't have a plan to change things.

We've all heard the expression, "You can't be all things to all people." Yet in the world of financial planning, as long as a prospect has a pulse and a free hand to sign an application, most financial consultants will welcome him or her into their practice. We all justified this strategy by believing that someday, they could turn into fabulous clients. The exercise of really getting to know our practice made clear that this strategy created more "wait and see" clients than clients who could make our business profitable today.

Can you think of any other profession that offers the same service to everyone without regard for the revenue they generate? Is it possible to treat your clients fairly, but not equally?

Statistically, we understood our firm's points of vulnerability and it was time to make some hard decisions. We printed the names of all clients and placed their client category after their names. We pictured their faces while we read their names, we could recall their unique stories, and reflected fondly over most of these relationships. But reminiscing wasn't going to solve our problems. We agreed that the Other client category needed to phase out of our practice. In addition, we agreed that, moving forward, we would only serve clients who could produce at least $2,500 in annual revenue to the office. Our five-year goal was to move that number to more than $4,000, annually.

I'm not sure exactly how we came up with this number, but here are some factors we considered:

- Average number of hours needed to serve a client face to face
    - Annual review
    - Review preparation
    - Periodic incoming questions from the client
- Overhead costs
    - Employment costs
    - Printing and postage costs
    - Entertainment/sales promotion costs
        - Client appreciation events
        - Newsletters
        - Philanthropic support
- General overhead

Planner Exercise: *What costs exist for every client you serve? No matter the service you provide to each client, there are certain tasks, costs, and time factors associated with each relationship. How would you quantify your cost per client? Consider looking at the total expenses at your firm (including your salary) and dividing it by the number of households you serve. For example, if your expenses are $350,000 and you have 700 clients, your cost per client is $500.*

Try doing the same exercise by taking your net profit and dividing it by your number of clients. Chances are that number is less than you may have ever imagined. As I said earlier, the Moss Adams study displayed a net profit per client of $41 in our practice.

No longer could we afford to deliver our quality services to clients when they were generating only a few hundred dollars or (in many cases) less per year. The average client in this group of 125 was generating about $61 in gross revenue to the firm. If our hourly billing for financial planning advice was $200 per hour, we were losing money before the client had actually arrived at our office. That's because, in advance of his meeting, our staff would need to be calling him for an appointment. We needed to update his financials from the last time he visited with us. We needed to build an agenda for the meeting, and we would need to explore what questions we'd be asking the client during our session.

But in the back of my mind, I kept hearing voices. They whispered:

"Marc, these are really nice people."

"Marc, your dad has been serving these people for over 30 years; are you about to throw them into the streets?"

"Marc, someday they could be great referral sources."

"Marc, what if they inherited a ton of money. How would you feel if they weren't your clients any longer and they ended up working with someone else?"

The more I wrestled with the voices, the clearer the vision and values of our firm became. Suddenly, I began to feel more and more comfortable with facing these voices head on, and living with the consequences. I believed that, in the end, as scary as it felt, we were doing the right thing for the firm. We were putting the interests of clients we could serve best, first!

With the voices at bay, we decided to take the next step.

REMOVING WHAT NO LONGER FIT

Now that we had agreed to address the client segment of our firm, we considered the following options:

- Keep and reassign them
- Fire them
- Ignore them
- Sell them
- Refer them

Keep and reassign them. Much has been written about bringing on a junior planner to assist with less profitable clients. We had attempted this strategy twice before, and learned that it would be too costly, and most importantly, would not be consistent with our core values. By simply allowing a junior planner to serve them, there would still be a tendency for these clients to want to poke their heads in our doors and ask us questions. But even more frightening was facing the return of all of these clients if our junior planner chose to leave our firm. We'd be back to square one.

Fire them. We couldn't simply fire them. These were clients we deeply cared about. We had lived through a range of experiences with each one of them. We knew we would see them in our community and in other social settings.

Ignore them. One of firm's core values is integrity. Ignoring these clients couldn't be an option. Yet, truthfully, prior to acknowledging that integrity was a filter we would apply with every client, we had to admit that there were more than a few clients we had forgotten over the years. Moving forward, we agreed never to allow it to happen again.

Sell them. Frankly, I was not interested in profiting over their departure. I wanted to sleep well at night. I also realized that if I sold these clients to a buyer, the only way the buyer could recoup their costs would be to sell these newly acquired clients something else. In this case, two people would immediately profit from the transaction, and neither would be the client.

Refer them. I felt good about this option. In fact, it gave us the opportunity to interview investment professionals in my community and better understand the value they felt they could deliver to clients. If they held themselves out as financial planners, but were solely interested in dealing with managing a client's investment portfolio, I elected not to use them. I felt that if someone carried the title of financial planner and only managed investments, that I was doing a disservice to my clients and to the profession. I wanted to hand these clients to someone who said his or her primary function was to deliver investment solutions to clients. Because, as we soon found out, planning had nothing to do with our Other clients' perceived relationships with our firm—these clients valued the investment relationship most.

We identified two investment professionals in our community. One was affiliated with a major wirehouse and one was affiliated with an independent broker-dealer. Each was excited about the free referral.

THE COMMUNICATION PLAN

With Kevin's help, we developed a communications campaign that was designed to publicly introduce our firm's vision and values, while at the same time, initiating a strategy designed to streamline the types of clients we planned to serve in the future.

Below is phase one of the communication strategy we initiated. On January 1, 2003, we mailed the following letter to our entire client base (450 letters). It was designed to recap the services and benefits we had delivered to our clients over the course of the year, but most importantly, it also stated: *If we've learned anything, it is that our clients benefit the most when our discussions center on financial planning issues—not simply investment advice.*

January 2003

To: Friends and Clients

From: Barry M. Freedman CFP®, Chairman
*   Marc S. Freedman CFP®, President*

The New Year is a good time for reflection and rededication. It is also a great time for us to say thank you for your continuing trust, referrals, and relationships. It goes without saying that the past 12 months have provided elements of excitement, challenges, anxiety, and temptation—and through it all, you, our valued clients, have maintained confidence and patience in our financial planning approach.

This past year we concentrated on planning, education, and innovation, all in an effort to improve the quality and depth of our relationship with you. The attached "Reflections on 2002" recaps our past year and shares a glimpse of the services and programs we offered to you, our valued client.

If we've learned anything, it is that our clients benefit the most when our discussions center on financial planning issues—not simply investment advice.

That is because equity-based investments are just a part of a sound financial plan. When we focus our collective dialogues around your changing goals, dreams, and variations in your everyday life, planning has become even more meaningful.

A commitment to financial planning first has been at the heart of what we've delivered since 1968 and today, it resonates even louder. Our pledge to all of you in 2003 is an enhanced focus on the big picture by addressing all the elements that affect your financial life.

For the past several years our highest level of service and attention has been focused on our Strategic Asset Management (SAM) clients and

---

their families. These SAM clients pay one fee for an integrated financial planning and investment advisory service. This integrated service provides many benefits to our participating clients. Here are just a few items that our clients say are their favorites:

- **Ongoing counsel and guidance for all financial matters.** *You know you can lean on us for trusted advice during times of crisis.*
- **Tax saving strategies and year-end tax planning.** *Keeping more of what you earn is still a patriotic motive.*
- **Invitations** *to client appreciation events, our advisory council, receipt of our in-office crafted newsletter, and other special seminars and events.*
- **Saving time and reducing frustrations** *by having a certified financial planner professional to partner with your other advisers (accountant, lawyer, mortgage broker, etc.). We guide you through interpretation of their language.*
- **Holding family meetings and your organization's committee and board meetings in our office.**

For those who do not presently participate in (or qualify for) the SAM program, we have some very exciting news for you. We are pleased to announce a new fee-based relationship that will provide the range of services we want to offer to all our clients. In a few days, some of you will receive a separate mailing explaining this new opportunity.

Finally, we want to encourage you to stay in touch. No question is too small or too silly, if it is one that concerns your financial goals or objectives. As our mission statement says, we want:

"To build relationships as we build financial futures… We are in touch with our clients' goals and expectations. We are always accessible, always communicating, anytime, anywhere…."

We wish all of you a happy, healthy, and prosperous new year—2003!!!.

* Strategic Asset Management (SAM) is offered through Linsco/Private Ledger

We reaffirmed our commitment to planning and noted that some clients would be receiving a second letter introducing them to an exciting new service available to them. This letter would be sent one week later to 125 clients.

The day I dropped the second letter in the mail, I felt sick to my stomach. It was the day our clients would be faced with our firm's re-engineered purpose and they would be forced to make a decision. We had decided that, effective January 1, 2003, our minimum annual financial planning fee would be $1,500. However, since these clients had been affiliated with our firm for so many years, we would offer an annual retainer of $750 each year while they continued to maintain investment accounts through our firm. We hoped that these clients would recognize the value of our relationship and be willing to pay an annual fee.

Here's the second letter we sent. Before you read it, take a guess at how many people accepted our offer? The over/under in the office was 18. I guessed that only three people would take us up on the offer.

January, 2003

Mr. & Mrs. John Doe
123 Main Street
Anytown, USA. 12233

Dear Jane and John:

About a week ago, we wrote to you about the services we expect to provide to each of our financial planning clients. In the letter, we talked about our belief that financial planning is best delivered when we integrate and regularly assess all aspects of your financial life, not simply investments.

Traditionally, this financial planning service has been bundled into our investment advisory service. As you may know, most of our clients pay an annual financial planning and investment advisory fee through their

---

Strategic Asset Management (SAM)* account. This provides them with not only investment management, account maintenance, and periodic reviews; but most importantly, it includes ongoing dialogue, analysis, and strategic thinking by integrating all elements of their financial life in an effort to help them achieve their individual short- and long-term financial goals.

Based on our strong belief that every one of our clients should have an ongoing financial planning relationship, Freedman Financial has made a business decision to offer a "fee-based planning service" to all of our non-SAM clients. Additionally, we will no longer work with clients who do not have a planning relationship with us.

In 2003 and beyond, we want to provide you the same high quality service that we deliver to our SAM clients. These could include...

- Revisiting the "big picture" of your financial life to help visualize long-term goals and dreams.
- Rediscovering that financial planning is a fluid process and tinkering with changing variables as events change in your life.
- Annual discussions on changes in your financial goals and objectives.
- Trusting and comforting dialogue when "sudden money" and crisis planning issues arise, such as coping with a death, an inheritance, divorce, layoffs, early retirement, etc.
- Analysis of employer-sponsored retirement plans and benefits to be sure that investment and insurance selections are in line with your goals and risk tolerance.
- Having access to objective professionals to tackle problem solving issues such as home refinancing, buying or leasing an automobile, etc. This saves time, money, and frustration.
- Acting as liaison to your accountant, attorney, insurance agent, etc. We can help you interpret the meaning of their offers and recommendations.
- Receiving our personal newsletters, invitations to seminars, client appreciation events, and eligibility for our scholarship program.

The above and many more services are available to our fee-based clients.

We've learned that our best client relationships flourish when we understand and advise you on the multitude of elements affecting your financial life.

Most new clients pay an initial first year fee for financial planning advice. For some time now, our initial planning fee has been approximately $1,500, and was based upon our hourly rate of $200. For those whose relationship, after the initial planning session, developed into SAM clients, the services mentioned above become an ongoing part of the continuing relationship with our firm. We, however, never charged for ongoing planning services to our non-SAM clients, yet tried to be as attentive as possible to your needs. We believe we can no longer operate in this capacity.

Therefore, effective January 1, 2003, we must institute an annual financial planning and advisory service fee so that you will be entitled to a high level of advice and service from both our professional and administrative staff. Moving forward we expect this fee to be approximately $1,500 per year for new clients. However, since you have been a valued client of our firm and already have an established account relationship with us, we are pleased to offer our financial planning service to you at a discounted annual fee of $750 per year, or at an hourly rate of $200.

We sincerely hope that you recognize the value of quality financial planning advice and will want to continue to have our professional and administrative staff available to you as planners, advisers, and partners throughout your financial life.

Enclosed you will find a response form, which we ask that you immediately return to our office. As always, please feel free to contact our office with any questions. We look forward to continuing to build a long and successful financial planning relationship with you.

Sincerely,

Barry M. Freedman CFP®, Chairman
Marc S. Freedman CFP®, President
Enclosure: Response Form

* Strategic Asset Management (SAM) is offered through Linsco/Private Ledger

Mr. & Mrs. John Doe
123 Main Street
Anytown, USA. 12233

Financial Planning Response Letter
Please return this form to us in the envelope provided, indicating your level of interest and desire to continue to having us serve as your financial planner.

_____ **I/We** *look forward to receiving a higher level of financial planning advice and service from your professional and administrative team and agree to pay an annual fee of $750. Enclosed is my check for $750 made payable to Freedman Financial. Please schedule an appointment for me/us so that we can begin the process of reviewing my/our goals and objectives.*

_____ **I/We** *look forward to receiving a higher level of financial planning advice and service from your professional and administrative team. Please schedule an appointment for me/us so that we can begin the process of reviewing my/our goals and objectives. During our meeting we can establish a fee-based payment arrangement.*

_____ **Thank you, but no.** *I/We fully understand your commitment to a client base that you can plan, advice, and partner with. However I/we do not feel the need for that high level of service. Therefore I/we agree that: (PLEASE CIRCLE ONE)*

- *We will arrange to have our existing investment account transferred to an investment professional.*
- *Please assign our account to another representative who you think may be able to address our needs.*

Name _____ *Address* _____

City _____ , *State* _____ , *Zip* _____ ,

Home Phone _____

Office Phone _____ , *Email* _____

Signature: _____

Eleven clients agreed to send checks for $750 (11 * $750 = $8,250) —almost completely offsetting the entire $10,000 annual revenue stream we had been receiving from our group of 125.

To our great surprise, many clients called us to say, "What took you so long to do this?" or "I always wondered how you were able to provide your financial planning services for free—no one works for free, you know."

Others called, confused. They would say, "I thought that the investment company was paying you each year." When I explained the compensation received from 12b-1 fees on their account, they were surprised. "That's all? How can you run a business?" they would say. "You'd have to have thousands of clients."

And yes, there were a couple of clients who were furious. One was a client who paid $1,200 in 1999 for financial planning advice. The primary implementation strategies focused around repositioning employee retirement plans, refinancing strategies, adjustments to payroll withholding, and more. He was under the impression that he paid a "lifetime" financial planning fee, yet, when he reviewed our contract he realized that the advice was good for one year. Our mistake was that we continued to provide him (free) advice over the phone for several years. I suspect that, deep down, we hoped he'd turn into a substantive client for the office.

Many of our clients signed the form either indicating their desire to move the account on their own or authorize assignment to an investment representative. We happily introduced these clients to the representative we felt would serve them best, and all of them appreciated our gesture.

In reality, what we believed would have been a squeamish period in our office, became invigorating. From here forward, we could screen each new client with clarity and refer poor matches to qualified people when needed.

Admittedly, not all 125 people responded to the first letter. Follow-up letters were needed and others asked, "What will I get if I pay you on an annual basis?" That led to our preparation of a financial planning tune-up letter that we still periodically reflect on today.

**Financial Planning
Annual Tune-Up**

1. **An annual face-to-face review.** *Once a year, we will meet with you to discuss changes in your financial life.*
2. **Review of short- and long-term goals and dreams.** *Events are always changing in our lives. Annually, we will revisit your goals to assess congruence with your strategies*
3. **Ongoing upkeep and charting of your net worth.** *A clear, refreshed picture of your collective worth helps refocus one's planning.*
4. **Analysis of education funding.** *The cost of educating children increases every year. You need to be ready for this significant expense in your life.*
5. **Analysis of retirement funding.** *The retirement phase in your life encompasses a multitude of components. We'll be sure that you understand the details and help you focus wealth accumulations strategies.*
6. **Analysis of spending needs in retirement.** *During retirement, it is important to revisit the components that provide*

---

*resources to you. We will keep an eye on taxes, distribution
rules, and regulatory changes, all with a goal of providing maximum income with limited tax liability.*

7. **Analysis of investments and/or insurance held by our
firm or through your employer's retirement program.**
*The market environment is constantly changing and you need to
be sure that your asset allocation and capital needs continually
reflect your goals, objectives, and risk tolerance.*

8. **Open access via phone/e-mail to discuss personal
finance decisions.** *Periodically, issues will arise that require
you to bounce an idea off us. Feel free to pick up the phone or
e-mail us at any time.*

9. **Receipt of Freedman Financial newsletter Managing
Expectations.** *We have been crafting our own newsletter for
over ten years. It contains relevant stories and personal perspectives on the financial planning landscape.*

10. **Invitations to client seminars.** *We are committed to building life long relationships with our clients. These seminars are
designed to educate you and keep you informed about changes
in today's marketplace.*

Planner Exercise: *How might a communication campaign that
heightens your awareness of key target markets and frees you from
unprofitable clients work at your firm? Could it be worth a try?*

The transformations in our practice still amaze me each day.
When you have clarity in your purpose, your ability to share messages
about your firm becomes not only easy to convey, but inspirational to
those who truly want to know.

Throughout the remainder of this book, we will share stories
and practical ideas that will help you better connect to both clients
and prospects today. Once you find that "secret sauce" that makes
you a genuine financial planner, your clients will recognize your
new passion for life, and they will want to help you spread your

message. In fact, I bet that your clients will tell you, "I only wish I had done this sooner." Once you take the time to reevaluate your firm and run it as a business, I'm certain you'll make the same comment to yourself.

SUMMARY

1. Rather than seeking new clients to serve, identify the clusters of clients in your current mix that reflect people you'd most like to serve.
2. Create a list of adjectives that best describes your core clients.
3. Craft a paragraph that illustrates what makes these clients so special to your practice.
4. Identify unprofitable pockets and craft a strategy to stop serving those who demand your attention but don't contribute to your bottom line.
5. Discover your personal values and vision for your firm.
6. Implement a communications campaign that honestly conveys the future plans for your firm, and offers alternatives for those who can't be part of the journey.

16 | *Simple Practice Management Ideas You Can Implement Today*

OBJECTIVES

1. Explore roadblocks that prevent planners from introducing great ideas
2. Introduce ten powerful ideas that build genuine relationships with clients
3. Present an overview of the remaining chapters in Section IV

Promoting your services and yourself as a trusted financial planner is not easy. Still, it's something most planners think about, tinker with, and obsess over every day—I know I do! But in the end, how can you really ever be certain that your strategy was effective?

WHY PLANNERS HAVE TROUBLE LAUNCHING A GREAT IDEA

How many times have you woken up with a great idea for your business, but as soon as you walked in the door of your office, distractions appeared? The fabulous idea that emerged while you were in the shower has slipped into a netherland as the sound of the ringing phone, your staff's questions, and reminders of the unfinished business from the previous day creep into your morning activities. It's no wonder that some of the best ideas are "stolen."

Face it: large financial institutions have enormous budgets, intellectual capital, and teams of MBAs dedicated to developing marketing strategies designed with an eye toward enhancing the company's bottom line. Perhaps it is easier to rely on the successful ideas of others rather than finding time to develop marketing strategies that are unique to your practice. Of course, we all think about building a marketing plan, seminar, direct mail program, or advertising campaign to attract a new breed of clientele, but when it comes time to actually implementing it, those pesky "issues" appear again. Maybe this time your computer catches a virus, the Internet goes down. Maybe a client calls with a referral. Maybe your assistant calls in sick. Maybe you have a tee time.

Ideas don't often emerge in a vacuum. Nor do ideas appear when we tie ourselves to our desks and bury ourselves in paperwork. However, great ideas can happen when you expand your knowledge and commit yourself to your profession. You need to find thinking and imagining time. And you need to build it into your work week. Be an environmental scanner. This is a phrase I learned from Heather Almand, director of public relations at FPA. Environmental scanning means to gather information from your surroundings to better achieve a sustainable competitive advantage. Whether you choose to attend conferences, read financial publications, rely on a client advisory council, or simply meet with your colleagues, environmental scanners seek to find that edge. I think you will find that this book contains a collection of those ideas.

To kick things off, I would like to introduce a top ten list of simple, yet effective service/marketing ideas that could be implemented within two weeks in your practice.

10 POWERFUL SERVICE IDEAS YOU CAN IMPLEMENT NOW

1. **Answer the Phone!** How do you feel when you call any business and your first impression is introduced by a voice-operated answering service? Remember, your clients hate voicemail as much as you do. I think we all would agree that if a live voice answers the phone, we are a bit more careful with how we pose our questions or offer our opinions. No matter the size of your firm, if you suggest to your clients that great service is a priority, ensure that a live voice always answers your phone during regular business hours.

    There will, of course, be times when a client asks to speak with someone who is unavailable in the office. Here is how we tell our staff to respond to the caller's inquiry:

    "I'm sorry, Mrs. Client. Mr. Smith is unavailable at the moment. Is there something I might be able to help you with?"

    If the client insists on speaking to Mr. Smith, simply say, "I'd be happy to take a message for you and deliver it to him directly, or would prefer to leave your message on his voicemail?"

    This is when voicemail holds a value in your office. If there is no way to reach the person you are calling, and your client would prefer to leave a personal message rather than a note with the receptionist, they will appreciate voicemail as an option.

2. **Tell Your Story on Hold.** Periodically, we need to place a caller on hold. What do they hear? Is your phone system plugged into a radio station? Do you have music playing on a loop? Do you use hold time as an opportunity to share information about your practice?

    Several years ago, we were introduced to the concept of having simple messages about our firm recorded with pleasant music playing in the background. With today's technology, these sound files can be easily created and used instead of your traditional hold music. Below are messages you will hear if you call our office.

"*At Freedman Financial, we're your planner, adviser, and your partner. When we embarked on our mission to deliver peace of mind through sound, genuine, and personal financial planning, we agreed to live by our core values and beliefs. They permeate everything we do. Our foundational core value is planning. In order to best help our clients envision their goals and dreams, we maintain a relationship that continually addresses your entire net worth and your spending needs—not just your investment account.*"

"*At Freedman Financial, we don't just deal with your finances, we strive to understand your personal history and your lifelong goals. We know that money is a personal issue, and your financial affairs need nurturing, dedicated service. We develop a road map to get you from where you are now to where you hope to be.*"

3. **Put Some Color on the Walls.** If your office is laboratory white, go out and invest in a few gallons of paint that add warmth and character to your office. We changed our conference room from China White to Sedona Red. Our clients immediately noticed and responded with great positive feedback. We went on to add colors to each person's individual office and allowed them the opportunity to select from a palette of colors that best matched their style.

4. **Find the Right Music.** Know your client. If they are generally 60+, hip hop and gangsta rap should probably not be your office's background music of choice. Electing to find a radio station that suits a wide array of genres works well, but beware of the sponsors who advertise on the station. I recommend adding satellite radio as an option. You can select from genres you want and most stations are completely commercial-free.

5. **Express Your Appreciation.** Each time a referral is sent by a client, center of influence, friend, or relative, I recommend expressing your appreciation by sending a personalized note along with a gift. There are plenty of options for less than $50 that can be delivered to the referrer's home or place of business. Here are a few that we use—and rest assured they are not paying me to endorse their products.

   • Wine Country Gift Baskets—This company offers a wide array of gift baskets that can include gourmet items, chocolates, wines, etc. www.winecountrygiftbaskets.com

   • Hershey's—Who wouldn't like a tower of chocolate delivered to them? You can also personalize a one pound bar of chocolate with a message of your choosing. www.hersheys.com

   • Gift certificates—Can't decide what to get the person who has everything? Send them a SuperCertificate from Gift Certificates.com. The recipient can select from hundreds of popular retail and dining establishments and redeem their super certificate for a gift card. www.giftcertificates.com

6. **Recognize Important Events in People's Lives.**

   • Birth—When a client has a baby, we contact Taggies. This online company personalizes the cutest, softest blankets and toys anywhere. Client are so appreciative when they receive the gift. Especially when it's for a second, third, or fourth child. If you have children, you know that gifts and support seem to diminish with each child you have. www.taggies.com

   • Milestones—Retirement, 50th anniversary. We generally rely on the Web sites listed above to commemorate milestone events, as well. However, if we learn that a client is holding a special dinner with family and friends, or if they are traveling to celebrate this event, we contact the hotel or restaurant and have something delivered to them in their honor. Ideas can include chocolate-dipped strawberries and champagne, dessert on us, flowers delivered to the room, and more. Always be sure that your gifts are under $100. You wouldn't want your compliance department dinging you for lavish gifts to a client.

- Death—If ever you learn that a client or a relative of a client has passed away, you should visit www.legacy.com. Here you can search for information on funeral arrangements, and where donations can be sent. In addition, there is an opportunity to write a personal message in a guest book.

  We always send a condolence card to the children and spouse of a loved one who has died. In addition, we have made arrangements with several caterers to have prepared dinners delivered to the home of the grievers, but we choose to do so two or three days following the funeral. Generally, well-wishers bring food, support, and stories to share with those who have lost a loved one, but then the house gets quiet. The gesture of sending a meal or two that can be simply heated in an oven is greatly appreciated and remembered more than a spray of flowers.

7. **Support Your Clients in the Community.** We are all approached for donations to support charitable causes. We let our clients know that they can count on a contribution when they are raising funds for something important to them. It might be the promise of an advertisement in a program book, a check to support them on a walk-a-thon, or the straight purchase of a gift.

One year, we were approached by a local church for whom we managed an endowment. They told us that a TV/VCR combination was stolen from their community room. They simply brought it up during one of our meetings, and never expected that on a Sunday morning, we would be delivering a new TV/VCR to replace the one that was stolen.

Your simple gestures of kindness make lasting impressions.

8. **Recommend Books and Give Them Out When You Can.** Our clients have come to know that our office stocks up on books that we think will be of interest to our clients. In fact, during our seminar on non-financial issues pertaining to retirement, we gave all of the attendees a copy of Mitch Anthony's book *The New RetireMentality*.

   In addition, we have recently recommended the following books:

   - *The Wealthy Barber,* by David Chilton. This common-sense book on becoming financially independent is mailed to all individuals who apply for our scholarship. Even if they aren't the winner, we want to be sure that we provide them with a tool that could lead to making smarter financial decisions.

   - *The Social Security Fix-It Book,* by Alicia Munnell. This booklet highlights ways that the Social Security Administration is reviewing fixes to its current system. It also explains, in cartoon-like graphics, the effect each decision would have on future beneficiaries of Social Security benefits.

   - *My Baby Boomer Book,* by Mary Lou Weisman. I found this hardcover book, which looks like a book you would give to a new mom, in a Naples, Florida, gift store. I couldn't stop laughing and thought my clients would enjoy a few giggles. We ended up contacting the publisher and buying 100 books at a discount. The subtitle of the book is "A Record of Milestones, Millstones & Gallstones." It is recommended for those ages 42 and up.

- *The Ultimate Gift* by James Stovall. This book, adapted for a major motion picture, tells the story of a billionaire who just died. Over the years, he had lavishly supported all of his extended family's material needs, but now that he has passed, his last gift to a family member will teach him about values. We have given this book to clients from 14 to 84. Everyone enjoys the story—and it's a lot better than the movie.

9. **Show Clients Your Portfolio**—I got this idea from a fellow colleague, Paul Fain III, of Knoxville, Tennessee. I believe you serve your clients best when they feel you are as open with them about your life as they need to be with you. Therefore, sharing your portfolio would only be appropriate. I know, I know, you've immediately assumed I am talking about pulling out a net worth statement and showing your clients the performance of your investments. I am not suggesting anything like that at all.

   What is a portfolio anyways? Isn't it a collection of examples that embodies your true passions and your greatest work? When I talk about your portfolio, I am talking about whatever is important to you. What excites you in the morning? What do you look forward to when you come home each night? My portfolio consists of my five children, my wonderfully dedicated wife, family vacations, my piano, my music, the Red Sox, the Celtics, karaoke, and of course, Disney. Pictures and stories of my portfolio are how I connect with my clients when it's time for stories, examples, and reflections. What would be in your portfolio?

10. **Make it Memorable.** Challenge yourself to present your role as a financial planner through a fresh new lens each day. Perhaps it means visiting an auto dealership with a client. Maybe

it means driving a client to the bank to help her pay off her mortgage. Could it be a phone call you make to your client while he is recuperating from surgery, or perhaps a report that's printed in 14-point type rather than 10-point type because you know your client has been having trouble with her eyes? Whenever you can surprise your client in a way that says "They really care about *me*," you've created a service standard that results in lifelong relationships.

No matter what you do for your clients, they will appreciate it as long as they can see the sincerity in your eyes and feel the warmth from your heart. Whatever motto you live by in your office, make sure you revisit it and instill it in the lives of each employee and every client. Our motto remains, "To exceed our clients' expectations by paying attention to detail." I hope the ten ideas above were examples that reflect our commitment to our motto.

To be very candid, the ideas and stories throughout this book could have only emerged after attending industry conferences, listening to colleagues, and being a conscious scanner. If I've learned anything about planners and marketing, it is that we are our own devil's advocate. We can always find an excuse. Too many academics, consultants, business coaches, and trained professionals have written books, courses, audio tapes, and DVDs on helping you identify where you want to go—and how you should get there. Instead, I hope that Section IV of this book not only will give you ideas about what to do, but bring you behind the curtain and show you how we do it. In Chapter 17, we will introduce you to the importance of understanding the difference between internal and external marketing. In addition, we'll share a story about service promises and consider whether there really is a difference between marketing and service.

In Chapter 18, we'll introduce you to a marketing strategy that will help you learn about your competition while indirectly offering tools on how you market yourself.

In Chapter 19, the founder of our firm and my mentor, Barry Freedman, will share the successful strategies he has employed through seminar marketing techniques. This is the first time he's ever collected all of his thoughts on seminars and put pen to paper. It is my great honor to include one of his greatest contributions to our profession in this book.

Chapters 20 and 21 are dedicated to what I believe is the greatest marketing resource a planner could ever rely upon—a client advisory council. In Chapter 20, we will share the process our firm took to develop and maintain our advisory council. Chapter 21 is dedicated to a selection of great ideas and opinions they shared with our firm. I hope that, through these stories and experiences, you will find a desire to construct an advisory council of your own. The value they bring to our firm is indescribable.

Chapter 22 will present the notion of advertising your firm via cable television. It is rare that we see planners using television media as a means of promoting their firm to the public. We'll discuss how we've used television media in the past, and the challenges we faced as we looked to construct our commercial.

Finally, in Chapter 23, we will attempt to wrap up all the wisdom, ideas and stories into a top ten list of changes you should consider if you seek to serve the mass affluent effectively.

My ultimate goal is that by the conclusion of this section, you will renew your passion about what service really means to your business and begin building your own set of strategies that ignite new ideas, new opportunities, and new connections with those you already serve. Enjoy.

SUMMARY
1. Recognize that the most effective marketing ideas can be implemented for little money and minimal effort.
2. When you offer a service where clients can feel safe under your leadership, you will succeed in earning clients for life.

17

There's More to Great Service than Saying You Offer It

OBJECTIVES

1. Discuss why planners need to back up their words about service with deeds
2. Raise the notion that service and marketing are one in the same
3. Present differences between internal and external marketing strategies

HOW DO *YOU* DEFINE GREAT SERVICE?

Have you ever run into a financial adviser who says he delivers terrible service to his clients? Of course not! In fact, when I travel and visit with financial advisers around the world, they are always telling me that the number one quality that distinguishes them from their competition is great service. So, how do you define great service anyway?

I remember sitting on a panel in Boston with two other financial advisers at a "Top Producers Meeting." We were asked to share ideas on how we separate ourselves from our competitors. The first adviser on the panel pulled the microphone close to his lips and boasted nonchalantly, that he had created a system called "Gold Level Service." In fact, he had even provided the moderator a colorful PowerPoint slide that said

GOLD LEVEL SERVICE

Surprisingly, neither the moderator, nor anyone in the audience, pressed harder to find out what he meant by "Gold Level Service." Feeling quite good about his statement, he began to pass the microphone along to the panelist sitting beside me.

Just as the moderator was about to ask the next adviser to share his compelling example, I couldn't contain myself. I leaned forward into the microphone and said, "Since no one else will ask, I will. I'm intrigued by your comments. What *is* Gold Level Service?"

The microphone slowly slid back to this adviser. He once again grabbed the mic stand firmly and tapped the top of metal mesh to insure that the volume was still on. He took a deep breath and offered his definition of Gold Level Service. Honestly, I expected a well-prepared answer from the adviser, as I had to believe he had been asked this question many times. In addition, he was clearly prepared for questions about service from the moderator because it was built into the day's slide presentation.

In 1998, this planner managed over $250 million in client assets and had a client minimum of $5 million. To my astonishment, he explained that Gold Level Service meant promising to return a client's phone call within 24 hours.

"*And?*" I wondered.

But there was nothing else. Was that all it would take to deliver better service than anyone else? Could this adviser's "Gold Level Service" be the difference between great advisers and ordinary advisers? Could it be that the larger your firm gets, the more marginalized definitions around service become?

What do you do to differentiate yourself from your competition? Go ahead. On the lines below, list three service standards you believe that you do better than anyone else. This shouldn't be hard. Just list the three items that jump into your head.

1. _____
2. _____
3. _____

Did you have difficulty with this exercise? Have you ever really thought about your unique value proposition, that "special sauce" that separates you from your competition?

As I mentioned in Section 2, first impressions are critically important when building trust-based relationships. Clients make impressions about you the minute you walk in the door or they walk into your office. Is your hair combed? Have you tucked in your shirt? Is your desk clean? Are your shoes polished? Does your breath stink? Does your office have a funky aroma? All of those impression points are reflections of you, and your client has processed them before you even said hello.

Why is it that the most obvious, yet simplest details are often overlooked? What if we thought about service and marketing through the same set of criteria? Think about it, when you send a thank you letter to your client, is that a service item or a marketing item? How about when you answer the phone? Is this an expression of great service or marketing? I think they are deeply intertwined. So says Roy Diliberto.

MESHING MARKETING AND SERVICE

Roy Diliberto is a widely respected and outspoken advocate for genuine financial planning—or as he calls it "financial life planning." Recently, I read an article he wrote in the June 2007 issue of *Financial Advisor Magazine*. It discussed an idea in which I've always believed. It's the concept that marketing and service are not two separate roles. In a business that's dedicated to placing the interests of clients first, it's only reasonable that exceptional ongoing service would naturally breed marketing opportunities that continually fuse clients with your firm. It's probably why practice management tracks at conferences burst with attendance. We all register in the hope that we'll gather one great, simple idea that is destined to transform our business with little effort.

WHEN MARKETING/SERVICE GETS PERSONAL

We've all heard the expression that it takes money to make money, but when you are a small business owner, clients count on your accessibility, your family counts on your salary, and your staff counts on your leadership. With so many pressures, how can you find time to focus on the metrics of your business and monitor the effectiveness of marketing campaigns? Instead of well-thought out marketing strategies, we rely on quick-fix ideas that have the potential to create results. Not to mention, they appear to have the greatest chance of delivering an immediate return on the investment.

If marketing and service are interdependent, could it be possible that focusing first on developing service and marketing strategies that cater to the needs of your existing clients could be more valuable and less costly than an external (potentially expensive) marketing strategy? Sure, a combination of both would be best, but neglecting the opportunities that exist within your own office is a mistake that too many planners make. Surprisingly, though, these internal marketing opportunities are not only the most effective, but usually the most memorable.

INTERNAL VS. EXTERNAL MARKETING

There are sections in your local bookstore exclusively dedicated to the subjects of marketing and client service. Rather than send you there, I'd like to offer my view of this broad subject by simplifying it down to two categories: internal and external marketing. Consider implementing some of these ideas for your practice, but definitely add your creative pixie dust; after all, the best ideas start as a big hunk of clay and take greater shape when the wisdom of others is added to the sculpture.

1. Internal Marketing—Think of internal marketing as any experience, system, process, or impression from your office. Generally, these marketing ideas serve your clients either while they are visiting with you in person or by phone, letter, or e-mail. Here are a few to consider…

    •   **Be Our Guest:** How do you and your staff present yourselves when clients enter your office? Do you still wear a jacket and tie, a well coordinated suit, or a smart ensemble that screams *"executive"*? Perhaps you have found yourself dressing more casually these days. Is that because you want to or because your clients aren't as comfortable with you so dressed up? Do you create an atmosphere that inspires your staff to display a certain air of professionalism or informality? Do you instill a certain sense for what it means to exceed a client's expectations while paying attention to details? Incidentally, these little impressions make powerful statements about who you are and how you want your firm perceived.

        Let me offer an example of what I mean. If you've ever planned a family vacation to Disney World, you know that when you are telling your kids about the trip, all they want to talk about is making sure they get to go on their favorite rides. Yet, when they return from the trip, all they (and you) want to talk about are the experiences and impressions that made for lasting memories.

That magical shift in a person's perspective from talking about "grains of sand" (the little stuff), to reflecting on larger stones (what really matters) is why Disney is so successful at achieving its primary objective, which is: "To exceed our *guests'* expectations by paying attention to detail." What do you do in your practice to make lasting impression on your clients?

- **"Who are you?"** It is important that you can clearly articulate the vision and purpose of your firm.

  When a client asks what we do at Freedman Financial, we say that "we deliver peace of mind through sound, genuine financial planning." When someone asks about the future goal of our firm, we tell them that "it is to be the most visible, credible independent financial planning firm on the North Shore." How would you answer those questions?

  What does your firm do?

  _____

  _____

  What is the goal of your firm?

  _____

  _____

- **Conduct a Competitive Analysis:** Who are your competitors? What do they do that's different from you? What could you learn from them? I find that members of the financial planning community are some of the most sharing professionals in the world. Yet, we also respectfully continue to be competitors of one another at the same time. I think that's one of the reasons this profession is so great.

How might you build a competitive analysis about the planning firms in your region? If you are committed to building a practice that better serves the community, wouldn't it be helpful to know how your competitors present themselves to the public? In Chapter 18 of this section, you will learn about how we perform an annual survey to understand our competition.

- **Understand Your Target Market:** Can you be all things to all people? Is there a certain segment that you serve better than others? Remember our metaphor in Chapter 1, that talked about your favorite crayons in the box? Are there certain colored crayons that you work with best? Do you focus more of your time and efforts on courting a certain clientele, or do you simply hope that new prospects will somehow be representative of the clients you'd prefer to serve?

- **Rely on the Greatest Marketing Department of All:** Have you ever considered what value the wisdom, creativity, and honesty of your existing clients offers you? Don't they know about your business better than anyone else? If they don't, shouldn't they? Have you every considered a client advisory council as a source of feedback and ideas that could be presented to you from a completely different angle? What stops you from asking the difficult questions about your practice to your clients? In Chapter 20, we will share lessons and stories about how a client advisory council could be an important component of your marketing plans.

2. External Marketing—How will people know that your firm exists and what services you offer? Sure, prospects can learn about your firm through a Web site, but doesn't everyone have one of those? Here are a few ideas to consider when you want your message to reach new prospects and/or add greater visibility to your firm's branding initiative.

   - **Your Unique Collection of Deliverables:** What tangible marketing materials do you have that you could send to an interested prospect or even a client if they asked?
     - Company brochure—This simple, mailable document should be a clear reflection of who you are and what your firm seeks to deliver. Think about the following questions:
       - What is your firm's mission?
       - What clients do you seek to serve?
       - What services do you offer?
       - Why should a prospect hire you?
       - How can a prospect contact you?
     - Newsletter—This piece is a means of touching your client and telling them more about issues of relevance, as well as items of importance occurring in your office.
     - Reprints—If you've ever been quoted, do you proudly make these pieces accessible to clients?
     - Personal bios—Who are you and what's your experience in this business? Do you update your biography regularly?
   - **A Credible Voice**—Whether you choose to write a column for your local paper, appear as a guest on your local news station, write a book, or become a

> regular resource for a reporter, it is important that
> you position yourself as a credible individual in
> your profession and your community.
> - **Seminars**—Ever since the emergence of the finan-
>   cial planning profession, seminars have been a core
>   method of introducing prospects to both your firm
>   and the issues that may be affecting their lives. In
>   Chapter 19, my father, Barry Freedman will share
>   his thoughts on how to deliver effective seminars to
>   the mass affluent.
> - **Advertising**—Whether you consider direct mail,
>   cold calling, print ads, television commercials,
>   or a host of other advertising solutions, you
>   need to do something. How will you know what
>   method to choose, and which market will you
>   choose to reach?

What marketing and service components do you implement
in your practice to speak to the core of your business? Do you
advertise yourself in random publications hoping that one of the
strategies will work, or do you focus you efforts on ensuring that
you affiliate with marketing concepts that align with the core
values and beliefs of your firm? If you can't articulate your core
values, you may find that those who gravitate from your marketing efforts will define your values for you. Is that what you
want? Do they serve as building blocks that help you to imagine
what your business will look like in two, five, or ten years? If
they don't, how will you ever know when you get there? Could
your competition be doing it more successfully than you? How
would you know?

In the next chapter we will provide one type of roadmap for
planners to use that allows them to better understand how marketing and service standards are delivered by their competition.

Oversold and Underserved: A Financial Planner's Guidebook to Effectively Serving the Mass Affluent

SUMMARY

1. Challenge yourself to identify your definition for great service.
2. Allocate more resources toward retaining clients than searching for new ones.
3. Commit to a few simple ideas that will change the service dynamic of your office.

18

Remaining Competitive When Marketing Your Firm

OBJECTIVES

1. Develop a sense for how financial planning is marketed by others
2. Present a low-cost strategy to understand the planner's competitive landscape
3. Offer ideas on how planners can market their firms

When someone asks "Who's your competition?" what do you say? I know that many financial planners believe that competition for their services doesn't even exist, because they believe they offer a relationship unparalled by anyone else in the community. While we would all like to think that we deliver financial planning better than the next person, like it or not, the public gets to choose with whom they will work. They often make selections based on criteria that would puzzle most logical people, but nevertheless they make a decision that works for them. So, why wasn't it you? Is it possible to understand how others in the financial services arena position themselves as financial planners? Could you gain an edge if you understood how your competition tells it's story and presents itself to the public at large?

No, I am not suggesting that you head to your local costume shop or make-up artist and interview planners in disguise. Nor am I suggesting that you rummage through a planner's trash in search of client lists, though we've caught people actually doing this at our own office complex. Instead, I'd like to offer a low-cost idea that will help you compare how your competitors create first impressions versus the approach you take.

EXAMINING THE COMPETITION

Each summer, we hire a college intern to tackle a variety of marketing initiatives in our office. The activity that creates the most excitement and interest is when we ask this student to send an e-mail to up to 100 financial advisers in the local community. The intern is asked to draw from professional association Web sites, search engines, brokerage firm sites, etc. The only specifications are that the adviser must live within a 20-mile radius of the office, and they must hold a professional designation in the field of financial services. Even though our client radius is less than 15 miles from our office, the added mileage parameter allows the intern to consider metropolitan Boston as part of the inquiry. In addition, we believe that the public deserves advice from a competent, financial adviser, thus the presence of a professional designation was important in our eyes.

This year, Tara, our intern, had a great personal story and I thought it would produce some interesting responses. What I have learned was that no matter how complex and/or how simple the situation, the response rates have always been roughly the same. Here's the letter she e-mailed:

> *Hi, my name is Tara H. and I am a graduating college student who is looking to work with a financial adviser in my community. I found your name over the Internet and I am hoping that you could send me some information about your background, the types of clients you work with, and how you work with them.*
>
> *I am 21 years old and I am the beneficiary of a trust that will be paid to me upon graduation from college. My parents have always managed the money in my trust, but they are now ready to turn it over to me, and admittedly, I am a bit nervous. They have asked me to find an adviser with whom I could build a long-term relationship.*
>
> *I look forward to receiving additional information from you.*
>
> *Sincerely,*

Tara provided her home mailing address, phone number, and an e-mail address. What kind of responses do you think she received? How would you respond if you got this e-mail?

Of the 96 people she e-mailed, 56 advisers (about 60 percent) responded. Yet only 19 people (about 20 percent) followed up by sending information in the mail. From that group of 19, there were 15 people who sent a beautiful, four-color, corporate brochure that highlighted the virtues of the insurance company or financial institution they represented. Only 6 of these 15 people included a personalized letter of introduction along with the brochure. What surprised me the most was that, of the 96 people Tara e-mailed, only 4 people sent a personal, customized information packet about their firm, their background, and their personal qualifications.

We've been doing this exercise for three years now, and the numbers generally don't change. Typically, a ratio of 1:2 planners will respond to an e-mail inquiry, and less than 20 percent of planners will actually send information by mail about their firms.

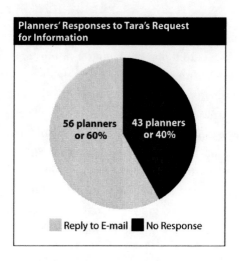

What's worse is that most planners who send information mail a generic brochure about the large financial institution they work for and include their business card with a brief cover note similar to the one below:

> *Dear Tara:*
>
> *Enclosed is the information you requested. Please contact me to schedule an initial consultation.*
>
> *Sincerely,*

By the way, we're still waiting for a follow-up call or e-mail from any of the people who sent Tara information. Of those who responded by e-mail, about 10 percent sent a second e-mail to follow up.

How would you feel about trying this exercise? What could you learn? How much would it cost you? We've learned that it doesn't matter whether you are an independent adviser, wirehouse broker, life agent, a member of a large financial planning firm, or a one-man shop, it is very rare that an adviser has spent much money or time building a piece that effectively promotes themselves and the services they offer. Could this be an opportunity for you? Do you have a customized brochure that differentiates you from your competition? What do you send to a prospect when they are seeking information about your firm? If you don't have collateral material about your firm, how can a prospect distinguish you as a financial planner? You need to be able to provide a resource, whether it's print-based or Internet-based that provides an interested prospect with information on who you are, what you do, and why you are different.

RELYING ON TEMPLATES TO PROMOTE YOUR PRACTICE
When I first began writing this book, almost three years before its publishing date, I thought that maintaining a Web site for a firm dedicated to building face to face, locally-based relationships was a waste of time, energy, and money. I have since had a total reversal in my opinion on this topic. With each year that passes, more and more people are using Web-based tools and realizing the power and immediacy of the information available to them. Age no longer matters. We have 70 year old clients with pages on Facebook, and most adults use the Internet from their cell phone as much as they do their personal computer. We live in a wireless world and information can be collected with a few simple keystrokes. As such, building a Web site via a template can be a rather simple task.

Planners can retain professional marketing firms who have developed compliance-approved templates, well written content, and an array of graphics that could compete with Madison Avenue advertising agencies. The cost is reasonable and the turnaround time is quick. Yet, how much differentiation in your services and messages might you have if the same people you compete against are pulling from the same template options, selecting from among the same boilerplate copy, and relying on the same set of resource hot keys that can be included in your site? It is very possible that your desire to build a custom Web site could be nothing more than a standard overlay with a color palette that best blends with your corporate logo. If you intend to maintain a Web site that expresses your firm, spend some money and hire a firm that would jump at the challenge to build a Web site that's different. Make sure they are ready to listen to your firm's story and how you differentiate yourself from the competition. Don't let them sell you a pre-packaged solution system—especially when you know the same system could be sold to hundreds of other planners around the country. Or, better yet, if you have the skills, try building a Web site on your own.

More than anything else, find quality time to craft copy that describes:

- Your firm's story
- Your people
- Your services
- Your clients

Relying on cut and paste paragraphs will no longer work in a world where customization and innovation drive the world of marketing. With the ability to Google words and phrases, how embarrassed might you be if a prospect came in with a printout from four other financial advisers who described their firms and their services exactly the same. If you truly wish to differentiate yourself from your competition, be certain that the messages of who you are come from you—not a template.

The same holds true with any marketing material you mail to a prospect who has inquired about your services.

DESIGNING A MARKETING KIT, FROM LOW COST TO HIGHLY EXPENSIVE

Today, more and more financial advisers are solicited to purchase pre-packaged marketing kits. Many of them are quite good, but rarely are they a true reflection of your business. Instead a marketing firm sends you a template questionnaire and asks you to answer a few qualitative questions. The marketing company scores the answers to your questions and steers you toward a series of color palettes and design templates that their "artificial intelligence" has determined would best describe you. Wait a second—doesn't that sound like the way many advisers use risk tolerance questionnaires to select the proper asset allocation of a client portfolio? This isn't a great example of truly customized work.

If you truly want to differentiate yourself, try building a marketing kit that includes your personality, your words, and your messages. This is one true way to say what you want and present yourself in the manner you wish. You needn't do it alone, but you should find someone who will ask you tough personal questions about your existing clients, your firm's goals, and what statistical measures (both qualitative and quantitative) would suggest that your effort was worth it.

In Chapter 6, we introduced you to our disclosure kit. This customized collection of information allows prospects to gather answers to questions that are unique to our firm. (See appendix.)

Our disclosure marketing kit is just one of many. If you do nothing else, take a moment to write down a list of items available in your practice that would help a client better understand who you are and how you can help them. In addition, take some time to call a few planners in your community. If you want to share ideas with other planners, talk to your local Financial Planning Association chapter and ask for members to bring copies of their literature and leave them on a table for you and your peers to review. You'll not only get some great ideas, you'll probably find some planners who act, think, and manage their businesses like you do, and what could be wrong with that?

SUMMARY

1. Understand how financial planners are promoting their services in your marketplace.

2. Examine how you market yourself to the public-at-large.
3. Craft your company's story and include it in all of your marketing materials.
4. Insist that your Web site be a reflection of who you are and not how others believe you should appear.

19 | *Lessons in Seminar Marketing—Thoughts from a Rat in the Barn*

by Barry M. Freedman, CFP®

OBJECTIVES

1. Provide a "soup-to-nuts" menu for conducting successful seminars
2. Share stories you can use in seminars to stimulate audience thinking and elicit appropriate responses
3. Provide advice on presentation skills that you can use both one-on-one and in the seminar environment

Deena Katz is one of our profession's most notable planners who consistently shares her wisdom and practice management lessons with anyone who asks. In 2001, she published an interactive workbook entitled, *Tools and Templates for your Practice* with Bloomberg Press. In the early part of the book she refers to my father, Barry Freedman, CFP®, as one of our profession's pioneers in developing, presenting, and successfully training others in the virtues of seminar marketing.

She writes, "Barry Freedman…is one of the best seminar presenters I know. His presentation style is warm, comfortable, and knowledgeable without being overwhelming or complicated."[1]

It is with this endorsement that I am delighted to include him as a guest author for this chapter. Over the next several pages, Barry will share, for the first time in writing, his notes, stories, lessons, and wisdom with you. I hope you enjoy learning from him as much as I enjoyed his mentorship and guidance.

Lessons in Seminar Marketing
by Barry Freedman CFP®

Early on, when gas was inexpensive and business was conducted at the kitchen table, we were trained to spend hours on the phone cold calling for appointments. We also used pre-approach letters and collected names in a raffle bowl at a home show or other places where a large number of people gathered. Back then, we were trained to believe that the law of large numbers would produce enough leads to put us in front of enough people to develop some sales. But it didn't produce much in the way of lasting relationships. Nor did it allow us to develop a client base within a relatively modest geography. We drove everywhere to follow the lead and hope for the sale.

SEMINARS—THE CONSISTENTLY SUCCESSFUL SOLUTION

I started in this business more than 40 years ago. Many products, systems, and theories have come and gone, yet one staple that remains constant in creating new relationships with prospects and maintaining deep connections with existing clients is the power of seminars. What surprises me is that more and more planners seem reluctant to commit to this approach. If you're reading this chapter, perhaps you've considered introducing seminars as an integral component of your marketing plan, but pulled back at the last minute for some of the following reasons:

- It's too expensive
- There is too much organization required
- I've seen others fail at seminars
- I've got enough leads and referrals
- I'll never run out of people to send direct mail
- I'm petrified to speak in front of a group

Someone once told me that "successful people do the things that failures refuse to do." I would suspect that many of you reading this book have probably experienced some level of success in your businesses, but perhaps you're looking for a newer way to develop long-term client relationships that will take you out of the prospecting business forever. Properly developed seminars can be the key to your success. How so? The simple answer is that a client-centered business is a high touch business. While you may see your clients in your office once or twice a year, those meetings are usually focused on the financial stuff of the clients' relationship with the firm. Group meetings, with many different kinds of people, provide clients (and prospective clients) an opportunity to see and learn a lot more about the you, your firm, your staff, and/or your family in a completely new environment. It also allows your clients and their guests to learn something of value about an issue of general importance. Finally, many of your clients are likely to run into friends, neighbors, and even total strangers who have similar interests.

I cannot ever imagine a day when we would not be planning our next seminar or client appreciation event. After awhile, your clients come to expect these events, and without your asking, will bring prospects, friends, family, business associates, etc., as their guests.

DEVELOPING A SEMINAR MARKETING PLAN

There are five steps to mastering the seminar marketing process. Once you learn, understand, and focus on them, nothing else will matter. However, failure to focus on all of these factors will surely lead to poor long-term results.

1. **Commitment.** Seminars and other forms of client meetings will only succeed if you commit to doing a large number of them over a long period of time. You cannot simply "try it to see if I like it."

During my first few years in the business, I elected to plan seminars for late afternoons and evenings on Mondays and Thursday. I would commit to running these meetings every month for five consecutive months. We reserved a room at a local highway motel, arranged for the room to be set up a certain way, and purchased names for a continuing mailing of seminar prospect letters. We also ran seminar ads in our local paper. Before a meeting, we would arrange the room, set up a reception table, prepare handouts, and then wait for people to arrive.

During one of my early seminars, I found myself with only three people in the room, an elderly couple (the woman arrived in a full-length mink coat) and my divisional manager, who showed up to offer me encouragement. I needed to react to the moment and refused to allow myself to let this prospect see my disappointment in the poor attendance. Acting off the cuff, I couldn't bring myself to conduct the formal, organized seminar I had planned. So instead, I focused on this one couple and had a conversational meeting with them for about an hour and a half. Yes, they ultimately became clients and, before they passed away, provided many referrals to us. Were we discouraged? Of course. We expected the 13 to 15 people who had made reservations. There are probably lots of reasons why more people didn't show up, but the important thing was that more seminars were planned. Subsequent seminars went well, and we grew from there.

There is no substitute for a well organized seminar development plan. It will take time, money, and assistance from others. You cannot afford to take the time to do it all yourself. So, yes, money will be needed for personnel, mailing lists, postage, printing, newspaper ads, room rental, and possibly A/V equipment, refreshments, handouts, and a take-away. If money is a problem, then you have to make a business decision. Can I put together a business plan for this style of marketing that can show a profit, such that a loan will make sense? There may be times in your practice when borrowing money to finance a marketing plan makes sense.

So what's really involved in committing to seminar development?

A. **Determine What Type of Seminar You Want to Deliver— Public, Product, Client, Corporate, Etc.**
   It is a mistake to think that the primary reason for your seminar is to educate your audience. Educating your audience should *not* be the single, overriding communications objective. In fact you are really there to make four more important impressions:
   1. You are there to sell your audience on the urgency and significance of action.
   2. You are there to sell your audience on the fact that you care, can be trusted, and that you are willing to listen to and empathize with them.
   3. You are there to sell your audience on the fact that you will work with them over many years to ease or eliminate their pain and help them accomplish their dreams.
   4. Most importantly, you are there to sell your audience on the need to schedule a personal interview in your office.

315

When you're speaking to existing clients, instead of to a group of prospects, product seminars can be effective. The last thing the mass affluent prospect wants in an adviser is one who is product-focused. So save product seminars for client groups who already understand that you are not solely focused on specific products.

When we decided to add a new asset class to our client portfolios, we introduced it with a seminar and invited a wholesaler to address our clients with the concept of the asset class and then the specifics of his offering. We also wrote an article in our newsletter and sent e-mails introducing the asset class to our client base, since not all clients attend seminars. Here again, we made a commitment to ensure that all our clients were made aware of our asset allocation decision.

We continue to use this approach when making major changes in asset classes. These client-focused seminars are held either in our conference room (12–18 people) or at a local hotel.

Many years ago, we developed a process for attracting employers to conduct employee financial education seminars. The material we presented was geared to three topic areas: pre-retirement, estate planning, and general financial planning. We provided agreements to limit the company's liability and all other forms for employer and employee to sign between each other to assure that all understood the desired outcome. Our goal was to provide education and then to offer employees the opportunity to meet one-on-one with us to consider the development of a financial plan. The plan fee could be paid by the employer, the employee, or some by both, and would be discounted to those who attended the seminar. All of this seemed to assure a large number of prospects...and it did. However, the development time from initial approach to the company to a face-to-face meeting with a prospect took so long that we decided to focus our future seminars on publicly marketing to the aging mass affluent, and work directly with the prospect rather than through his or her employer.

Once you decide on your target market, you still have several additional factors to consider.

B. Target Your Market—Age, Income, Location, Etc.
While it might be nice to think you could master all markets, it's probably not wise, especially if you are in a boutique practice. Larger practices can and do develop professionals who specialize in certain kinds of issues and they market to those professionals' specialties.

We understood that our market was the mass affluent. We sought sources of prospects by age, area, income, etc. We purchased lists and used the same list over and over again for many years. We focused our list purchase to a specific geography, and as a result of that focus, 90 percent of our clients ended up living within 15 miles of our office.

We used several sources to attract attendees to each seminar. The direct mail letter was the most voluminous and time consuming. We learned early on that the percentage of those replying to our direct mail offer was very small. However, we also learned that, like any other form of advertising, repetition works very well in direct mail marketing. Just because a recipient did not respond positively to the first direct mail piece, it didn't mean they were not interested. *They simply were not interested at that time.* So we mailed to the same list two or three times in a two- to three-year period. We found that the percentage of positive responses increased over time from the same list of prospects. This is another example of consistency and persistence paying off.

C. Schedule—Number, Dates, Time, Place, Size, Etc.
Your commitment to a large number of seminars over a period of time is key to making a seminar system work for you. We typically

chose a mid-afternoon session that began at 2 p.m. and would follow it the same day with an early evening meeting that started at 7 p.m. We ran the same seminars twice in a day, on two different days per week (usually Monday and Thursday) for about four months over several years. Why different days? We simply could not know if our prospects had other commitments on the night of our seminar, so we gave them a choice.

All of our public seminars were conducted at a local hotel meeting room. While schools, public and private, might offer free accommodations, they are usually not as well equipped, nor are they as comfortable as local hotels. Parking may also pose a problem at public schools, since the parking lots are usually a considerable distance from the entrance. The senior mass affluent market could be put off and possibly offended at having to deal with a less than efficient facility. We decided that the savings was simply not worthwhile.

THE IDEAL ATTENDANCE

While large numbers of attendees may seem desirable, they can also be a curse. A planner who attended one of my seminar training sessions had recently added a local public radio advertisement to his list of attendee sources. The results were overwhelming. In a room set up to accommodate a maximum of 50 people, there were almost 100 attendees. While some were simply turned away, those who did fit in were squashed into an environment that was quite uncomfortable. The results of this seminar were not nearly what they would have been had he stuck to the plan. What plan? I believe that you should try not to have to accommodate more than 20 potential household prospects per seminar. That will produce between 30 and 40 people in the room. That's a very workable number and can accommodate a lively discussion.

2. **Sources of Attendees**
   A. **Direct Mail—Consider Lead Time, Number, Costs, Who Does the Work?**

We mentioned the use of direct mail lists and how valuable they can be. Other considerations are costs and how well equipped your practice is to handle the amount of work required to manage a direct mail seminar marketing effort. While outsourcing the direct mail effort is possible, it is not easily controllable. The work required is quite specific. Mail needs to be prepared and mailed about six weeks before the seminar date. A follow-up mailing should arrive two weeks before the event. The mailing must include a response request, either a piece to be mailed back to the planner, an e-mail address to be contacted, phone number to be called, or all of these. Someone must track all responses and follow up with potential attendees with a mailing that includes a confirmation of the reservation (perhaps a ticket to be brought with the attendee for use in a raffle or other free drawing). This is certainly not the kind of work that the planner should do, so be prepared to have someone work with you.

B. **News Releases—How, When, Where**

Befriending newspaper editors, reporters, etc. is always a wise move in a narrow geography. When planning a seminar event, news releases can be quite effective if you can get them into the paper. We found that while we would send releases to all the local papers about two weeks before each seminar, they were only sporadically published. We learned that the papers would use them when and if they needed to fill space. While you might think that advertising in a particular paper would help to find space for a free news release, it isn't so. In most papers, the advertising department probably doesn't have any communication with other departments that would affect the placement of a news release.

Focus your news release mailing to very local and neighborhood newspapers, even free papers. Avoid the major city papers unless you have no choice. They simply won't run the release, and if they do, it's unlikely to be placed in a spot where your target market is likely to see it.

C. **Personal Mailings—Clients, Centers of Influence**
As you accumulate seminar respondents to mailings, ads, etc., you should begin building a list of people that you will want to continue to contact for future seminars. Some will have responded to an invitation by indicating that they cannot attend but want to be kept apprised of future meetings. You will want to develop another letter to be sent periodically to these people, reminding them of their indicated interest and informing them of the next event. This type of mailing can go on for years.

Your centers of influence can also be a deep well of seminar attendees. Many professionals, accountants, lawyers, bankers, brokers, etc. are reluctant to refer prospects directly to you. However, they are more likely to refer someone to a public seminar.

Many of our professional contacts continue to provide periodic lists of possible seminar attendees and we accommodate their request not to call any of these people unless they respond positively to the seminar invitation.

D. **Referrals—Lists, Corporate, Rosters, Etc.**
For several years, our entire marketing thrust was through seminars. So when we were provided with a direct business referral, we were likely to invite

the prospect to our next seminar rather than simply contact them for an immediate appointment. Why? We had created a process with our staff to follow up with seminar prospects who indicated an interest in visiting with us after the seminar. The volume was large enough that any other administrative methodology was disruptive to the flow in the office. We didn't change that process until we were large enough to add staff.

Once the community realizes that you are a credible source of quality financial information and you become known in the community as a seminar moderator, you then seek additional prospect lists from within the community. This may be lists from the local Chamber of Commerce, Rotary, Kiwanis, HHH, major corporate employers, religious affiliation rosters, etc. This further develops your mail prospects, and may, in time, eliminate the need for purchasing lists.

E. **Newspaper Ads—When, Size, Shape, Content, Where Placed**
    Where the cost is not prohibitive, newspaper ads can be very effective if created and placed properly. We learned early on that each newspaper ad must have a response coupon along with a telephone and e-mail contact. After much trial and error, we settled on a specific size, shape, and content of the seminar ad. The effectiveness was so overwhelming that, for years after we stopped running the ad, we had people come up to us and say "I see your ad in the paper all the time."

    We learned that maximum ad response was achieved with a two-column by six-inch block that contained the picture of the speaker in a semi profile position, looking into the body of the ad; a simple title next to the picture; then a series of four to six bullet points of what was to be covered at the meeting. Information about the seminar time, date, location, phone, and e-mail info was next. At the bottom was a coupon to be torn off and returned by mail.

Placement of the ad is very important. While you might think the business section would be best, we found that the entertainment section was the most effective, followed by the sports section, and then any other section available. If possible, you want your ad placed on the bottom open corner of the page. This makes it easier for the reader to simply tear off the coupon without ripping apart the whole page.

F. **Related Professionals—Attorneys, CPAs, Insurance Agents, Bankers, Etc.**

It was important to us, in the early years, to have a local allied professional attend each seminar. We would introduce the professional at the beginning of the seminar and indicate that he or she would be available during the Q & A session if a question arose that would be more appropriately answered by that professional. Most of these professionals are also building their businesses, so finding one to attend was not a problem.

3. **Pre-Seminar**

A. **Organize Respondents—Attendees vs. Non-attendees**

We've been discussing the vast number of resources being used to attract possible attendees. So it becomes vital that the person you select to coordinate all the factors that will influence your seminar be extremely well organized and able to multitask. The organization of both the positive respondents and the positive non-attendees is a vital component of your seminar marketing activity over the weeks, months, and years.

B. **Confirm Reservations at Least Twice—By Mail, E-mail, or Phone**

While the initial confirmation may seem obvious, it's the phone call or e-mail 24–36 hours before the seminar that will assure the best results. This step must not be missed.

C. **Confirm Location Concerns, Equipment, Lighting, Entrances, Exits, Power Supply**

The day of the seminar, someone must physically check out the seminar room, even if you've used the same room for months. Your obligation is to make the seminar room as accommodating as possible. There should be nothing left to chance. The entrance should be as close to the rear of the room as possible, so that late arrivals will disturb neither you nor the other attendees.

The lighting should be set to accommodate your needs, including your audio/visual set up. If you are using a projection screen, you do not want a ceiling light directly over it. It may be necessary to unscrew one or more bulbs if wall switches are not set up to your needs. It is better to use a higher lumen bulb in your projector rather than dim or turn off lights over the audience. You want them to be able to take notes comfortably.

If there are power cords on the floor, they must be taped down to prevent accidents. At one of our early seminars, while we were still trying different hotels in the area, we had an incident that brought home the need for taping. We failed to realize that there was a live phone on the wall behind the speaker's podium. When the phone rang in the middle of the seminar, we had no choice but to answer it. It appeared to be an important call for a woman seated about halfway back in the room. As she came forward, down the center aisle, she tripped on an untaped electric cord and fell forward, hitting her jaw on the edge of the table next to the cord. After taking the call she left the room. Several days later, we were notified that her facial injury included the loss of two teeth, and she insisted that we pay for her loss. Fortunately we carried liability insurance for just such an occasion. You, too, will want to carry a liability insurance policy.

The most comfortable form of seminar seating is what is called a "herringbone" configuration. Additionally, narrow tables in front of a row of three to five chairs makes for comfortable seating and note taking. There should be an aisle up the middle of the room with the tables and chairs at an angle from the center facing the middle of the room (herringbone or chevron configuration). An odd number of chairs in each row will make it more comfortable for singles to sit closer to the front of the room.

A registration table should be outside or just inside the entrance. The assistant should have a list of attendees to acknowledge their attendance and provide a handout package. Do not simply leave handout material at each chair. Make sure

Optimal Room Arrangement

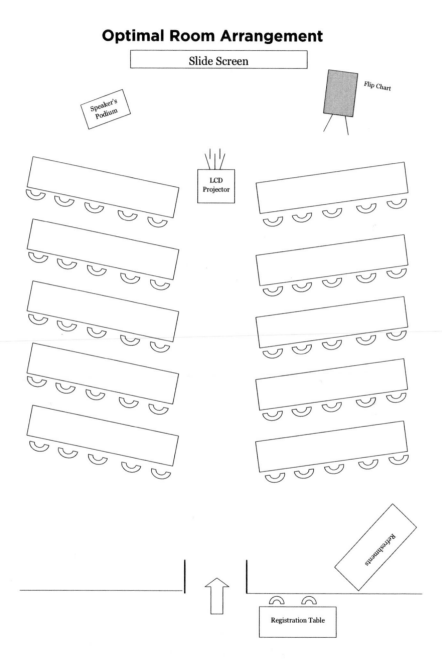

someone greets each attendee, acknowledges their reservation, and perhaps suggests a place to sit.

It is generally best to provide light refreshments throughout the seminar. Coffee, cold drinks, cookies, etc., are more than enough, and should be available from the rear of the room. Some attendees are more comfortable with refreshments during the seminar rather than waiting until the end. There is no good reason not to accommodate them, so be prepared.

One final note before conducting the seminar: In addition to the chairs and table set up for the attendees, it is just as important that the front of the seminar room be set up to accommodate as much learning as possible. Unless you are like some of my relatives from the Middle East, you probably read from left to right. Therefore the speaker's position should be to the audience's left (stage right). The projection screen should be in the middle and a flip chart (if necessary) to stage left (audience right). This is the most comfortable position for adults to receive information from a speaker.

During Marc's very first year in our practice, we attended an IAFP international conference in Toronto, Canada. I was to deliver a training presentation titled "Do's and Don'ts of Seminar Marketing." Marc and I visited the room where I was to deliver the presentation the afternoon before the presentation. The room was set up to accommodate several hundred attendees. Due to the size of the room, a rising platform was set up at the front with the podium in position and all electrical cords appropriately taped down. However the podium had been set up on stage left (audience right). This was to be an important presentation for me, and I wanted nothing left to chance. It was well worth the considerable time to find a union worker to reset the room because now the presentation room showcased a noticeably different set up from the other session rooms at the conference. I was delighted to receive positive feedback from attendees who observed that it was easier to follow our presentation because the room was set more intuitively.

4. **Conducting the Seminar**
    You must be in total control of all aspects of the seminar environment, from lighting to podium location, etc. In addition, there are certain other items that will assure a successful seminar.

    A. **Ground Rules, Smoking, Breaks**
        Warm up to your audience—and warm them up to you—by introducing yourself to people as they walk into the room. Make people comfortable. Try to find a common bond (for example, you're both golfers or tennis players, you have children in the same school or a common friend). Let them know you are a caring person by taking the time to get to know them before you start the formal presentation.

        In most cases, it is best to have someone introduce you rather than introducing yourself. Your credentials and experience are more comfortably presented by someone other than you; if you tell your audience about them, it could seem self-serving. Next, walk up to the front of the room directly down the center aisle. Turn to face the audience, and make an opening statement. This may be the only time during the seminar when a prepared remark is appropriate. This opening statement should be very brief. It should contain a thank you for attending and then a comment about what the audience should hope to accomplish during the presentation. At this point, indicate some ground rules—things like smoking, cell phones off, whether or not there will be a break, where refreshments are located, how long the session will last, how you will handle questions (at the time of, or at the end).

B. **Commitment Card—Seminar Evaluation Form and Gifts**

The seminar evaluation form is vital to the success of the seminar, so you must explain what is expected of the cards each attendee was handed when they arrived. Hold one up, explain how it will be used. If you're asking for referrals on the card, be sure to indicate that the referrals will be invited to a future seminar, not contacted directly. It can also help if the attendees know at the beginning of the seminar that they will receive a small gift in exchange for their comment card at the end. The gift need not be anything costly—it may be something as simple as an investment terms booklet or a giveaway from your b-d, custodian, insurance, or annuity company, etc.

C. **Appropriate Use of Humor**

Most financial planners are not gifted speakers, much less good storytellers or comedians. So how does one use humor in a seminar and make it effective, especially when most attendees appreciate a good story? In fact professional speakers will tell you that their audiences remember the stories more than they do the content of the seminar. I found that the only way to use stories effectively is to use the same ones over and over again. Practice them. Write down the punch lines and don't be afraid to tell the same story(s) at each seminar, even to attendees you know have been to your previous seminars. If the story is appropriate to the discussion and well told, those who have heard it before will still laugh and appreciate it.

For example, there are three stories that I have used over and over at just about every public presentation I have ever made. I cannot take credit for their development since I'm sure I heard them at someone else's seminar and decided that they would work for me.

The first is helpful to clear the air about experts, especially when there may have been audience questions at the very beginning of the seminar that appeared to test the knowledge of the presenter.

It's the story of the petroleum geology professor who decided to take his timely message on the road rather than continue to earn a living as a college teacher. So he hired himself a chauffeur and a limousine and took his talk to college campuses around the country.

After several weeks on the road and as they were approaching the next presentation location, the chauffeur turned to the professor and said, "You know professor, there ain't no justice in the world. Here you are taking this simple message all over the country and making money hand over fist and I'm barely eking out a living as your chauffeur."

"What would you expect?" asked the professor, "I've trained with this knowledge for years. However, if you think you can do what I do, then pull the car over there and we'll change clothes. We're about the same size. I'll get into your chauffeur's uniform and you'll get into my blue serge suit."

They pulled up to the lecture hall. The president of the college ushered the chauffeur (dressed as the professor) to the podium, while the professor took a seat in the rear of the auditorium. Since the chauffeur had heard the professor's speech so many times he delivered it flawlessly. However, at the end, the president of the college came to the podium to thank him for his presentation and then turned to the audience and asked if there were any questions for the professor.

A young man stood up. He had a pile of books under his arm and asked, "If we were to drive up to a northern city in the state of Maine—say Caribou—and drill down to where a dinosaur died there, thousands of years ago, and then pull up the drill bit, how far would we have to drill, what strata would we be at, and what would be the viscosity of the oil we might find?"

Unperturbed, the chauffeur, still playing the role as the professor, said, "Young man, I've been on this lecture tour for several months and have taken all kinds of questions. Frankly, it's unusual to have to respond to such a simple, silly question. In fact, it's such a silly question that I'll defer to my chauffeur in the back of the room."

Another ice breaker story is intended to quash anyone's fear that the seminar is just a sales pitch in disguise.

A successful businessman was fond of throwing lavish parties at his Florida home. One particular evening, he came to the edge of the swimming pool and announced to the large number of guests that he had an offer to make to any man in attendance. As he spoke, the lights came on in the pool and the guests could see several live alligators swimming around. He then introduced his guests to his absolutely lovely daughter. He claimed that he would give his daughter's hand in marriage or $100,000 to any man who would swim the length of the pool. The lights dimmed and several minutes later there was a loud splash in the pool. As the lights came up, a man, who had indeed swum the length of the pool, came up over the edge. He was beaten, bloody, and exhausted, but alive. The property owner came to him and stated that he was a man of his word and would indeed give his daughter or $100,000 to this man. The disheveled-looking man spoke to the host and said, "Sir, I do not want your daughter's hand, nor do I want your $100,000. What I want is the name of the person who pushed me into the pool!"

You would then go on to say that our intent this evening is not to push anyone in any particular direction but to share ideas, etc.

The final story we have been telling for years is about the pioneering families who developed our western states. They traveled in groups in covered wagons, heading west. After a particularly long day of traveling, one such family began looking for a place to settle down for the night. A heavenly voice came to them and demanded they get off their horses and begin walking. They reluctantly obeyed. A few minutes later, the heavenly voice came to them again and demanded that they pick

up some of the pebbles and stones at their feet,
remount their horses and ride off into the night.
Again, they obeyed.

After finally settling down for the night the
heavenly voice appeared to them again and said,
"You have obeyed my commands well. In the morning, you will be both glad and sorry." Sure enough,
as they were preparing to ride off again the following morning they put their hands into their pockets
and found that the pebbles and stones they had
picked up the night before had turned into diamonds, rubies, and emeralds. They thought about
the words of the heavenly voice, that in the morning they would be both glad and sorry. Glad they
had picked up so many and sorry they hadn't picked
up more.

You might state as your closing remark at your
seminar that "As the months and years go by after
this seminar, you too might be both glad and sorry.
Glad that you picked up on some of the ideas you
heard here today and sorry that you didn't do more!"

5. **Presentation Skill Development**
Finally it is important to be as professional as possible in front
of the audience. There are several excellent presentation
training skill courses you can take. While they may take different approaches to the training, including video feedback,
they all should at the very least teach you the following:

A. **Control Tension**
Why, according to the *Book of Lists*, is speaking in
public the number one fear of Americans today?
Before terrorism, lying, loneliness, before dying of
cancer? My own experience in this area is that tension is related to several factors:

1. **Unrealistic Audience Expectations**
    Audiences are becoming increasingly passive.
    Just think about how Americans watch televi-
    sion. I believe audiences are watching you
    the same way they watch television. So, don't
    be so concerned about how much they will or
    can absorb. Keep your expectations realistic.

2. **Narcissistic Illusions of the Presentation
    Process**
    When we get up to speak, what do we think
    people are looking at? Our hair, face, what
    we have on, our legs, shoes, and more impor-
    tantly, audiences seem to look beyond that
    into our hidden inner vulnerabilities, those
    secrets we all have. Maybe there's something
    about me they're going to find out, that
    they're not going to like.

    You must consider what audiences are
    really concerned about. Audiences don't care
    what you look like or sound like. All they care
    about is what you can do for them. If you go
    into the presentation with a service mental-
    ity, "How can I help you solve a problem?"
    then your concern for service will relieve
    your concern about yourself. You'll be more
    effective at promoting what you are there to
    discuss, and tension will disappear.

3. **An Unnecessary Fixation on Words**
    Trying to memorize a speech is certain death
    to a seminar presenter. There are too many
    opportunities for interruptions to fixate on
    words. Ideas, not words, communicate mean-
    ing, especially ideas that are visually presented.

We've also learned that it's virtually impossible to make a letter-perfect presentation. According to Irving Goff, author of *Forms of Talk*, some form of communication error is made every 4.6 seconds. That's potential for 15 errors per minute.

There's a convention in extemporaneous talk that allows your audience to ignore those errors in word order, choice, and pronunciation. So when you go to a script, the tension level increases dramatically. Avoid the script. Audiences want to believe in you. If they can trust you, they are more likely to do business with you. If they don't think you're sincere, I don't care how good you look or sound, you're never going to get them to buy into your information. So get away from a fixation on words—focus on ideas. You'll be much less tense and in better control of your behavior.

B. **Move Appropriately**

Moving around the front of your audience is a controversial subject. I believe it sets up a level of distraction and don't recommend it. You might walk to an area of the room to respond to a questioner, but how do you get back? You have to turn around, creating a level of distraction. Movement works well for the presenter, not the audience.

C. **What to Wear**

Today's casual dressing styles make it difficult to understand what our dress does to our audiences' perception of the presenter. My experience is that your dress should not be memorable. Think about the news anchors on the network and cable TV stations.

They wear classic suits, fairly solid ties, and stylish shirts. They do not wear flashy colors or jewelry. They do not want to be remembered for what they wear, only for what they say. That's the perfect approach for a seminar presenter of financial information. Jewelry and pins should be avoided. They are a distraction, especially if there is any kind of direct light shining on the podium, the presenter, etc. Remove your name tag before approaching the podium as it is also a distraction and a light reflector.

D. **What to Do with Your Hands**

Consider what presenters do with their hands. First there is the "at-ease" position…this is the classic military stance with hands behind the back. Then there is the prayer position, and of course, who can forget the fig leaf?

In the course of presenter training, we generally videotape each participant. One particular trainee consistently rested his hands over each other in a classic fig leaf position. However, when he wanted to make a point to emphasize his comment, he would lift his hands slightly at the wrist. We called this the flashing fig leaf. The cure was obvious, but he didn't really realize how distracting it was until he saw himself on his training video.

What about putting your hands in your pocket(s)? If you must put your hands in your pockets, be sure to empty your pockets before the presentation and when you do place a hand in a pocket, push your jacket aside rather than lifting it up.

The most comfortable position for your hands is at your side, relaxed and natural, allowing you to gesture naturally with either one or both hands.

An acceptable crutch for new presenters is to stand behind a podium, but don't grab the sides and hold on for dear life. If you do, your knuckles will turn bright white. Be relaxed, with perhaps one foot to the side and behind the other. The podium is not a barrier for you to hide behind. It's a place for notes, a pointer, and a remote. You can and should move away from it to make a point or flip over a chart. There is no need to walk and talk at the same time. In fact it is more effective to walk, turn to the audience, make your point, stop talking, walk back to the podium, and then continue.

E. **How to Gesture and Where to Look.**
I do believe in gestures that reinforce the information. They make the information more believable. There are two types of gestures, symbolic (a representation of what you're talking about) and energized (reinforces the enthusiasm you have for the information). When gesturing, think in terms of a high strike zone. It's the area from the bottom of your chin to the tips of your fingers. Do not block your face. Arms can swing out at a 45 degree angle in front of the body about waist high. Gesture too wide and high and you could look like the flying nun. Time your gesture. "The point is…" (gesture), not "The point (gesture) is…" Don't look at the gesture. Hold it out there to transfer it from your body to the mind of your audience. It can take a while for a listener to process the information.

You're now relaxed, you know how to stand, you know how to carry your body, you know what to do with your hands, where do you look?

What do presenters do with their eyes? How about the presenter who appears to be talking to a dot on the back wall? He or she is apt to speak in a sing-song manner and may go cross-eyed. Then there is the presenter who looks from side to side, like he or she is watching a tennis match or a set of windshield wipers. Excessive eye movement can cause your mind to go blank, so your eyes go up. Why? Because that's where the brain is, and it appears you're looking for help. So where should we look?

Research indicates that you should look for about five seconds at each section of the audience. Move your eyes slowly from one area to the next and slowly back. Since most people are right-handed, that's the area of the room they tend to talk to. By dividing the room into pie-shaped sections and slowly talking to each section for about five seconds at a time, you will avoid the focus on one side of the room.

Many people will sit to a speaker's right side to feel they are getting more than those on the left. If the responses and questions come from one side, the tendency is to focus on those who are giving you, the speaker, positive reinforcement. Just because someone is smiling at you doesn't necessarily mean they are agreeing or even listening. Don't read messages into an audience's reactions that don't necessarily exist.

F. **How to Handle Visual Aids and the Flip Charts**
Regardless of all the technological advances developed for presentations over the past 20 years it still comes down to how an audience receives and responds to information. Whether it's rear projection, digital or LCD projectors, overhead projectors, laptop

or desktop computers, we've learned that certain colors are acceptable and some are not. We know that too many words on a slide or flip chart inhibit note-taking. So what's the most effective way to present material on a flip chart or PowerPoint slide? According to 3M Corp., a flip-chart or slide should have no more than six lines per slide and no more than six words per line. More slides are better than crushing all the data into a few. Blue, yellow, green, and red are the most effective colors. Stay away from white letters and white backgrounds, especially in poorly lit rooms. Stark, white light, like that which comes from an uncovered overhead projector, causes the pupils in our eyes to contract and affects the continuous intake of information. The use of a laser pointer from the podium to the PowerPoint or flip-chart is fine, as long as the presenter does not walk around talking and pointing at the same time. The most comfortable way for an audience to accept and retain the information from a flip-chart or slide is for the presenter to first touch or point to it, then turn toward the audience, then talk to the audience. Your back should never face the audience. As you touch the chart, you should turn slightly toward it, touching it with your left hand. Then turn full face toward the audience before you begin to speak. Remember, it's touch, turn, and talk.

When you are finished with a slide or flip chart remove it or flip it so that there is no additional focus time on the material you have finished talking about. Leave no room for distractions.

G. **How to Deal with Interruptions and the Q & A**
Now that you know how to look, stand, and ges-

ture, how should you deal with interruptions and the Q & A session? The theory of effective Q & A is to maintain control. Is the questioner seeking information or attempting to elicit an emotional response? The best technique is to listen to the entire question, break eye contact with the questioner, and then repeat, rephrase, or restate the question. There is no reason to simply rush in and answer the question just because you know the answer.

Do not evaluate the question by saying "that's a good question." Why? Because unless you're prepared to tell everyone who asks a question that theirs is also a good question, you have set yourself up to make someone feel that their question is not important. You want to stay in control of the Q & A period and pace yourself to handle as many questions as you want to.

We've learned that our thought speed exceeds our speech speed by about eight times. So by repeating, rephrasing, or restating the question, you have ample time to formulate an effective answer. Look directly at the questioner as you begin to answer the question, but as you complete the answer, make sure you are not looking at the questioner. Why? You'll want to avoid a follow-up, especially if it's an emotionally charged issue. If you do not know the answer to a question, go through the same steps, repeat, rephrase, or restate to be sure you fully understand the question, and then, rather than bluffing, say simply that you are not prepared to respond. However, you should offer to meet personally with the questioner or ask them to be sure to write it on the evaluation form and you'll get back with them after the session.

What about obnoxious or grandstanding behavior? If you are in control of the Q & A, have restated, re-phrased, or repeated the question, have looked away from the questioner, then the audience will be the best help to you. The majority of the audience will want you to do well and they will act to suppress inappropriate behavior.

We were at a local motor hotel in front of an audience of about 40 people, and, due to inclement weather, we started the presentation about a half-hour later than planned. One member of the audience spent the half-hour waiting on a bar stool adjacent to the seminar room and proceeded to drink too much. By the time we got to the Q & A, he had become rather loud and boisterous in his questioning. I made it a point to look away from him and the other members of the audience who were nearest to him managed to escort him out of the room. The audience wants you to succeed.

Of course, there can be no substitute for practice and training. These techniques need to be repeated over and over again until they become natural.

It's now time to close. Remember that you are there to sell your audience on a personal interview in your office. The most effective way to accomplish this is to hold up the seminar evaluation or comment card and ask everyone in the audience to do the same. Then ask for their comments about the presentation, the good, the bad, and what they might like you to talk about at future meetings. Also ask for referrals to friends, neighbors, business associates, etc., who they think might like to be invited to a future seminar. Also remind them that there is a place on the form to indicate their interest in a personal meeting with you in your office. Explain briefly what that initial meeting might feel like and what if any information you might want them to bring to the meeting. If you have any use for an information form prior to an initial meeting, have some handy to pass out to those who indicate an interest. Give people plenty of time to fill out the card. We found it helpful to offer a free gift in exchange for the comment card. You and/or an assistant should then walk through the audience handing out the free gifts in exchange for the comment cards.

It might also be helpful to tell a story while they are filling out the card. The one we have used for years goes something like this:

"I feel a little like the president of a dog food factory who at the annual sales meeting stood up and asked 'Who has the best dog food in the industry?' To which the salesmen, in unison, said 'We do!'

'Who has the best sales structure and marketing plan for the sale of dog food?' Again they said, 'We do!'

'And who has the best price structure for the sale of dog food?'

'We do!' they all said.

'Well,' said the president, 'If we have the best dog food, the best sales and marketing plan, and the best price structure for the sale of dog food, how come we're not selling more dog food?'

From the back of the room someone yelled 'Because the dogs don't like it!'

I don't want to stand here and compare you to the dogs, but if I don't know what you like or don't like about what you heard here today, then I cannot improve on it. That's why those comment cards are so important to us. Thank you for your candor."

Now pick up those comment cards and grow your practice with the kind of clients you want, within the area or market you want, and start building relationships that will last a lifetime.

Seminars have become the cornerstone for the development of our practice, and I am sure that with effort and commitment, you too can discover the prospecting success that emerges from these powerful presentations. But what if you already have a strong client base and you don't need to rely upon seminars as a prospecting tool? What if finding new clients isn't the answer, but keeping the ones you have is of greater importance? In the next chapter, I turn the reins back over to Marc so that he can share an incredible resource we developed in the mid 1990s and continue to rely upon today. It's called a client advisory council, and when you listen to the stories and hear about the guidance and frank advice they've given to us, I wouldn't be surprised if you embark on developing a council of your own.

SUMMARY

1. Have an orderly methodology for creating a successful seminar system.
2. When using seminars as a prospecting tool, seek to mobilize your audience rather than educate them.
3. Always incorporate the five-step seminar system into your planning.
4. Be a storyteller. Rely on time-tested stories that provide a memorable experience for your audience.

ENDNOTE

1. Katz, Deena. (2001). *Tools and Templates for Your Practice.* Bloomberg Press. p. 38.

20 A Client Advisory Council—A Planner's Unique Secret Weapon

OBJECTIVES

1. Introduce the value of a client advisory council
2. Share the steps needed to build an advisory council
3. Offer reflections and lessons we've learned from our advisory council

Besides your staff and possibly your family, who in your life is in a position to offer honest feedback when asked about the perceptions of your firm? Does anybody have a better read on your approach and passion for the business more than the clients you already serve?

Financial planning is one of the few professions where you can do your best work when your clients trust you. They gain that trust when you show a commitment to serving their needs, and from you being authentic and honest whenever they are in your presence. Most other professions keep the customer relationship at a distance. They simply seek to complete the transaction or service and then move on to someone else. Financial planners are different, and it's one of the reasons a client advisory council can deliver incredible benefits to your firm.

In the next two chapters, we will introduce you to what I refer to as the greatest marketing resource in a financial planner's toolbox: the client advisory council. I know it may sound intimidating, but it is the one unique marketing resource that is exclusively yours, and it is the differentiation point that can't be replicated anywhere else. Relationships you build with your clients are different from relationships other planners will develop with their clients. Your clients know you better than your prospects and they surely know you better than any marketing firm that might solicit you with their newest strategy for obtaining clients.

Just imagine if you had enough trust in the relationships you maintained with your clients that you could call upon them at any time for help in marketing, service, and other issues affecting your business, knowing they would offer well-intentioned perspectives and keep you grounded in the process. It can and does happen.

It is true that more planning firms are beginning to form client advisory councils, but in my opinion, they are not being formed fast enough. It's truly puzzling that many advisers find greater safety in throwing advertising dollars at an array of external marketing techniques than in allocating business development time and money to identify strengths that already exist within their practices and expand on them. Below are some of the reasons I believe advisers are reluctant to form an advisory council:

1. **No time**—You have a busy enough schedule already. Who is going to coordinate, schedule, and for that matter, form an advisory council for you?
2. **Lack of consistency in service and product offerings**— Perhaps your business has become one that serves all people without any parameters. In doing so, you have a client base,

but you've also formed a collection of people who might each describe your services differently.

3. **You're passionate about finding new market niches**—If you relied on the advice of your existing clients, they could distract you from attempting to capture the next hot client niche.

4. **You don't see the need to open yourself up to criticism**—By appearing vulnerable, you wonder whether your clients will rethink their opinions of you and see this as a sign of weakness.

5. **You don't want to report to anyone**—When you are a business owner, you get to make the rules and have the final say on all decisions. Perhaps you feel like you'd be held accountable, and that's exactly what you didn't want when you elected to become an independent adviser.

Each of the above concerns are valid, and they only scratch the surface on the number of reasons advisers are typically reluctant to get started. They are also some of the issues we struggled with in our own firm when we began thinking about forming our council.

If planners are truly sincere when they say they want to change the lives of people they serve, why wouldn't they ask their clients for advice on how they can serve them better? An advisory council, from my perspective, is all about learning how you can serve your existing clients better by listening to how your firm is perceived by those you serve.

AN ADVISORY COUNCIL IS BORN

In May of 1995, while attending the IAFP's (International Association for Financial Planners) Advanced Planners Conference in Washington, DC, my father and I found ourselves seated in a section of the lobby talking about our business and issues of the day. Somewhere in the discussion, our conversation steered us toward marketing ideas and the services we deliver to our clients. This is where the concept of an advisory council emerged.

We had heard of financial planning firms building boards of directors—groups generally composed of business leaders and high profile individuals in the community who acted as mentors to the owner of the firm. They offered to analyze the company's financials, share their perspectives on the "state of the firm," and collectively they would view this board work as an opportunity to build a prospecting network.

Many financial planning firms have found tremendous success and value by maintaining boards of directors. We felt differently. Ever since the inception of our firm, we had told our clients to introduce us to their existing list of affiliated professionals and we would be happy to work side-by-side with them. If we established a local board of directors, we were concerned that a conflict of interest could emerge and create the appearance that we were affiliating with a professional network in the community. We wondered whether our clients would see this as compromising our independent presence.

That day, we agreed that for a practice to better understand the nuances of our existing clients and the mass affluent clients we hoped to serve, we needed to connect more with our clients. After all, they were members of the community and they had a different, almost innocent sense about how financial planning, and our services in particular, were perceived in the community. We had confidence that they would provide a fresh point of view.

If the story below isn't a good enough reason to continue exploring why a client advisory council could be good for you and your firm, I don't know what will clinch it for you.

STAN M., ADVISORY COUNCIL MEMBER EXTRAORDINAIRE!

A few years ago, we asked members of our advisory council to think about how we could illustrate the role of a financial planner in a client's life. Stan M., a retired marketing director for a large defense company, offered the following vivid description, and in my opinion, he's nailed the answer to this question better than any planner I've ever met. "Imagine the silhouette of a human body placed on a large white screen. In the background, the faint sound of a beating heart can be heard through the sound system in the auditorium. As the sound of the heart beats louder, a glow of red appears where the heart would be positioned on the human body. With each pulse of the heart, the circulatory system begins to appear on the silhouette, and soon you can see each vein branching through the body from the tips of the fingers to ends of the toes. As the color on the screen grows more vivid, and sound of the heartbeat gets louder, you can actually see the flow of blood passing through the heart, through each extremity, and back again. That," he said, "is a financial planner."

A financial planner is like the heart of the human body. It sends needed resources to the extremities—always analyzing whether more or less antibodies are needed.

"Think of an investment broker as the hand, an insurance agent as a leg and an attorney as an arm on the body, for instance. Then imagine if one of these extremities became damaged. What would happen next? A specialist—that is, a broker, insurance agent, attorney, etc., would be contacted to care for the injured part of the body and make an assessment that would repair the extremity in need. But a financial planner would react differently to an injury. A planner would seek to reassess the entire body first and determine the level of care needed on the injury while attempting to limit undue strain on the rest of body. As the flow of blood runs through the body, the heart (the financial planner) assumes the awesome responsibility of managing the entire body's needs."

Is your jaw hanging open as much as mine did when I first heard this explanation? Just imagine what insights and perspectives your clients could share if you simply asked them.

CONSIDERATIONS WHEN BUILDING A CLIENT ADVISORY COUNCIL

As you begin to ponder what you might expect from an advisory council, ask yourself some important questions. Here are some we used:

1. What realistic expectation should we have for the group?
2. How often should we meet?
3. How will we determine what we'll talk about?
4. What criteria should we use to select our council, and how long will they serve?
5. While we would never violate client confidentiality issues, what firm-related information would we like to share about the firm? Is anything off limits?
6. What risks might be associated with building a client advisory council?

If I've learned anything from sharing stories surrounding the success of our client advisory council, it's that our way is surely not the only way. However, it has worked effectively for us since 1995. In fact, each year we take a photograph of our advisory council and mount it on the wall in our conference room. When prospects ask about what makes our firm different, we proudly showcase a group of real clients who are committed to helping both our firm and their fellow clients find something different. Prospects are impressed that you care enough to ask your existing clients for feedback.

IDENTIFYING CLIENTS FOR THE COUNCIL

How might you go about choosing clients for your council? We decided that we wanted to find people who would constructively share their perspectives on our firm and the financial planning landscape at large. We knew we didn't want clients who would "yes us to death," or seek to dominate conversations in a meeting.

We also determined that we wanted a council that represented the current demographics of our firm. But to do so, we needed to create a demographic snapshot of our client base. How easily could you construct a breakdown of qualitative and quantitative data concerning your entire book of business? It's not easy, but when you refine the data in a meaningful way, the results can be quite revealing.

In the case of our office, we decided to identify the number of existing clients (about 500 at the time) who lived within a 15-mile radius of our office. (When I refer to a client, this means all clients who live in one household.)

What we learned was that about 90 percent (about 450) of the households we served lived within the radius we built. That, in and of itself, was interesting, but we also knew that to find our first advisory council, we would need to filter 450 clients down to 12. Why 12? Honestly, I'm not sure. It just felt like a good number—there was no magic that went into that decision.

The next step was to identify the head of household and capture their age. With the allocation of client ages in front of us, we then constructed the chart on the next page. In this case, the client age represents the age of the head of the household. The 55–74 household age range represented about half of our client base.

We then decided to dig deeper. We wanted to see which of these households, by age, had paid for a financial plan first, prior to implementing investment strategies. We didn't hire our business coach to help us identify our statement of core values and beliefs which included our commitment to "financial planning first" (for a fee) until 2002. Instead, at the time, we accepted any client who sought our services—and we admittedly provided an excessive amount of free financial planning advice.

Oversold and Underserved: A Financial Planner's Guidebook to Effectively Serving the Mass Affluent

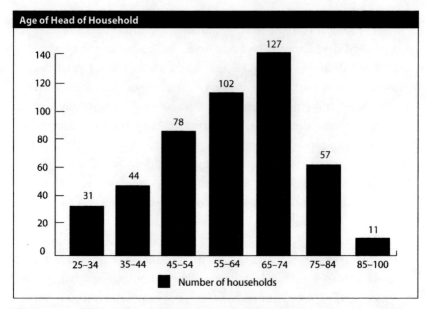

The next table gave us the answer to our question.

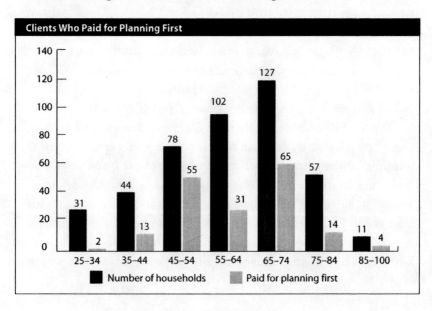

What we found interesting was that, of the 450 households, only 41 percent had actually paid for a financial plan. In fact, clients between the ages of 45 and 54 paid for financial planning services before implementing investment strategies at a greater rate than any other age category. It was also interesting to see that only about 30 percent of our clients ages 55 to 64 paid for financial planning first. Our retention rate for clients was easily in the 95 percent range, but when we looked at the clients who had left us over the past five years, all of them were clients who never paid for a financial plan. Frankly, they just viewed us as "the investment guys."

At the time, our financial planning fees ran between $500 and $1,500, and today our plan minimum is $1,500. We estimate our time at $200 per hour, and quote a maximum fee to each prospect.

A third criterion we wanted to determine was the total assets managed for each household, but in 1995, with a significant portion of our clients' money held directly at mutual fund and insurance companies, the work was simply too monumental. Today, advisers have that information available at the click of a button.

Upon the completion of our analysis, we decided that the minimum eligibility requirement for our advisory council was the following:

1. We must like the client. Face it: it's no fun taking advice from people you don't like.
2. Each member must have initially paid for a financial planning analysis. Since we realized that clients who paid for a plan fee provided roughly 100 percent retention rates, we believed they would be a solid resource.
3. Each member household must maintain a fee-based advisory account or have the potential to become advisory clients in the near future. With the likelihood that we would be continuing to transition existing clients into advisory programs and using the fee-based asset management approach as a

primary tool for new clients, it was important that we had clients who were familiar with the advisory program.

4. Finally, we wanted to be certain that our collective council mirrored the age distribution chart of those who had paid for a financial plan.

What criteria might you use to identify an advisory council? Would it be your best clients? Your most profitable clients? How about clients most likely to provide referrals to your office? There is no right criterion. Choose ones that work best for you.

IDENTIFYING MEMBERS FOR THE COUNCIL

After weeks of analysis, we identified a pool of candidates from each age group and began calling them on the phone. Some folks simply weren't interested, and others asked that we consider them in future years. However, the majority of people were intrigued and they wanted to learn more about what was expected of them. Many initially thought they wouldn't be able to deliver enough knowledge of the markets and economics to be great participants. This was never our expectation, nor was it a scheme to test their reactions on new product offerings before we attempted to offer them to other clients.

What reactions do you think your clients would have if you asked them to be part of an advisory council? What questions might they have for you?

We explained that we intended to build an advisory council of our clients to gather honest feedback and to bounce new ideas off, in the hope that their objective perspectives could lead to even better ideas. We would take this group out for dinner twice a year for an informal discussion on issues regarding their thoughts on service standards, seminar topics, marketing strategies, and more. We stressed that we wouldn't talk about what was going on in the market, our opinions on interest rates, housing prices, the election, or events in the news; it would simply be an open dialogue on how we, as their financial planners, could remain innovative and deliver the services *they wanted*—rather than products and services *we thought they needed*.

The 12 couples who composed our first advisory council were engineers, marketing managers, an attorney, a math teacher, a pharmaceutical salesman, a nurse, homemakers, retirees, a plumber, a liquor store owner, and more. They were definitely a wide cross section of our client base, and we were confident that this group fairly represented the clients we served.

PREPARING FOR OUR FIRST ADVISORY COUNCIL MEETING

In the previous chapter, my father shared his wisdom on presentation skills and setting the right mood for a meeting. With his experience as our guide, you can be certain that the slightest details were addressed *before* guests arrived at our first dinner meeting to ensure that distractions were kept to a minimum. Here are a few items of note that you might consider when you begin planning your first council meeting.

1. **Design an agenda.** Prior to your meeting, prepare a brief letter/agenda that describes where the meeting will be held, date, time, etc.

    If you intend to gather rich content from your attendees, I strongly recommend limiting your agenda to no more than two items. Some great items for conversation at a first advisory council meeting might be:

- What service standards have you come to expect from our firm?
- What is your understanding of the roles each of our staff plays in the office?
- If someone were to ask you to describe our firm and what we do, what might you tell them?
- If we could change one thing in the way we serve our clients, what would it be?

2. **Accommodate meal choices in advance.** Try to select a few choices that will appeal to the broadest array of attendees and include the dinner choices with your client's invitation to the dinner. This will allow you to record their entrée choice when they call to RSVP for the meeting. Provide as much detail as possible about the menu choices and encourage them notify you of any dietary needs that you should share with the restaurant in advance.

    One of the greatest and most embarrassing distractions at a meeting is having to stop conversations so that each person can special-order their meals. Try preparing color-coded cards that indicate each guest's meal choice and alert the server, in advance, to any guest with special requests. This not only will save you time but it will reinforce to your clients that you heard their requests and have honored them.

3. **Configure the right mood.** When hosting a dinner meeting where conversation is encouraged, one key but often forgotten preparatory item is the configuration of the room. Often, restaurants want to build a "U-shape" or a long rectangle for meetings, but in the case of advisory council meetings, you should try whenever possible to either have *round* tables of seven to nine people, or a giant square table. If you want great dialogue, you need to create an environment that allows it to happen. You want your attendees to be able to see other's faces and react to body language. If your guests can't see the face of the person who is sharing an idea, it can lead to misinterpreting the full context of the comment. Think about how many times you've read a story in a newspaper and immediately developed an impression about what you thought you read, but then you hear the same person quoted on television and, because of the dynamics of their voice, their facial expressions, and surrounding environment, you establish a completely different

impression. Always try to see the faces of those you want to hear at your meetings.

4. **Make a decision about alcoholic beverages.** If you choose to make bar service available for your clients, pick up the tab. Remember, they are your invited guests and they shouldn't have to lay out cash at the bar for beverages.

5. **Discuss your agenda with the waitstaff.** Be sure you have orchestrated a plan for when courses will be served and when dishes will be cleared. Ask them to avoid removing items when you begin speaking. When the plates are fully cleared, be sure that water glasses and pitchers of water remain on the table.

6. **Respect your guests' time.** It is very easy to lose track of time, especially when conversation is lively and guests are enjoying themselves. However, a critical lesson in managing an advisory council is to announce a start and finish time, and never, ever, go longer than you promised. Your clients are already honored to be a part of this group, and they really hope their contributions are worthwhile and appreciated. Out of respect to you, they are also unlikely to leave your meeting before it's over, even if they promised the babysitter they'd be home at a certain time. They will stay for you and pay the consequences later. Do whatever it takes to be respectful of their time. They have great respect for what you do for them, and it's something you never want to take for granted.

7. **Assign a note taker.** Invite a member of your staff to take minutes at the meeting. This person should also prepare a written recap and mail it to members of the council.

8. **Relax and have fun.** Remember, no one forced you to create this council. You have developed it with the hope that your clients will provide useful feedback and an honest perspective on questions you have for them. Be sure to

let your guard down and try not to be their planner for the moment. Instead, try to be a student who is seeking wisdom from those who know you best.

As with most well-laid plans, there will always be surprises. Below is a story that highlights a recap of our first advisory council meeting. While it may not have gone exactly as I planned, the end result was compelling enough to lead us to believe that our client advisory council would be an invaluable tool for a very long time.

Our first meeting was held at a hotel in Lynnfield, Massachusetts. We chose this facility because it was centrally located, it was a landmark that dated back more than 100 years, and was easily recognized by our clients. During the first 45 minutes, we greeted our guests, introduced them to other council members, had a cocktail, and enjoyed hors d'oeuvres. We covered all costs for our clients, including any liquor.

THE MEETING BEGINS

During the salad course, my father Barry stood up and welcomed the group. He reaffirmed our commitment to seeking guidance and direction from members of our council and promised that we would listen intently and capture their ideas.

There were a couple of agenda items we had provided in advance, but Barry surprised both me and the group by testing them with a surprise anecdote and question instead—not an unfamiliar tactic for my father, and one I've grown to respect rather than fear. For the first time publicly, he shared his thoughts about slowing down from the business a bit—*at our very first client advisory council meeting*. About half of the clients in the room had known Barry for well over ten years, and all of them had been with the firm for at least three years.

Dad explained that he hoped to take six weeks away from the office in January and February of 1996 and rent an RV so that he and my mother, Phyllis, could travel cross country. He promised he would call into the office regularly and check in, but it was clear that Marie, our executive assistant and jack of all trades, and I would be the primary people at the office. Remember, in 1995, cell phones, e-mail, and the Internet were far from common features in our lives. It was clear that Dad was looking for feedback from the group before he could feel comfortable taking this extended time off.

While the salad plates were cleared, he kept talking. Though he periodically asked questions, they were more rhetorical in nature, because he never paused long enough to entertain answers from the attendees. While I have always respected my father's skills as a public speaker, I had to appreciate the fact that even the most highly trained speakers get nervous sometimes.

Finally, Barry stopped talking. The quietness hung for a few moments, and then sporadic comments percolated. I think he was looking for strong positive or negative feedback, but the clients seemed not to be fazed by the announcement. In fact, our client advisory council collectively encouraged Barry to enjoy himself. They suggested he visit the Grand Canyon; the Petrified Forest; Branson, Missouri; and Niagara Falls.

This became lesson number one from our client advisory council. *Never fear telling the truth to your clients. Worrying about sharing what's on your mind creates far more angst for you, and in the end, your clients will never know, or care for that matter, about the extent of struggling you endured.*

Surely, I thought, after dinner was served, the conversation would grow more intense. After all, we weren't looking for a bunch of yeses, "I agrees," and polite applause.

As our guests ate dinner, I noticed that conversations at the four round tables had become quite lively and sociable. Barry and I sat separately at tables with our clients, and tried our best to facilitate the conversation and not offer too many of our own personal opinions. We encouraged our clients to weave our agenda questions into their conversations during meal time and they did.

Our questions were:

1. What services do you believe Freedman Financial offers?
2. What types of services and/or informational meetings would be of value to you and the public?

Once the final plates were cleared, Barry began to lead the discussion by asking for feedback on our questions. Suddenly, this group of cordial and professionally unassuming council members began sharing their thoughts. It's possible that a few drinks lowered their inhibitions a bit, but they were truly interested in sharing ideas and learning from one another.

In response to our question, "What services do you believe Freedman Financial offers?" we learned that several council members expressed a hope that we would offer life insurance and long-term care solutions along with our array of financial planning and investment management services. *Hmm,* we thought—*that's interesting.* We always make recommendations on risk management issues in the financial plans we write. How were they not aware that they could implement insurance strategies through our office? We learned from more than one advisory council member that they had taken our financial planning advice and implemented our insurance strategies elsewhere. What a great first learning!

The second question, "What types of services and/or informational meetings would be of value to you and the public?" became the ah-ha moment of our meeting. It assured us that our decision to build a client advisory council would pay many more rewards than we could have ever imagined.

One client suggested that we build a reference library of tall of the videos and tapes we've gathered on topics pertaining to financial planning issues. Just recently, we had talked with our clients about ethical wills after a nonprofit organization had sent a copy of the tape to our office. A council member who had recently watched the video in our office suggested that we list available reference items in our quarterly newsletter and allow clients to borrow the tapes (now likely DVDs) from the office.

Another client wondered why we didn't share our new marketing brochure and disclosure kit with existing clients. He had recently referred his neighbor to our firm and saw our kit on his coffee table. In 1993, we had revamped our logo and briefly shared this announcement with our client base solely through our newsletter. It never occurred to us that our existing clients would want to see our new brochures, etc. Honestly, the pieces were developed for new prospects—people who we hoped would pay for financial planning first, and then elect to implement strategies with us. In retrospect, could there have been a subconscious reason we neglected sending this new information to our existing clients? Was it possible that we subconsciously believed that many of our existing clients were not familiar with, or even interested in, paying for financial planning advice, let alone learning about our assets-under-management services? Could it be that by *not* sending the brochures to everyone in our client base, we were placing *our* interests ahead of our clients? It was a humbling question from our council. They were offering honest feedback and they felt great about having a forum to share their thoughts.

What if you asked your clients questions about your practice? How do you think they'd respond? Consider the following:

- Do your clients have a comprehensive grasp on the services you offer?
- Do your clients wonder whether the services you perform for them and the specific products you advise are the same for everyone?

KEEPING YOUR ADVISORY COUNCIL FRESH

It's important that your council always include new faces and honor others who have served their time. Consider building a three-year rotating council, and at your very first meeting, place all your members' names in a hat. By drawing the first third of the hat's contents, you will have established a council class that will serve three years. The next council class will serve two years and the last council class will only serve one year. You might promise those whose service will end in less than three years that they will be included as part of the pool of candidates when you appoint your next council class the following year.

OFFER REPORTS FROM THE COUNCIL TO THE REST OF YOUR CLIENT BASE

Whether you communicate with your clients via newsletters, over the Web, or just cordially in review meetings, always remind them about the council and maintain interested client names so that you will have a pool of candidates to draw upon each new year.

A TOKEN OF YOUR APPRECIATION

At the conclusion of a council class's term, be sure to find time during your last meeting to recognize them for their time and service. Since our council's inception, we have given an engraved mantel clock to each outgoing council member. It simply states, "Freedman Financial Client Advisory Council Year X to Year Y." If you're truly looking to build lifelong relationships with your clients, never miss an opportunity to say thank you.

OTHER ADVISORY COUNCIL STORIES AND IDEAS

For more than 13 years, our client advisory council has continued to be the single most valuable marketing idea we've ever used. Over the years, there have been stories, lessons, ideas, and challenges that remind us that our firm is not cut in stone, but rather it transforms itself around the needs of our clients. What never changes, though, is our core values and beliefs, and with this foundation, we can adapt in changing times while keeping our principles intact and our clients' interests at the forefront.

In the next chapter, you will find a collection of true stories that have come from our advisory council. It will provide you with a sense of the diversity in questions we ask, as well as the sincere and honest perspective our clients are willing to share with us. I hope you found this chapter's introduction to building a client advisory council valuable, and that it encourages you to construct one on your own. Remember, your clients have different perceptions of you and your firm, and it is through these perspectives that you will emerge as a planner who stands behind the statement, "We listen to our clients."

SUMMARY

1. Establish a client advisory council.
2. Determine what results you hope to discern from your council.
3. Develop a membership roster that reflects the current demographics of your firm.
4. Share the results of client advisory council meetings with the rest of your clients.
5. Remain a facilitator of the discussion at your meetings—let your clients offer the opinions and advice.

21 | *Great Ideas from Our Client Advisory Council*

In Chapter 20, we shared both stories and strategies on how you might consider building your own advisory council. With more than 13 years of experience in maintaining an advisory council, I thought I'd share some of the more memorable feedback that they've shared with us. Some ideas have produced wonderful results, while others—well, let's just say we should have never introduced them.

CLIENT SCHOLARSHIP

One of the great ideas that emerged during our very first advisory council meeting took us a few years to develop. Today, it is one of the most successful and rewarding programs we run.

Our advisory council wanted to teach kids about money, and we decided that a scholarship program could be a great first step. Now in its ninth year, our scholarship is awarded to a high school senior with aspirations of attending a college or university within the year following graduation. Eligible applicants must:

1. Be the child, grandchild, or great grandchild of a client who maintains an advisory account in our office
2. Complete a scholarship application
3. Provide a 500-word essay that answers the question "What Does Financial Responsibility Mean to You?"

We explain that this scholarship is not needs-based, and the winner will be awarded a check for $1,000 made payable to the institution of higher learning they plan to attend. You can find a copy of our application form in the appendix.

The winning applicant is selected by a subcommittee of our client advisory council. Each member is provided a copy of the applicant's information. In advance of the meeting, we remove any names of the applicants as well other information that could identify them. Remember, 90 percent of our clients live within a 15-mile radius of the office.

We hoped that the essay question would give our clients an opportunity to initiate a conversation with their children and grandchildren about what it meant to be financially responsible. Some of the essays have been wonderful. We share two in sidebars in this chapter.

2007 Scholarship Winner—
"What Financial Responsibility Means to Me"

I am a firm believer in the old proverb, "money cannot bring happiness." However, I do think that money can convey a great deal of responsibility and judgment. I learned at a young age the value of a dollar and great saving methods. I have always had a vast knowledge about financial responsibility and can often be found helping others in this department. My name is Xxxxx Xxxxxxxx and I plan to attend Xxxxxxxxxxx in Xxxxxxxx, XX this upcoming fall. At Xxxxxxx I will be double majoring in economics and education, as well as competing on their women's varsity tennis team.

Throughout my life I have had quite the array of jobs. Whether it was the stuffed animal store during my sophomore year, the disc jockey company during my junior and senior years, or the residential camp counselor position for the past two summers, I can easily say that my favorite job was the small business I started. At age 14, the beginning of my freshman year, I decided to use my talent—tennis—and create a business out of it. I photocopied dozens of flyers that read, "Xxxxx Xxxxxx: Tennis Instructor... call for cheap lessons!" Soon enough, I had a few neighbors sign their children up and I quickly learned the basics of business. After a few content customers and several referrals, I was able to increase my rates and found myself with a great pocketful of change. At this point, I could do two things with this money: spend it all that night, or put it away in the bank. After careful consideration I decided to put most of the earnings in my savings account, and leave out a small sum so I could buy the new tennis shoes I was eyeing. Although it was important for me to save since college was in my near future, I had learned the value of hard work and found it necessary to treat myself with a small portion of the money. I also realized though, that it was essential to put the rest away into my bank account.

My tennis business was not the first time I saved money. Ever since I was little, I would deposit my birthday checks, babysitting money, and any other loose change into my account. Every six months, I would make the trip to the bank and I would give all of my money, except for a small amount that rested in my piggy bank, to the teller. Now, as I receive paychecks more frequently than I did when I was 11, I make that trip to the bank every month. When I entered high school and gained more financial responsibilities, I began to manage my bank account more carefully. I researched all of the programs available to me, and I decided to transfer most of my money from the saving accounts to a CD. This way I still have a savings account that I put money into every month, but also a CD that I place most of my funds into every year in order to earn greater interest.

I will never forget my father's face when I told him about this plan; he could not believe a 15-year-old girl thought of this on her own. I could sense how proud he was of me while I explained to him my reasoning and why it is I need to save now. I enlightened him with the need to put aside money for the costs that a car entails, books for college, necessities for living after college, a future family with a future down-payment of a house, and one day, retirement. My dad looked at me pleased, knowing that I had the ability to be financially responsible and independent. As it is, the sky is truly the limit for me, and I would never let not enough money saved up to stop me from accomplishing great things.

Establishing a scholarship is a statement of your firm's commitment to invest in the future of others. Not only will it breed goodwill for your firm in the community, it will also be a means of getting to know the next generation of clients.

For years, we've been encouraged by our advisory council to run a session for clients and their children so that the dialogue around money could be better understood. This year, we used resources available through the Financial Planning Association (FPA) as well as a few mutual fund and variable annuity companies who have already created exceptional PowerPoint presentations on basic financial planning lessons. The interest from our clients has been enthusiastic, yet finding a time when parents and 18+ year old children can schedule time together is a challenge unto itself. Among those who have attended the sessions, the response is overwhelming. We've heard stories about children who were avoiding participation in their 401(k) plans, but because of the session, were now inspired to participate. We've learned of children who have consolidated their credit cards and other who have been asking their parents to teach them more about personal finance.

Once again, our advisory council's collective wisdom has helped create a retention-based marketing program that keeps generations of families connected to the firm.

ADDRESSING THE NON-FINANCIAL ISSUES SURROUNDING RETIREMENT

A few years ago, I attended LPL's National Conference where world renowned demographer, Ken Dychtwald, Ph.D. introduced a presentation entitled "Your Power Years™: A Preview of Tomorrow's Possibilities." It is without a doubt one of the most entertaining, consumer-friendly presentations I've ever seen, and it is written so that advisers can deliver it with ease. I immediately decided to obtain a license to present the program which included invitations, guidebooks, and posters. The presentation was created in conjunction with Vanguard Funds, so it further added credibility to the show.

Just as I returned from our annual meeting, I met Mr. Callum, who you may recall from Section II, Chapter 7. He asked, "Can you help me with the non-financial issues I will encounter in retirement?" With this powerful question and my license to present "The Power Years," we went on to create a Saturday morning program that brought in over 170 clients and their friends. We thought about advertising this program to the public, but our advisory council cautioned us about the return on our investment. We were serving a full breakfast, and the room would only accommodate 200 people. They wanted to be sure that as many of our existing clients (and their friends) would have the opportunity to see the presentation, which we showed them in advance during an advisory council meeting. I think they made a smart decision, as the outcome of this session resulted in a new interest in retirement income planning for many of our existing clients.

The "Your Power Years" presentation can be viewed at www.yourpoweryears.com or www.agewave.com.

We decided to seize upon Mr. Callum's request to build a workshop that would have lasting benefits to both our existing clients and the public at large. In addition to the "Your Power Years" presentation, we did two specific things:

1. Created a nonprofit exhibit hall
2. Published a retirement resources booklet

CREATE A NONPROFIT EXHIBIT HALL

In preparation for our "Your Power Years" session, we decided to identify as many small nonprofit organizations, clubs, and lifelong learning centers as possible and invite them to our session. We sent the letter below to more than 125 organizations that we found via the Internet and through chambers of commerce or other community resources. Surprisingly, after an additional follow-up letter, and one follow-up call, only 15 organizations agreed to attend (only 12 showed up). Why? Many people thought we had a hidden agenda. No matter how hard we tried, they couldn't believe that we simply wanted them to be part of our event with no strings attached. We explained that our goal was for our clients who were seeking volunteer opportunities in the community to meet some of the vibrant nonprofits in the area. Incidentally, we specifically didn't invite national nonprofit organizations who might have a local chapter. We felt that they could have the potential of overshadowing many smaller groups.

The letter we sent to local non-profit organizations in our community appears on page 370.

**2003 Scholarship Winner—
"What Financial Responsibility Means to Me"**

Financial responsibility is a vital tool for success that can assume many forms and requires both hard work and knowledge. The way in which individuals manage their finances reflect their values and goals. Careful management of assets can help people to effectively provide for themselves and others.

I believe that being financially responsible involves taking care of needs before wants. Responsibility means that someone can separate necessity from desire, and then make the things that are truly important the priority. Once our basic needs are met, then we can look forward to the "extra" things to fulfill our wants. Saving and investing are valuable methods to assure that needs are met. By gradually saving, we can provide ourselves with some stability, even when circumstances are trying. Also, by investing wisely and taking reasonable chances, but not needless ones, we can further our opportunities to make the most out of what we have.

As a student, I am limited in my financial contributions to my family. My part-time job can cover some simple expenses, but in reality, I am still dependent upon my parents for many of my financial needs. Nonetheless, I can practice financial responsibility in a different way by striving to place myself in a position for financial success. I am convinced that the key to this goal is my education. By working hard and completely dedicating myself as a student, I can set myself up for future occupational and financial success. More immediately, academic accomplishments can help me to contribute to the payments for higher education. Scholarships, for instance, allow me to assume some fiscal responsibility toward my college education, something that is extremely important to me.

Financial responsibility is not an individual endeavor that affects only a single person. Rather, the ways in which one manages their finances influence many people, including family, friends, and the greater community. The ability to provide for family and loved ones often offers great personal satisfaction. Also, as parents teach their children effective ways to spend and save their money, they pass on valuable knowledge that their kids may continually utilize as they become older. Once people can offer secure support for themselves, their families, and their friends, I believe they have a social and financial obligation to assist those in the community who are not as blessed. Unfortunately, a very unequal distribution of wealth exists in most areas. By offering time and monetary contributions to those most in need, we are working towards social justice, another important cause that I value.

Financial responsibility is a term that can be interpreted several ways. To me, the phrase indicates the knowledge to manage money well, a personal duty to set myself up for financial contributions through education, and an obligation that extends beyond the needs of the individual. A person with financial responsibility is fully equipped with the tools for success and personal satisfaction.

<Name>
<Address>
<City, State, Zip>

As the baby boom generation approaches retirement, many will be seeking opportunities to give back to their community. That's the reason why you have been chosen to receive this letter.

On March 31, 2007, our firm, Freedman Financial, will be hosting an event for our clients entitled, "The Power Years—A Preview of Tomorrow's Possibilities." This event is expected to attract about 200 of our clients, their friends, and family, many of whom are either approaching or beginning the first few years of their retirement.

We hope this venue will serve as both a celebration of our clients' successes as well as an opportunity to introduce them to you. We all know that there are many programs, services, and volunteer programs buried within our own community. Many of these groups—like yours—are often times overlooked, and we feel that this is an ideal opportunity to introduce many of the North Shore's diamonds in the rough.

Therefore, we hope that you will accept our personal invitation to join us at our event on Saturday, March 31, 2007. There is no cost to attend. It is simply an opportunity for us to introduce our clients (and their guests) to organizations on the North Shore of MA, with hopes of helping them create new relationships and foster a tighter connection with the community at large.

Due to space constraints, we can only accommodate 25 organizations and we ask that you attend with either one or two representatives. We will provide you with an eight-foot, skirted table. You will have the opportunity to display information and meet and greet our attendees.

The attached flyer provides information pertaining to the event. Please review it carefully and contact our office with any questions you may have. Booths will be reserved on a first come, first served basis.

Sincerely,

Marc S. Freedman CFP®

Even though we were a bit disappointed with the smaller than expected interest from nonprofits, for those that did attend, we made a conscious effort to express our appreciation for their presence and provided them with a token gift for simply being part of our event. Our 12 nonprofits were positioned around the perimeter of the room and they were given the opportunity to hand out brochures and any other material about their group. Representatives from each organization greeted our guests both before and after the presentation. Many connections were made and our clients expressed great appreciation to us for connecting them with local organizations they never knew existed.

PUBLISH A NON-RETIREMENT RESOURCES BOOKLET

One of the greatest ideas that I credit to our client advisory council comes from a brainstorming session we held one evening over

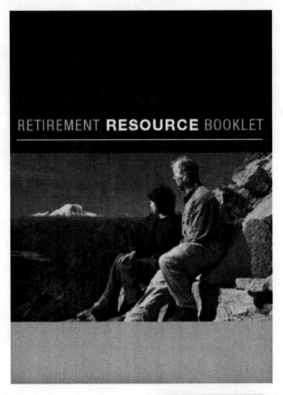

dinner. Our goal was to collect random ideas that could be part of a resource booklet that both clients and the general public could use. As we filled numerous sheets of flip chart paper, four themes began to emerge. They were:

- Finances
- Family
- Friends and Fun
- Fitness and Health

With these sections, we began to develop a booklet which served both as a marketing tool for our office, and as a public service to the community. In addition to providing a booklet to each attendee at our "Your Power Years" seminar, members of the community can find the booklets in local donut shops, barber shops, doctors' offices, and other places of business. Periodically, we visit these locations and refill the booklet box. Has it resulted in immediate new business for us? No, not really. But many people know of this booklet as a fixture in our community. The booklet can be viewed on the "Financial Planning Resources" page on our Web site (www.freedmanfinancial.com) and it can be printed as a PDF.

With some time and effort, I bet you could build a booklet that could serve your client base. How could you serve the non-financial issues in your client's life? What if your client asked you the question, "How can you help me prepare for the non-financial issues pertaining to my retirement?" Would you have an answer to the question? The Retirement Resource booklet is just one example of fulfilling that request.

A PERSONALLY CRAFTED NEWSLETTER

In 1994, before the establishment of our advisory council, we began publishing our own customized quarterly newsletter. Prior to this, my father would purchase pre-written newsletters that allowed him to slug in his photo and add a brief remark. The introduction of Microsoft Publisher led us to custom-creating a newsletter, and with my background in marketing, I was up for the challenge. While I was excited to serve as editor, publisher, graphic designer, printer, layout specialist, and photographer, the number of hours needed to create the finished product wore on my time, and took me further away from working with clients.

Years ago, we asked the advisory council how they would feel if we outsourced the newsletter rather than publish it in-house. Their response was quite clear. It was fine to outsource the layout, design, and printing, but the writing and tone of stories needed to come from us. They enjoyed the personal touch and simply written features that they said connected them with our office.

For more than five years now, we have been working with the same freelance writer, who happens to also be part of a three-generation client family. Our process for building a newsletter each quarter is as follows:

1. Liz, our writer, offers up a few ideas of general interest that would be used as a cover story
2. We submit our "Speaking Out" piece and "Marion's Corner"
3. Our staff collaborates on tidbit items
4. Liz edits our copy, completes the layout, and inserts graphics as needed
5. We edit the newsletter, make adjustments, and create a proof
6. We submit our newsletter to our compliance department for review
7. Within 48 hours, we receive edits and they approve a final copy
8. After Liz submits the copy to the printer, we can expect the finished product within five days

Our total cost for the newsletter is about $2,500 per issue, not including postage. We have chosen to send our newsletter first class. We decided that the time and energy needed to sort our newsletters wasn't worth the reduced cost in postage.

By the way, ever since we have hired a freelance writer for our newsletter, our advisory council has noticed the increased professionalism and freshness to each piece. Our newsletter remains a cornerstone communications piece in our office, and it's something our clients tell us they look forward to each quarter.

Following is an example of the cover from one of our earlier newsletters. Much has changed regarding the look and feel of our current newsletter. It now follows a more formal process and outline. Below are typical elements that our clients have come to expect in each issue:

1. A cover story of general interest (sample headlines are below)
   - Retirement—Here's Permission to Celebrate It Your Way
   - Keeping Up with Home Work (The Value of Paying for Services)
   - Getting to the Root of it All (Financial Planning)
   - The Tricky Business of Inheriting IRAs
2. A personal finance story that includes quick tips:
   - Secrets to Safe Online Shopping
   - Graduation Gifts That Last
   - How to Lower Home Insurance Costs
   - Tips on Buying a Vacation Home

3. A feature story relevant to Freedman Financial
   - A report from the client advisory council
   - Highlights from our client appreciation event
   - Reprint of the winning essay from our scholarship winner
   - Introduction of a new employee
4. Speaking Out—An editorial written by a planner on a current issue that affects the lives of consumers
   - The Right Priorities in an Upside Down Market—A warning to consumers on over leveraging themselves to purchase a home
   - Great Ideas Take Time—Wisdom from our advisory council
   - Downsize—Downshift—Reinvent—A personal reflection from Barry as he prepared for retirement
   - What is the Ultimate Gift?—Thoughts on instilling values into the lives of people we love
5. Marion's Corner—A relevant financial planning piece
   - A Crash Course in Credit and College Students
   - Climb a Bond Ladder as Interest Rates Rise
   - Highlights on Tax Law Changes
   - Long-Term Goals vs. Short-Term Noise
   - Capital Gains and Taxes
6. Tidbits and Highlights
   - Our travel schedule
   - Photos with captions from a client event
   - Shout-outs to an employee who passed an exam
   - In Memoriam—A list of clients who died over the year
   - Press releases of interest
   - Scholarship announcement

Today, our current newsletter looks highly professional, it folds in half (top to bottom) and is printed as a self-mailer. It is distributed

Winter 2008

In this Issue:

3 Marion's Corner: A Look at the Last Eight Years

4 Long Term Care Insurance—Points to Consider

5 Speaking Out: Securing your Retirement

New Face at Freedman Financial

If you've stopped by the office lately, you may have noticed a new smile behind the front desk. It belongs to Lisa Drown, Freedman Financial's official "Director of First Impressions." With over 20 years experience in administration, and 15 years in the financial world, Drown brings a commendable skill set to the position. But her outgoing, friendly personality may be her biggest plus.

"I feel comfortable here because I know what people are talking about when it comes the financial language, but I also understand what clients expect. I know how I would want to be treated, and that makes it easy to do the job," says Drown, who is also a Freedman Financial client.

Drown, who grew up on the North Shore and now resides in North Beverly, wasn't job hunting when she attended a Freedman Financial client event last fall. But in chatting with Marc and Marion, she learned that the role of executive assistant was open at the firm, and decided to apply.

At her previous job, as an executive assistant with a chemical company, Drown rarely interacted directly with clients. "I missed the financial aspects, and I missed the flow of people," she says. "Here, I get to use my social side."

In her spare time, Drown can be found pursuing outdoor activities with her husband Bill and their daughter Rebecca. "We like to hike, camp, and sail," she says. Drown, a two-year breast cancer survivor, also plays in a softball league with other moms in her daughter's school system.

Being a team player comes naturally to her, she says. Growing up, her family owned a retail hardware store, and the family's focus was on its success.

"My father would always say 'When it's your name on the sign, you've got to work that much harder,'" she says. "I can relate to the approach here because I had exposure to it growing up."

Seminar on Social Security

What's the future of Social Security? Come find out at an event Freedman Financial is hosting on April 8th at the Peabody Marriott hotel. Limited to 50 guests, the seminar will be held from 6 to 8 p.m. and will include coffee and dessert. All attendees will also receive a free copy of *The Social Security Fix-It Book* by Alicia H. Munnell. To reserve your spot, please contact our office.

FREEDMAN FINANCIAL
planners · advisors · partners

Eight Essex Center Drive · Third Floor · Peabody, MA 01960 · Tel. 978-531-8108 · 800-588-8108
Fax: 978-532-2666 · Email: freedman.financial@lpl.com · www.freedmanfinancial.com
Registered Investment Advisor · Securities offered through LPL Financial · Member FINRA/SIPC

to about 900 households, which include prospects, clients, centers of influence, vendors, friends, media members, and colleagues.

One thing that never changes on our newsletter is our statement of our core values and beliefs. It appears on the back fold and it says:

Planning is the critical first step to a secure financial future
Integrity is essential—our words must match our deeds
Competence can only be achieved through constant learning and skill assessment

The **Relationships** we build with our clients are for life
Innovation is the key to our success—we are dedicated to improvement, creativity and value
The **Personal touch** matters because the best relationships are built face to face

Our core values also appear on the desktops of each employee, in our waiting area, and in our conference room. In fact, our advisory council liked that we visibly share our core values so much that they inspired us to craft a laminated card that has our firm's information on one side and our core values and beliefs on the back.

Do you write your own newsletter or have you elected to use a mass-marketed template?

LESSONS LEARNED FROM OUR ADVISORY COUNCIL

Periodically, our client advisory council gives us the tongue lashing we deserve after we've made a possible error, or they caution us in advance of a mistake we might regret. Below are two ideas that didn't work for us—perhaps they will for you.

Client Spotlights

During a flash of creative brilliance, we thought it would be fun to include "Spotlights" on some of our clients for our newsletter. In one issue, we featured a client of ours who ran a successful disc jockey business. About four years prior to the printing of the story, he had come to us for financial planning advice and we both thought it would be a nice idea for him to talk about how financial planning had helped him better manage his financial future. In addition, we would promote his business within the story. Following is the page that appeared in our 2005 Spring issue.

We didn't have to even ask our client advisory council about the new feature to our newsletter on the evening we met for dinner. They were already anxious to discuss it. When they read the story,

Spotlight On ...

In this issue, we begin a new column that shines the spotlight on another branch of the Freedman Financial family - our clients. If you or someone you know deserve some time in our Spotlight, please contact us at freedman.financial@lpl.com.

Name: Greg Gates Plowman

Age: 43

Family: Married, one daughter, age 16

Hobbies: scuba diving, photography, white water rafting

Career: Owner of Entertainment Concepts, a full service disc jockey and event production company (www.djgreggates.com)

Greg has been in the entertainment business since 1974. His first break came at age 14, when he got his start as the disc jockey for his church youth group dance.

For Greg, it's the people who make his job rewarding. "Helping someone create the perfect wedding, being a part of a special anniversary or birthday party, lets me touch someone's life in a meaningful way."

Tricks to delivering the perfect event: "Good planning and a thorough understanding of the client's needs and goals. From Usher to Aretha, the right music creates the mood they're seeking to capture."

Financial goals: Greg's future includes financing his child's college education, saving for a vacation home, and preparing for retirement.

Length of time with the Freedman Financial family: "We've been with Freedman Financial for less than a year, but their expertise helped us get our finances organized and get on track with our goals."

Reasons for choosing Freedman Financial: "I was comfortable with Freedman from the very first meeting. My father-in-law has been a client for a number of years, and I'd known Marc through social circles. I've been very happy with their technique – the way they put people before products – and with their services. Their personal approach makes me feel confident that they understand my concerns for the future and have my family's best interests in mind."

Living wills — and the need for them – have made headlines lately. At Freedman Financial, we've found the booklet 'The Five Wishes,' put out by the company Aging With Dignity, to be helpful. We're happy to loan our copy of the corresponding video to our clients, and we'd be glad to help you consider the issues that go into writing a living will.

For more information, visit www.agingwithdignity.org

We've received six applications for our annual scholarship this year. Our Client Advisory Council meets April 12th to review the essays. **THE WINNER WILL BE PUBLISHED IN OUR NEXT ISSUE!**

5

they felt that we might have been selling advertising space to our clients. They were disappointed that we took space in our newsletter away from topics of financial planning interest and instead made an appearance that we were shilling on behalf of a client. Needless to say, this was the first and last "Client Spotlight" that ever appeared in our newsletter.

A High-Quality Service Directory

Just last year, we asked our advisory council how they would feel if we created a directory of businesses that delivered exceptional service and exceeded their customers' expectations. We explained that we would build the list by soliciting feedback from our existing clients and ask that they only submit the business names of people who they would not only recommend to another family member, but who overwhelmed them with their customer service, professionalism, and high-quality workmanship. We had heard of other advisers building similar directories in their communities, but wanted to test the idea with our council.

Initially, the response was favorable, but a series of questions emerged that hung unanswered. "Would Freedman Financial be willing to place its stamp of approval on a business by simply relying on a client's recommendation?" "What about clients that were currently tradespeople—how would they feel if a competitor was on the list and they weren't?" "Who would maintain the list and make sure that it was updated?" "Where would the list be maintained and how often would you look to make additions and deletions." Based on the litany of questions that multiplied during the conversation, we immediately backed away from the idea and thanked our council for their feedback. Frankly, we had never given the answers to many of the questions much thought, and upon further reflection, we agreed that a "high-quality service directory" could do more harm than good.

Advertising on the Radio

During another client advisory council meeting, we brought along a boom-box to get our clients' impressions about a 60-second radio spot that was created by a local radio station. The producers of the show had met with us, learned about our company, and felt that they could craft a message that would interest their listeners. Honestly, we weren't all that impressed by the radio spot, but we agreed that having a client perspective was more important. Think about it: how often do you like looking at pictures of yourself? You can almost always find a flaw. Perhaps, we thought, we might be doing the same.

When we told our advisory council that we were considering a radio ad on the local station, they actually seemed quite intrigued. So, we played the tape for them. When the voice over finished, they sat shaking their heads. There was almost a sense of disappointment that we thought they would actually like what they heard. They wondered why we would even bring something like this to them, since they agreed that the radio spot didn't closely resemble who we were as a firm. Our lesson from this meeting was that if we were to ever approach our clients again on marketing issues, we would need to be comfortable with the result first, before allowing them to offer feedback.

A year and a half later we tried again, on a television ad, no less. Because of what we learned from the radio ad presentation, we felt much more comfortable in the delivery of our television ad presentation. In the next chapter, we will walk you through the process we followed to create a brand-driven television advertisement that continues to be recognized by people in our community every day.

As I said at the beginning of this chapter, our client advisory council serves as a critical sounding board for ideas and issues that internally impact our firm and externally represent us to the public. I am forever indebted to them for their service, and I encourage every financial planner to have the courage to allow those you serve to share well intended advice when you need it most.

SUMMARY
1. Allow yourself to be vulnerable to your advisory council.
2. Consider ways in which you can brand your firm in the community.
3. Commit to innovative ideas.

22

A Lesson in Branding— Television Still Doesn't Understand Financial Planning

OBJECTIVES
1. Discuss our rationale for creating a television ad
2. Discuss the importance of going with your gut
3. Highlight the truths in ratings

COMMUNICATING THE MESSAGE (TELEVISION)
Have you ever considered advertising on television? This is the story of how a television branding ad was developed with the help of our advisory council after conceding that producers at the cable company couldn't understand the message we were trying to convey.

A few years ago, we set a long term vision for the office: "To be the most visible, credible, independent financial planning firm on the North Shore."

If you are not familiar with the North Shore of Massachusetts, this is a region that runs along the coast north of Boston and covers the western area about 15 miles inward. Many people are familiar with the city of Salem, which was home to the infamous Salem Witches of the 1600s. Other cities and towns in the region include Marblehead, Peabody (pronounced pee-buddy), Ipswich, Beverly, Middleton, and Andover. Over the years, we had learned that over 90 percent of clients who chose to work with us lived within a 15-mile radius of our Peabody office. So as we began thinking about strategies to promote our vision, we knew that our efforts needed to be focused. Advertising in newspapers such as *The Boston Globe* or *The Boston Herald*, the major newspapers in eastern Massachusetts, required us to solicit a demographic that far exceeded our criteria for attracting clients. Advertising on the major networks such as ABC, NBC, FOX, and CBS broadcasted to regions that we weren't currently serving, and was exceptionally expensive.

One afternoon, our phone rang and it was a salesperson for the local Comcast affiliate. She had seen a print ad we were running in a regional magazine and wondered whether we would be interested in exploring television advertising. We invited Sue in for a meeting, more to listen than anything else. However, by the end of our conversation, we began to realize we could segment a television message not only to the particular client demographic we wanted, but we could actually regionalize our advertising and focus on cities and towns we served, and no others.

As an incentive, Comcast was willing to build the television ad for us, and at a one-time cost of about $8,000, I thought it was a good investment for the firm as long as it was designed to be timeless and professional. My experience in viewing local ads was that they were cheesy, "come-on-down," used car salesman-esque. We knew we couldn't risk the credibility of our firm's longstanding reputation with our clients and the community, so we knew we'd have to tread carefully.

We scheduled a two-hour interview with Sue and Peter, a producer from Comcast, for an interview on our goals and objectives. We shared many stories and experiences about how financial planning created positive outcomes from clients we served. The follow-up questions posed by Peter encouraged our team that they got it. All we needed to do was patiently wait two weeks for them to draft a few ideas for our consideration.

The day I received the e-mail, I couldn't wait to see what they put together. I was excited because I thought we did a fabulous job conveying our differences in business practice, our commitment to our clients, and our dedication to celebrating our clients' successes.

However, as I read through the three story ideas, I felt my energy diminish and my stomach churn. I read the stories again, and began to think how the public would react to these ads. I couldn't help feeling a bit uneasy about each story.

Marion, who also was uncomfortable with the story ideas, reminded me that we weren't the client that the ad was designed to solicit. Thus, how could we be the best judges for what works on TV? We shared our concerns with the producer, and he was a bit surprised by our reaction to the stories. He thought that each vignette had the potential to be memorable and further connect our vision with our branding strategy. I won't say that he wasn't willing to make drastic changes to the options, yet, he really encouraged us to talk with others in the community and test their reactions.

Enter our client advisory council.

In fall 2006, we scheduled our council meeting to gather feedback on our consideration for using television as a medium to promote our vision. Our ad in *NorthShore Living,* the regional magazine where Sue learned about our firm, was being noticed by people in the community, and we wanted to share the work we had collected from Comcast and gather their feedback.

Below you will find the copy Comcast submitted to us.

Initially we read the introductory copy to the group below, and proceeded to read each story idea. We reminded them that the market we were targeting were mass affluent individuals who fell into our family stewards category (see Chapter 15.) These clients were generally married, over the age of 55, and had lived in the community for a long time. Together, they had been through many life events and, despite the anxiousness that comes with planning for retirement, they had a desire to celebrate their future as much as the past.

Here is the memo and story ideas we received. What reactions do you have?

To: Marc Freedman
From: Comcast

We believe that it is important to reinforce Freedman Financial's long-term presence in the community as a local family-owned business. This can be effectively presented by including an on-camera direct address by you as part of any message. Other recognizable members of the Freedman Financial team, including Barry Freedman and Marion Gilman, should also appear during this office sequence. I like to avoid using photographic portraiture on TV, so I'd recommend that when Barry and Marion appear in the commercial, we cut to them engaged in action pertinent to their profession: working with a client, consulting with each other about an issue, etc.

Your on-camera message would be simple, along the lines of "**At Freedman Financial in Peabody, we help families on the North Shore live their dreams through sound, genuine financial planning. We're your planner, your adviser…and your partner. Visit us online at freedmanfinancial.com.**" *This office sequence would appear at the end of a spot, after we've captured viewers' attention with an opening conceptual approach. Several treatments of these concepts are offered for your consideration below. These are not in full or final script forms yet. I'd ask you to choose the treatment you prefer and we'll work it into a full script.*

Treatment #1 is serious but lighthearted and emotional, treatments #2A, 2B, and 2C take a humorous approach. Treatment #3 uses a stylized interview/documentary approach.

#1: We open on a man and woman in their 60s, taking a walk along an otherwise empty beach. They're wearing jackets, long pants, etc. They're clearly happy together, enjoying each other's company. We hear emotionally uplifting music. After several seconds we hear a woman's voice say "**Paul and Carol have been together 42 years and have two married children.**" *We see them walking some more, then the voice says* "**Their son graduated medical school in Boston…and their daughter got a bachelor's degree in Arizona.**"

More walking and enjoying each other's company, then we hear "**Next up? Sending five grandchildren to meet a mouse in Florida.**" *Then we see the office sequence.* "**At Freedman Financial in Peabody, we help families on the North Shore live their dreams through sound, genuine financial planning. We're your planner, your adviser…and your partner. Visit us online at freedmanfinancial.com.**"

Some Humorous Approaches…

#2A: We open on a man looking for something in a closet. He's whistling then yells "**Honey, have you seen my toolbox? Never mind, I found it.**" *He starts whistling again.*

Cut to a ceramic piggybank on a table. We hear an announcer say: "*For years, Ted has told Ruth not to worry about money after retirement.*" *The whistling grows louder as Ted approaches the table. He stops whistling. Suddenly a hammer smashes down on the piggybank, and change spills over the table.*

We cut to a wide shot of Ted and Ruth looking at the carnage. He says, quite satisfied, "**This should get us through the next week and half.**" *Ruth looks a little frightened. Then the announcer says,* "**Looks like Ruth should start worrying. (PAUSE) How's your financial plan?**" *Then we see the office sequence and tag/signature, although for these humorous approaches it might make better sense to have an announcer read the copy and have you appear in the same way as Barry and Marion.*

#2B: We open on a man seated at a table at the end of his driveway next to the road. The table is covered with cakes. We hear an announcer say "**Bill and Maggie always assumed having enough money for retirement would be a piece of cake.**" *Cut to wide shot with Maggie standing near table holding a cake. She optimistically declares,* "**If we sell 2,750 cakes a month we'll be able to maintain our pre-retirement lifestyle.**" *Then we hear the announcer say,* "**How right they were. (PAUSE) How's your financial plan?**" *Deadpan, Bill reaches over to one of the cakes on the table, runs his index finger through the frosting and licks it. Then we see the office sequence and tag/signature.*

#2C: We open to the interior of a typical upper middle class kitchen. We see two middle-aged (50s) men and two women. The two women are seated across from each other at a table. We hear an announcer say, "**Bob and Kath Wilson left some valuable assets for their children.**" *One of the men then says,* "**Okay, we all know why we're here, so let's get started.**" *The women then lean across the table and clasp hands to begin arm wrestling. Then one of the men says,* "**C'mon honey, this is for the house!**" *The women start ferociously arm-wrestling. The announcer says,* "**Too bad they weren't specific. (PAUSE) How's your financial plan?**" *Then we see the office sequence and tag/signature.*

The Monologue Approach...
#3: Could look like this: We open on a shot of you (not looking directly at the camera, but at an unseen interviewer) saying something about Freedman Financial, then perhaps we'd go to an announcer and your logo. Next up you'd say something about your dad starting the company, then we'd see and hear him elaborate on your point. Then we'd cut back to you making a point about the professionalism and dedication of your staff, then we'd see and hear Marion talking about working with her clients. Then we'd go back to you summing things up and finishing with something similar to the office/tag sequence: "**At Freedman Financial in Peabody, we help families on the North Shore live**

their dreams through sound, genuine financial planning. We're your planner, your adviser…and your partner. Visit us online at freedmanfinancial.com."

FYI-For this particular approach, we could probably get away with a portrait-type shot of the team somewhere near the end of the spot.

Well, what did you think? Was there anything unique about these scripts? How would they be received if shown in your market? Which one do you think the advisory council selected? If you guessed, none, you'd be right. While there were a few giggles as we read some of the spots, they collectively felt uncomfortable about the "corny-ness" of some of the ads and the "typicalness" of the first spot.

We reminded ourselves of the radio presentation that we made to our advisory council. And we knew that if we didn't have something that we thought was worth sharing with them, they would remind us of the uncomfortable meeting just a few years ago.

GOING WITH YOUR GUT

What troubled us the most about the bad fit of television scripts was that we really felt like advertising via television was a strategy that aligned well with our long-term vision. So, after collecting feedback, thoughts, and suggestions from the council, we asked them to think about one final script idea….

I tried to set the stage for them. "We open with soft background music that expresses an air of nostalgia, warmth, and friendship. While music plays lightly in the background we watch a series of photographs appear on the screen. A voice over begins to read the script as examples of the following photos appear:

- A couple standing together on their wedding day
- Sharing cake at a wedding reception
- Birth of their first child
- First day of school

- Child getting a shot
- Child with a broken leg in a cast
- Family photo from Disney World
- High school graduation (Three generations)
- Helping elderly parent
- Elderly parent birthday
- Picture of couple on vacation laughing and celebrating
- Birth of grandchild

(Voice over) "..., *for richer, for poorer, for better, for worse, in sadness and in joy, through sickness and in health." Together you were there. But now your greatest challenge lies before your eyes...*

Open to a 55+ year old couple sitting in an upper/middle class kitchen. Piles of statements, booklets, tax returns, life insurance policies, etc. are scattered around the table. A mostly empty tattered cardboard box is nearby. Behind them hanging on the wall is a framed pad of paper with the writing "Days until Retirement." The couple seems depressed, overwhelmed, and confused.

(Voice over) "*Who will be there to guide you through the most important years of your life? How will you replace your paycheck? Is there a way to uncomplicate it all and build a plan that celebrates your success in life, and empowers you to enjoy retirement to its fullest?*

Cut to a clip of the Freedman Financial sign in the office, then to the entranceway of Freedman Financial and then a clip of the conference room with planners working on a case.

Voice over "*At Freedman Financial, we've been there, serving generations of clients like you since 1968, delivering genuine financial planning so that your hopes, goals, and dreams are more than wishes but a reality.*

(Review of previous family photos) "*Admit it, It's your real portfolio that matters. At Freedman Financial, we're committed to listening to you and placing your interests first. As your planner, your adviser, and as your partner, together, we'll be there.*"

Fade to Freedman Financial Sign and (possibly our team of planners)

For more information…

Did this commercial idea work differently for you? How so? When our advisory council heard this idea, they fell in love with the concept. They enthusiastically encouraged us to move forward with this ad. And then we broke the news to them. Comcast didn't write it.

We did.

When we called the producer the next morning and shared our council's reaction over the ads, he was both surprised and defensive. We then mentioned we had just e-mailed our draft of a script and requested his feedback.

About 30 minutes later we got a call from him. Initially he wasn't happy that someone was attempting to trump his idea, but as we reminded him of our objectives, he began to better understand who we were and what financial planners really do. Despite sitting through a two-hour interview, I sensed that he already had preconceived notions about our profession and actually thought this would be a rather easy project.

The Problem

Here was the major problem with our ad, as noted by the producer. We would need about 90 to 120 seconds to say what we wanted; and we only had 30.

After many conversations back and forth, Peter, the producer, merged his creative wisdom in television production with our script idea and developed a commercial which has made our advisory council, our office, and the community take notice. The script is below for your review, and I'm tremendously grateful to Peter for persevering in this endeavor. I think we both learned a lot about each other's respective businesses, and in the end, through authentic collaboration, we're both proud of the product we created.

Comcast

Commercial Script

CLIENT: Freedman Financial
TITLE: Together
PRODUCER: Willett
DATE: 09/18/06   *:30 AE: S.S.*

VIDEO	AUDIO
FADE UP TO PHOTOS OF A COUPLE AND THEIR FAMILY OVER THE LAST 40 YEARS OR SO, STARTING WITH A PHOTO FROM THE COUPLE'S WEDDING, THEN PHOTOS OF CHILDREN, ETC.	EMOTIONAL, DRAMATIC MUSIC UNDER FEMALE AND MALE VOICES, SOUNDS LIKE A COUPLE AT THEIR WEDDING CEREMONY. "For richer, for poorer; for better, for worse;
PHOTOS CONTINUE.	in sadness and in joy; through sickness and in health… (the couple's voices begin to fade out and female narrator's voice comes in)
PHOTO OF COUPLE TODAY. THEY ARE AT AN APPLE ORCHARD. WOMAN IS POINTING TO APPLE BEYOND HER REACH. PHOTO BECOMES MOTION PICTURE, MAN REACHES UP AND GRABS APPLE.	FEMALE NARRATOR VOICE: "Together you were there. Now your best years, and some of your biggest challenges, lay ahead.

VIDEO OUT	AUDIO OUT
FREEDMAN FINANCIAL SIGN. PLANNERS WORKING IN CONFERENCE ROOM. GRAPHIC: www.freedmanfinancial.com PLAN BEING PRESENTED ON LARGE SCREEN. COUPLE IN THEIR KITCHEN MAKING APPLE PIE WITH GRANDCHILDREN. CUT TO TAG PAGE: Logo (with planners*advisers*partners) Since 1968 FADE IN SMALL TEXT: Securities offered through Linsco/Private Ledger-Member NASD/SIPC	At Freedman Financial we provide families with genuine financial planning advice, putting their interests first. We'll develop a plan that celebrates your success in life… …so you can enjoy your retirement to the fullest. Freedman Financial. Together, we'll be there."

It took a good deal of time and energy, but ultimately we had developed a video clip that we were proud to show.

Could you imagine yourself running a television ad? It does carry a large price tag so be certain that you're ready to make an investment in your business that carries unknown results before beginning. Here are a few things to think about before venturing into television advertising:

1. What results would you like from your ad?
   - Immediate response
   - Brand recognition
2. What story would you like to convey more than others?
   - Client experiences
   - Your experience
3. Who should be in the ad?
   - Professional actors
   - You and/or your staff
   - Clients
   - Family
4. Repetition is powerful—How long will you stick with it?
   - One month
   - One quarter
   - One year
5. What is your budget?
   - Cost to produce the ad
   - Monthly cost for advertising
6. What's the message?
   - Is it timeless
   - Product/service specific
7. Will you have enough time to produce the ad in the event the product or service you are offering has a limited life?

They are all very important (and serious) questions to consider before embarking into the television advertising market. Honestly, we entered this opportunity rather blindly. We thought we asked all of the right questions, but in the end, you can never ask enough of them.

Ultimately, it was time to set our ad loose into televisions in the regions we had selected, but choosing where to place our ad, what time of day, what stations, and how often were all up for discussion.

CHOOSING YOUR SPOT—OH THE CHOICES

Advertising on cable television can be as specific or as general as you might want. Initially, Sue Stricker, our sales rep thought that our ads were best to run on CNBC, FOX NEWS, "The O'Reilly Factor," "Larry King Live," and "Hannity and Colmes." Once again the perception of a salesperson versus the perception of who we believe we serve hit a snag. We felt that advertising on CNBC and other shows that expressed strong opinions to viewers was opposite from the message created in our ad. We wanted to advertise on stations our clients said they watched, so once again we asked the advisory council. The majority of attendees mentioned TNT, TBS, The Food Network, The History Channel, A&E, HGTV, CNN, ESPN, and of course, the New England Sports Network (NESN, which is the station for the Red Sox). They concurred that CNBC and the like were *not* the best venues.

What was interesting was that we could buy two to three times as many spots on the stations our clients mentioned than the ones proposed by Comcast. That is, with the exception of NESN, which was outrageously priced.

We budgeted $3,500 for four months and ran almost 300 30-second spots per month throughout the North Shore community (at least 300,000 households.) We never expected our phone to ring off the hook. We simply wanted brand recognition in the eyes of our clients, the community, and our centers of influence.

The research and economic behavior patterns that monitor cable television viewership are beyond my scope of understanding. After three months' time, more than $10,000 in advertising spending, and almost 1,000 30-second ads, the recognition of our ad by the community was surprising small. While we never expected a line of new clients to be standing in our foyer, we did expect better recognition.

We thought that when we visited the supermarket, movie theater, coffee shops, and department stores, people who were at least familiar with our firm would say, "Hey, I saw your ad on TV." To Comcast's credit, they threw in an additional 100 free ads per month to see if recognition improved. It didn't seem to.

On March 31, 2007, after running our ads for three and a half months, we were about to host a client event on non-financial issues that affect retirees—what we referred to as our "Power Years" seminar (see Chapter 22.) Over 160 people attended this Saturday morning event, and it's the first time in a long time we actually received a standing ovation during one point in our meeting. It came when we showed them our commercial. They loved it, yet only nine people in the room had seen it before that morning. What's worse is that 85 percent of the people in the room were Comcast subscribers and were part of the regional demographic where we were advertising.

I couldn't get over the proud feeling our client base expressed when they saw our ad, yet I wondered why (essentially) no one was seeing it. We then decided to do something I never expected I'd agree to.

THE POWER OF RED SOX NATION

The introduction of Tivo and DVR (digital video recording) has virtually become mainstream in households across America. Despite the multitudes of programs and hundreds of stations, DVR allows us to watch what we want, when we want it, in a time-compressed format. What I mean is that DVR subscribers are conditioned to fast-forward through commercials and watch an hour-long show in 40 minutes and a 30-minute show in 20 minutes. The visibility of television ads has been marginalized by a fast-forward button. Except for one kind of programming.

Laura, my wife, asked me one evening, "What is one program you'd never want to Tivo?" Without even giving it much thought, I immediately said, "the Red Sox."

When you live in the Boston area, the Red Sox command daily conversations. It's rare to find anyone in Massachusetts who doesn't know the score of last night's Red Sox game, own a Sox t-shirt or hat, and have a favorite player. Whether the Red Sox are in first place or last (a rarity), Fenway Park (home of the Red Sox) is always sold out.

We had grown accustomed to paying $8 to $50 for each 30-second ad. The Red Sox charged $218 for 30 seconds per region, and we were advertising in three regions.

So, instead of spending $3,500 per month in three regions of the North Shore, we decided to focus on only one, and chose to advertise solely on one Red Sox game per week from April to the All-Star Break in July—a total of about 13 commercials. We also agreed to double our visibility with two spots per week from mid-July through October. The local Comcast affiliate owns the commercial space on NESN that appears immediately following the end of the sixth inning.

Within the first two weeks of advertising exclusively on NESN, we received more phone calls, comments from passersby, and recognition by the community than we had in the previous three and a half months. Amazing. That simple change in strategy has not only saved us money, but it has helped us fulfill our goal of being the most visible, credible, independent financial planning firm on the North Shore.

Whether you elect to advertise on television or not, I hope the story offers a glimpse into the challenges you might face if you choose to head in that direction.

The impressions you create for the visibility of your firm can become lasting impressions and set perceptions of your services before a client ever enters your door. Be sure that every marketing endeavor you choose aligns with your values and your firm's goals. Your reputation as a financial planner, especially one who serves the mass affluent marketplace in a local community, depends on your integrity becoming an extension of every action and every statement you make. Be careful, but when the time is right, be bold, because there is a market segment that needs you more than ever—they simply have to figure out how to find you.

Before we close this book, I hope you will press on and read the final chapter. It includes one of my favorite client stories as well as our top ten secrets for achieving success as a financial planner.

I hope that you have enjoyed reading this book as much as I have loved putting it together. It was much harder than I ever thought, but the final product has become more heartening and rewarding than I would have ever imagined.

SUMMARY

1. No matter how you choose to brand your firm, make sure that it represents messages you want—not what others think you should be saying.

2. Be bold, but be compliant. We all want to market ourselves in ways that differentiate us from others. Just be sure that your creativity to market is reviewed by your compliance officer first. You don't want to imply promises that you can't keep.

3. Marketing yourself professionally costs money. Be sure you feel comfortable with the money you want to spend. Before you venture into a major marketing initiative be sure that you are prepared to spend the money needed to fulfill your objectives.

23 The Secret Sauce to Becoming a Great Financial Planner in the Eyes of the Mass Affluent

If you've read the entire book from cover to cover, I wish to extend my deepest appreciation. Writing a book was much harder than I ever imagined and I hope that when you close this book, you will hold a new sense of appreciation for the role you as a financial planner can play in the lives of your clients. You *can* change lives. You really can. And sometimes all it takes is a simple thank-you to make a difference.

In the days, months, and years ahead, I hope you will continue to use this book as a resource and guide to help you grow an authentic financial planning practice. Consumers desperately need your leadership because, as you know, it is rare that financial literacy and planning skills are taught as part of the regular curriculum in most schools around the country.

I would like to leave you with two final thoughts.

The first is a list of ten ideas for financial planning success. Though there are hundreds of possibilities that could have been included, I hope you'll enjoy this list of ten.

Second, I would like to close with a true client story of appreciation. I want to share it because I truly appreciate your reading this book. It's taken more than three years for it to all come together and I am incredibly honored that you were interested enough to crack the cover and learn from one of your peers.

Thanks again.

TEN SECRETS FOR FINANCIAL PLANNING SUCCESS

1. **Be Aware of Your Clients' Five Senses.** First impressions go a long way. Whether you visit with clients in their home or they come to your office (my preference), be sure you are consciously aware of what your clients will see, smell, touch, taste, and hear.

2. **Reconnect with Wholesalers.** The product vendors from days of old are long gone. These professionals are well trained to help you build your business and they are equipped with educational tools, real-life stories, and a wealth of resources you should not ignore. No longer do they lead with a "fund of the month" or tempt you with golf balls and sporting events. They want "sticky" business, and by aligning with you, they can offer an element of support you probably never even realized.

3. **Create an Advisory Council.** Your clients know you better than any prospect. Rely on them for advice and don't be afraid to ask them tough questions. The more honest you are with them, the greater appreciation they will have in your genuine desire to serve their needs.

4. **Rebuild Your Tax Planning Knowledge.** Sign up today for a tax planning refresher course. Taxes play an important role in everyone's lives. Your clients will appreciate your

wisdom when you can review their returns and offer a perspective they never considered.

5. **Become an Active Member of the Financial Planning Association (FPA).** If you are sincere about the value of financial planning and advancing your professional knowledge, there is no better resource than FPA. Join a chapter, steer a committee, write a column, or simply attend a conference or symposium. You'll be amazed at the hundreds of different business models available, and you will meet people from around the world who share your passion about financial planning.

6. **Get the Facts—All the Facts.** Make a promise to yourself that you will commit to understanding every financial element of a client's life before agreeing to implement any investment and/or insurance strategy. When you and your client are clear on their net worth, goals, and cash flow, you are positioned to truly place their interests first.

7. **Always Consider the Art as Much as the Science When Planning for a Client.** If we lived our lives in a vacuum, every analysis and projection would have a high probability of coming true. Fortunately (yes, fortunately), life happens, and that's what makes financial planning vibrant. Do your best to resist letting academic theories and statistical analyses prevent your ability to listen intently to your clients' emotions and fears. What looks great on paper can keep your client from sleeping well at night.

8. **Better Understand the Effects of Health Care Costs, Medicare, and Social Security**. As your clients age, they will be looking to you for answers on retirement programs and medical benefits offered through the Social Security Administration and other non-government-related entities. As a financial planner, you need to maintain a clear understanding of the operations of these programs so that you can effectively integrate them into your planning and recommendations.

9. **Document, Document, Document**. Commit to a daily activity of capturing every conversation, phone call, and e-mail. Be sure these notes are easily accessible and can be readily formatted for printing in the event an auditor asks for your notes. We live in a society where litigation and arbitration cases can destroy a planner's career if proper recordkeeping is unavailable to justify your actions. Be prepared.

10. **Be a Financial Planner**. *Be honest now*. Do you find that you spend most days researching investments, comparing client portfolio performance to benchmarks, or monitoring the daily gyrations in our economy? If so, when do you find time to *be a financial planner?* The greatest financial planners in our profession consciously commit to making sure they balance their time and honor every component of the financial planning process with equal attention. Use the formula for financial planning as your guide.

THE POWER OF APPRECIATION

I'll never forget the afternoon when Julia and James Howland visited our office. The Howlands had been clients of our firm since the early 1980s. Jim had worked in an iron mill and performed hard labor for almost 40 years. The rigors of the iron mill were tedious and the work conditions were often unbearable. Jim arrived in a wheelchair pushed by his dedicated wife of over 50 years. As they entered my office I noticed that his hands were badly calloused and worn, his skin had turned as tough as an overcooked skirt steak. It was clear that Jim's health was further deteriorating. Sitting proudly by his side was Julia, his life companion. She was a woman who had surely helped him through some of the most challenging days, and was his strength when he needed it most.

Jim was now retired. He never made more than $45,000 per year in his lifetime. Julia worked odd jobs and added about $15,000

annually to the family's income. They lived in the same home on
Cherry Street for over 40 years, and brought up two children on
their modest income.

When they retired, Jim was given his share of the company's retirement plan—$85,000. Fortunately, with only a modest income, they
had been able to accrue about $200,000 in personal investments. These
assets, the equity in their mortgage-free home, and about $19,000 in
combined Social Security income was all they had, financially.

They were visiting our office for a scheduled annual review of
their financial life. It just so happened that the meeting was about
one week following our most recent client appreciation event.

After moving beyond the small talk, we began to review their
ongoing income needs and the money they had been drawing from
their accounts, when Jim's head sunk into his chest. Julia and I both
grew silent. I actually thought Jim may have fallen asleep. After a few
moments, what appeared to be erratic breathing turned into a whim-
per. Jim's gigantic, leathered, and worn hands rose high over his head.
They shook for a moment and then dropped heavily upon his head.

I sat in silence a bit longer, and Julia placed her hand on Jim's
back to comfort him. She was aware of what was bothering him and
she encouraged him to share his story with us.

Jim lifted his head slowly; his eyes were red and swollen and his
nose was red. He began:

"For 39 years I gave my heart, my life, and my left pinky to that
place (referring to the iron mill), and they treated me like crap! Never
once did anyone say thank you. Never once was I congratulated for a
job well done—in fact, they never even recognized my last day at work.
Why did I work so damn hard? For what? Look at me—my knees are
so weak I can barely walk and my hands are so stiff and calloused I can
barely feel the fur on my dog. Then, to make matters worse, they hand
me a form and ask where they can send my retirement check. $85,000.
That's it. For years they wouldn't tell me or even your dad what I was
entitled to. All they said was that I would have a retirement benefit.

And then, we get invited to your party last week. Here I am sitting among 200 of your clients and I feel more appreciated there than I did for all the years I worked. Do you know how many times you said thank you last week? I know it's not much, but I never imagined how much it would mean to me until I heard you guys say it." And then he asked a question I have never forgotten: "Why do you people do stuff like that for people like me?"

I didn't quite understand what he was asking, but then Julia helped. She told me that for decades, all Jim wanted was appreciation for the work, years, and service he gave to the company. He never got positive feedback or even the slightest hint of appreciation. When he attended our appreciation event, he was so overwhelmed with our simple gesture of thanks that it touched him deeply, and it's something he couldn't shake from his head.

As Jim wiped his tears and then offered a wisecrack about my tie, it left an impression on me that the simplest gesture of human kindness engenders the most basic connections between people.

So there it is, the final secret to truly serving your clients well and helping them fulfill their goals and dreams. Simply say thank you, and say it with a smile. Your ability to deliver peace of mind through genuine financial planning is yours for the taking. There is more business out there than all of us could collectively handle. Find the clients whom you can serve best and bring the very best out in them. In my opinion, the mass affluent need your help more than ever before. They are underserved and oversold, and they need your guidance, wisdom, and sincerity right now. So, close your eyes and imagine what greatness you will bring to those you serve today and those lucky few folks who will soon benefit from your great service. You have the power to change lives. As a financial planner, you are the leader your clients are seeking in their journey for financial peace of mind. Never ever take that responsibility for granted, for if you stay true to yourself, great rewards will find you and those you serve.

Good luck!

Appendix
Forms & Templates

AUTHORIZATION TO FURNISH INFORMATION

To: Freedman Financial Associates Inc. Date: _____

    Barry M. Freedman, CFP®
    Marc S. Freedman, CFP®
    Marion B. Gilman, CFP®, MBA
    8 Essex Center Drive, 3rd Floor
    Peabody, MA 01960

    Re:

I/We hereby request and authorize the above to obtain any information necessary to prepare certain financial, investment and insurance recommendations for my/our consideration.

Any attorney, accountant, investment adviser, insurance agent, bank, or trust officer is hereby requested and authorized to furnish any and all information, papers, documents, or copies thereof which may be requested.

Any employer is requested and authorized to furnish any and all information regarding employee benefit programs for which I/we may be entitled now or in the future.

Any life, health, or casualty insurance company with which I/we have insurance is hereby requested and authorized to furnish any information regarding my/our policies, including any policy service, change, or surrender forms.

Any physician, medical practitioner, hospital, clinic, or other medical or medically-related facility, insurance company, or other organization, institution, or person is hereby authorized to furnish any information in their possession concerning my/our insurability and that of my/our immediate family.

Because this is a multipurpose service form, a photographic copy of this Authorization shall be as effective and valid as the original for a period of one year.

Client: _____

Client: _____

SCHOLARSHIP PROGRAM APPLICATION

Name: _____

Address: _____

City, State, Zip: _____

Telephone: _____

Date of Birth: _____

E-mail: _____

Academic Information:

Name of High School/Prep School: _____

Overall Grade Point Average: _____Class Rank _____out
of _____
(If overall grade point average is not available, a transcript of grades
is required)

Verification of Academic Information:
(The above information is mandatory and must be verified by a high
school guidance counselor or principal.)

Signature of high school official: _____

Printed name of official: _____

Telephone number of official: _____

Future Academic Plans:

Accredited post-secondary institution: _____

Signature of Applicant _____

(Section to be removed before selection process)

Name of Freedman Financial client and relationship to you

_____

Return the following information by March 31, 2008 to Freedman Financial

8 Essex Center Drive, Third Floor
Peabody, MA 01960

1. *Completed application*
2. *Attach a 500-word essay answering the question "What does financial responsibility mean to you?"*
3. *A list of community service work, extracurricular activities, and work experiences*

FACT FINDER
CONFIDENTIAL INFORMATION

	Client	Spouse
Name	_____	_____
Home Address	_____	_____
Date of Birth	_____	_____
Place of Birth	_____	_____
Soc. Sec. #	_____	_____
Home Phone	_____	_____
Occupation	_____	_____
Employer	_____	_____
Work Address	_____	_____
Work Phone	_____	_____
E-mail Address	_____	_____
Cell Phone or Beeper	_____	_____
Mother's Maiden Name	_____	_____

SOURCES OF INCOME *(please attach a copy of recent tax return)*

Base Salary	_____	_____
Expected Bonus	_____	_____
Soc. Sec. (Annual)	_____	_____
Pension	_____	_____
Other	_____	_____

CHILDREN

Name and Soc. Sec. # _____

Date of Birth _____

Est. Annual Cost Of College _____

1st Year of College _____

Earmarked Funds _____

What % will you pay? _____

Name and Soc. Sec. # _____

    Date of Birth   _____

    Est. Annual Cost Of College _____

    1st Year of College _____

    Earmarked Funds   _____

    What % will you pay? _____

Name and Soc. Sec. # _____

    Date of Birth   _____

    Est. Annual Cost Of College _____

    1st Year of College _____

    Earmarked Funds   _____

    What % will you pay? _____

FINANCIAL PLANNING QUESTIONS

PLANNING OBJECTIVES *(Please rank in order of preference)*

	Client	Spouse
Reduce Income Tax	_____	_____
Build Wealth	_____	_____
Retirement Comfort	_____	_____
College Funding Strategy	_____	_____
Reduce Estate Taxes	_____	_____
Adequate Life, Long Term Care & Disability Ins.	_____	_____
Purchase a Home	_____	_____
Purchase a Vacation Home	_____	_____
Leave a Legacy to My Children	_____	_____
Other (Specify)	_____	_____

INVESTMENT EXPERIENCE

What do you consider a reasonable rate of return on a long-term investment portfolio? _____ %

If your investment account dropped in value, at what percent would you be concerned? _____ %

What investments would you consider? *(Circle all that apply)*

      CDs   Stocks   Mutual Funds

      Bonds   Annuities   Partnerships

      Other, please explain _____

What is the BEST investment you ever made? _____

What is the WORST investment you ever made? _____

If you are considering changing your current investment adviser, please explain why; _____

ESTATE PLANNING

Do you have a will?   Client_____ Spouse_____

                       Dated _____ Last Review _____

Who is the guardian for your children? _____

Who is the executor under your will?

  Client_____ Spouse_____

Does your will contain a trust? _____

  If so, who is the trustee? _____

Have you exchanged powers of attorney with anyone? _____

  If so, who? _____

Do you have current health care proxies?_____
Do you have any trusts?_____
Why did you establish them?_____
Are any inheritances expected?_____ When? _____
How much?_____

ASSETS – *Tell us about what you own*
Indicate Ownership: C = Client, SP = Spouse, JT = Joint, T = Trust

---

Liquid Assets *(If more convenient attach statements instead of completing)*
   DO NOT LIST IRAs, 401(k)s, and other retirement plans.
   They will be listed on Page 4

Checking/Savings—Bank Name _____
   Ownership _____
   Current Value_____
   Interest Rate % _____
Money Market—Bank/Fund Name_____
   Ownership _____
   Current Value_____
   Interest Rate % _____
Cert. of Deposit—Bank Name _____
   Ownership _____
   Current Value_____
   Maturity Date_____
   Interest Rate % _____
Brokerage Accounts—Name_____
(Attach Statement)
   Owner _____
   Current Value_____
   % Stocks_____
   % Bonds/Cash _____
Mutual Funds *(Description)* _____

Owner _____

# of Shares _____

Cost Basis_____

Current Value_____

Dividends Reinvest? Yes_____ No_____

Stocks/Bonds Held by You *(Description)* _____

Owner _____

# of Share_____

Cost Basis_____

Current Value_____

Dividends Reinvest? Yes_____ No_____

Stock Options *(Indicate Owner)* _____

Date Vested _____

Option Price_____

# of Shares _____

Current Value_____

ISO or Non-Qualified_____

Limited Partnership *(Description)*_____

Owner _____

Total Cost_____

Purchase Date _____

Annual Income_____

Any Write Offs or Tax Credits? _____

RETIREMENT ISSUES

At what age do you plan to retire?_____

At what age will your spouse retire?_____

How much annual income, in today's dollars, will you want in
    retirement? $_____

Do you plan on working after retirement? Yes_____ No_____

Earning $_____ per year

How many years will you work? _____

Have you verified the status of your Social Security benefits?

    Yes_____ No_____

    If yes, what is the full monthly benefit you can expect?

    Client?_____ Spouse? _____

Do you expect to have any debts in retirement? Yes_____ No_____

Explain: _____

Do you have any aspirations to make seasonal location changes?

    (i.e., Winters in Florida?) Yes_____ No_____

Explain_____

RETIREMENT PLANS

CLIENT

Type: *IRA, ROTH IRA, 401(k), 403(b), Pension Plan, Profit Sharing, SEP, SIMPLE IRA, Tax Sheltered Annuity, etc.*

Type _____

Where Invested _____

Current Value_____

Your Annual Contribution _____

Employer Contribution _____

% Vested in Plan_____

SPOUSE

Type: *IRA, ROTH IRA, 401(k), 403(b), Pension Plan, Profit Sharing, SEP, SIMPLE IRA, Tax Sheltered Annuity, etc.*

Type _____

Where Invested _____

Current Value_____

Your Annual Contribution _____

Employer Contribution _____

% Vested in Plan_____

Any specific information you would like to add?

_____

REAL ESTATE PROPERTY

HOME
    Address _____
    Owner _____
    Month/Year Purchased_____
    Purchase Price _____
    Cost of Improvements _____
    Current Market Value_____
    Mortgage Amount _____
    Mortgage Date _____
    Interest Rate/Years Remain _____
    Monthly Payment (principal and interest) _____
    Annual Property Tax_____
    Homeowners Insurance _____
    Co-op or Condo Fee _____

OTHER #1
    Address _____
    Describe: Vacation home, investment prop. etc. _____
    _____
    Owner _____
    Month/Year Purchased_____
    Purchase Price _____
    Cost of Improvements _____
    Current Market Value_____
    Mortgage Amount _____
    Mortgage Date _____
    Interest Rate/Years Remain _____
    Monthly Payment (principal and interest) _____
    Annual Property Tax_____
    Homeowners Insurance _____
    Co-op or Condo Fee _____

RENTAL PROPERTY

If you receive rent from your properties, indicate here

Monthly rental income $ _____

When do you intend to raise the rent?   _____

How much will you raise it? $ _____

When did you last raise rent?   _____

Management fees you pay $ _____

Repairs and maintenance costs $ _____

Utilities paid by you $ _____

POTENTIAL REAL ESTATE PURCHASES

Do you have plans to change your residence in the near future?

Yes_____ No_____

Explain_____

Do you have long term plans of owning a vacation home?

Yes_____ No_____

Explain_____

PERSONAL PROPERTY (Other than real estate)

	Owner	Est. Value
Car #1	_____	_____
Car #2	_____	_____
Furniture & Jewelry	_____	_____
Collectibles	_____	_____
Other—Describe	_____	_____

LIABILITIES *(Not real estate)*

List All Loans and Debts *(Auto, School, Credit Cards, etc.)*
  Describe _____
  Amount Due _____
  Monthly Payment_____
  Est. Payoff date_____
  Interest Rate_____

DO YOU HAVE AN EQUITY LINE OF CREDIT?
  Yes_____ No_____
  Credit Limit _____
  Bank Name _____
  Outstanding Balance _____
  Original Date _____
  Interest Rate_____
  How Paid? _____

FINANCIAL ADVISERS
(Please provide name, address, & phone number)

Accountant_____
Attorney_____
Banker _____
Casualty Ins. Agent_____
Financial Planner _____
Life Insurance Agent _____
Stockbroker _____
Trust Officer_____

v

BUSINESS INFORMATION

Name of Business _____
    Estimated Book Value_____
    Percent Ownership_____
    Is there a Buy/Sell Agreement? _____
    Notes Payable to Bus. ?_____
    What are the terms?
    Original Amount _____
    Length of Note _____
    Interest Rate_____
    Original Date _____
    Payments (Monthly, Annual?) _____

INSURANCE

Please bring policies and or company benefit statements as well as your most recent premium notice. (Attach another sheet if insufficient space)

Life Insurance
    Company Name & Policy Number _____
    Face Value _____
    Policy Date _____
    Cash Value _____
    Annual Premium _____
    Policy type—whole life, term, universal life, group, etc.
    Insured_____
    Owner _____
    Beneficiary_____
    Amount of Loan Due _____
    Interest Rate_____

Disability Insurance: Client   Spouse

Name of Insurance   _____   _____
   Carrier
Monthly Benefit   _____   _____
Annual Premium   _____   _____
Through Company   _____   _____
or Personally Owned
Waiting Period and   _____   _____
Length of Benefits

Medical Insurance: Client   Spouse

Name of Insurance   _____   _____
   Carrier
Annual Deductible   _____   _____
Annual Premium   _____   _____

Auto Insurance: Client   Spouse

Name of Insurance   _____   _____
   Carrier
Annual Deductible for _____   _____
   Collision/Comprehensive
Annual Premium   _____   _____

Homeowners Insurance: Client   Spouse

Name of Insurance   _____   _____
   Carrier
Amount of Deductible   _____   _____
Annual Premium   _____   _____
Amount of Umbrella   _____   _____
   Coverage/Premium
Replacement Value   Yes_____ No_____

LIVING EXPENSES

COMMITTED EXPENSES—*Expenses you cannot readily reduce.*

	Average Monthly Expense	or	Estimated Annual Cost	Anticipated change (Y/N)
Rent (not mortgage)				Y/N
Renter's Insurance				Y/N
Gas, Oil, Auto Repair				Y/N
Utilities, Water, Sewer				Y/N
Telephone				Y/N
Online Expenses				Y/N
Medical, Dental				Y/N
Other Insurance Premiums				Y/N
Groceries				Y/N
Clothing, Dry Cleaning				Y/N
Personal Care				Y/N
Alimony/Child Support				Y/N
Support for Relatives				Y/N
Education/Day Care				Y/N
Job Related Expenses				Y/N

DISCRETIONARY EXPENSES—*Expenses that are possible to reduce, if needed.*

	Average Monthly Expense	or	Estimated Annual Cost	Anticipated change (Y/N)
Annual Vacation(s)				Y/N
Entertainment (Theater, Sports, Outdoor Activities)				Y/N

Dining Out	_____	_____	Y/N
Cable Television	_____	_____	Y/N
Gifts	_____	_____	Y/N
Babysitter	_____	_____	Y/N
Kids' Activities	_____	_____	Y/N
Hobbies	_____	_____	Y/N
Subscriptions	_____	_____	Y/N
Pocket Money	_____	_____	Y/N
Charitable Contributions	_____	_____	Y/N
Lawn Care/Snow Plow	_____	_____	Y/N
Home Improvement	_____	_____	Y/N
Other	_____	_____	Y/N

Planning any major expenses or unusual fluctuations in your expenses?

Describe_____

_____

Is there anything else we should know about your expenses?

Describe_____

_____

YOUR THOUGHTS

This space is reserved so that you can prepare any questions you may have for us.

_____

_____

_____

_____

_____

_____

_____

FINANCIAL PLANNING/CONSULTING SERVICE AGREEMENT

This is an AGREEMENT ("Agreement") entered this _____day of _____, 20_____ by and between Freedman Financial Associates, Inc., a corporation duly organized under the laws of the Commonwealth of Massachusetts whose principal office is located at 8 Essex Center Drive, 3rd Floor, Peabody, Massachusetts 01960 (hereinafter Called "FFA" and _____ with residence or place of business at _____(hereinafter called "Client").

WHEREAS the Client has requested that FFA provide financial planning services and advice with respect to his or her personal financial planning situation; and

WHEREAS FFA is engaged in the practice of providing financial planning services and advice to selected Clients:

NOW, THEREFORE, in consideration of the mutual covenants and promises contained herein, and other good and valuable consideration, the receipt and sufficiency of which are hereby acknowledged, it is hereby agreed as follows:

1. Responsibility of the Client. The Client hereby agrees to submit to FFA any and all pertinent data with respect to his or her financial and investment situation so as to enable FFA to study and analyze the Client's financial position and make recommendations to the Client, all within the context of the Client's stated financial needs and objectives as set forth in Exhibit A attached hereto.

2. Confidentiality. It is hereby agreed by FFA that any and all data submitted in accordance with Section 1 shall be treated confidentially. FFA may make such data, financial plans and advice given by FFA to the Client available to any professional adviser employed or retained by the Client to assist in the implementation of the financial plan and advice given by FFA.

3. Basis of Advice. FFA hereby agrees to study and analyze the Client's financial and investment situation including, but not limited to, such matters as Client's assets (including ownership thereof), insurance needs, tax planning needs, investment portfolio needs, existing employment benefit plans, and present and future financial needs, goals, and objectives. If requested, and in accordance with Exhibit A attached hereto, FFA will prepare a written financial plan for the Client.

4. Implementation. It is agreed that the Client may choose any person or entity to implement the advice and recommendations, provided orally or in a written financial plan prepared by FFA. The Client retains absolute discretion over all investment and implementation decisions. FFA shall cooperate with any attorney, accountant, banker or broker designated by the Client with regard to implementation of any recommendation.

Upon written request, instruction and/or direction from the Client, FFA will be available to implement part or all of the recommendations provided in the financial plan. To the extent such implementation, in whole or in part, is requested by the Client, FFA, its employees, agents, or affiliates may, and in most cases will, receive commissions in connection with such implementation. The receipt by FFA, its employees, agents, or affiliates of such commissions shall be in addition to any fees charged to the Client pursuant to Exhibit A, attached hereto. FFA hereby discloses to the Client that its employees, agents, or affiliates may be affiliated as registered representatives of a broker-dealer and, if so affiliated, will receive commissions from said broker-dealer for securities transactions effected in connection with implementation of the financial plan and advice provided to the Client. Furthermore, employees, agents, or affiliates of FFA may also be licensed as agents of one or more insurance companies, on whose behalf various insurance products may be sold to the Client. In the event the Client purchases such insurance products, FFA, its employees, agents or affiliates may receive sales commissions from an insurance company.

5. Compensation to Freedman Financial Associates, Inc. For services performed under this Agreement, the Client shall pay to FFA a fee in the amounts and payable as set forth in Exhibit A, attached hereto. Any fees computed on an hourly basis will be in accordance with the rate(s) as set forth in Exhibit A. FFA may increase the amount of the fee only upon thirty days advance written notice to the Client. The fees and rates set forth in Exhibit A do not include out-of-pocket expenses as may be incurred by FFA in connection with providing services to the Client under this Agreement. The Client acknowledges that FFA has explained to him or her the method(s) of compensation set forth in Exhibit A and that he or she understands the method of compensation.

6. Liability. The Client hereby agrees that neither FFA, nor its agents, employees, or affiliates shall be liable for any loss incurred in connection with any of the investments recommended or made by FFA, either as set forth in the financial plan or otherwise provided to the client. The foregoing shall not limit FFA's liability for losses occasioned by reason or willful misfeasance, bad faith or gross negligence in the performance of its duties under this Agreement.

7. Assignment. This Agreement shall bind and inure to the benefit of the Client and FFA and their respective legal representatives, successors and assigns, except that neither FFA nor the Client may delegate any of their obligations under this Agreement or assign this Agreement without the prior written consent of the other.

8. Termination. The Client or FFA may terminate this Agreement without penalty within five business days of the date of the Agreement, or any time thereafter by delivery of a notice as provided in Section 10.

9. Arbitration. In the event of any dispute or disagreement between the Client and FFA arising out of, or in relation to the interpretation, application, or meaning of this Agreement, or respecting compliance with its provisions, the Client and FFA will meet in good faith to attempt to resolve such dispute or disagreement. If they are unable to resolve such dispute or disagreement through such meetings, within thirty days after receipt of written notice by either party from the other that such a dispute or disagreement exists, such dispute or disagreement will be submitted for arbitration to the American Arbitration Association ("Association") at its office in Boston, Massachusetts, or such other location as is mutually agreed, in accordance with the procedures, rules, and regulations of the Association. Any judgement upon the award rendered by the arbitrator may be entered in any court of competent jurisdiction. In any such arbitration, each party will bear its own costs and expenses, including attorneys' fees and administrative expenses in connection with the Arbitration. Unless mutually agreed to by the parties in writing, there shall be no obligation to arbitrate changes in or additions to the terms of this Agreement and no arbitrator shall have the power to add to or subtract from the terms of this Agreement. All arbitration proceedings will be conducted in Boston, Massachusetts.

10. Notices. Unless otherwise specified in this Agreement, all notices, instructions, and advice with respect to the security transactions or any other matters contemplated by this Agreement shall be deemed duly given when received by FFA in writing at the address first above written or when deposited by first class mail addressed to the Client at the address appearing above, or at such other address or addresses as shall be specified, in each case, in a notice similarly given.

11. Miscellaneous. This Agreement: (i) may be executed in any number of counterparts, each of which, when executed by the Client and FFA shall be deemed to be an original, and all of which counterparts together shall constitute one and the same instrument; (ii) shall be governed by and construed under the laws of the Commonwealth of Massachusetts applicable to contracts made, accepted, and performed wholly within the Commonwealth without application of principles of conflict of laws; (iii) constitutes the entire Agreement with respect to its subject matter, superseding all prior oral and written communications, proposals, negotiations, representations, understandings, courses of dealing, agreements, contracts, and the like between client and FFA; (iv) may be amended or modified, and any right under this Agreement may be waived in whole or in part, only by a writing signed by the Client and FFA; (v) contains headings only for convenience, which headings do not form part, and shall not be used in construction, of this Agreement; (vi) is not intended to inure to the benefit of any third-party beneficiary; (vii) may be enforced only in courts located within the Commonwealth of Massachusetts, and we each hereby agree that such courts shall have venue and exclusive subject matter and personal jurisdiction, and consent to service of process by registered mail, return receipt requested, or by any other manner provided by law.

12. Force Majeure. Neither the Client nor FFA shall be responsible to the other for delays or errors in the performance or breach under this Agreement occurring solely by reason of circumstances beyond our control, including acts of civil or military authority, national emergencies, fire, major mechanical breakdown, labor disputes, flood or catastrophe, acts of God, insurrection, war, riots, or failure of transportation, communication, or power supply.

13. Receipt of Written Disclosure Statement. The Client hereby acknowledges receipt from FFA of a written disclosure statement which is either Part II of Form ADV or a similar document containing at least the information so required by Part II of Form ADV.

IN WITNESS WHEREOF, the parties have executed this Agreement on the day and year first above written.

CLIENT SIGNATURE(S);
FREEDMAN FINANCIAL ASSOCIATES, INC.

X_____

_____
PRINT NAME

X_____

_____
PRINT NAME

Freedman Financial Associates, Inc. is a Registered Investment Advisor in the Commonwealth of Massachusetts. Barry M. Freedman, CFP®, and Marc S. Freedman, CFP®, are Investment Adviser Representatives of Freedman Financial Associates, Inc.

Designed for use in Massachusetts. Applications may vary according to state and federal regulations, and expert advice about its use should be sought.

Exhibit A
Attachment To Freedman Financial Associates, Inc.
Financial/Consulting Agreement

CLIENT OBJECTIVE(S)

The investment and/or financial planning objectives of (Client) in connection with the Agreement with FFA are as follows:

SERVICES AVAILABLE

There are three general categories of FFA services you may choose among. Indicate choice(s) by "X."

☐ FINANCIAL PLANNING SERVICE

FFA shall prepare a written financial plan for (Client). FFA will be compensated for its efforts in preparing said plan at the rate of _____ dollars per hour. It is FFA's best estimate (such estimate not intended to be binding) that _____ hours will be required to prepare the financial plan. However, in no event will FFA's compensation for preparation of the financial plan exceed _____ dollars. Receipt is hereby acknowledged by FFA of the sum of _____ dollars as a retainer paid and to be applied to the compensation for preparation of the financial plan. FFA will refund any prepaid amounts not expended in connection with the services to be provided or in the event of termination of the agreement.

☐ CONSULTING SERVICE

Client wishes to retain FFA for the purposes of providing consulting services to the Client. The consulting services may include such advice, financial planning, or review of the Client's financial situation, or related matters as the Client may request, including in-person or telephone consultations. Compensation to FFA for providing consulting services will be at the rate of _____ dollars per hour. Receipt is hereby acknowledged by FFA of the sum of _____ dollars as a retainer paid and to be applied to the compensation for the consulting services requested by the Client. FFA will refund any prepaid amounts not expended in connection with the services to be provided or in the event of termination of the Agreement.

☐ PERIODIC REVIEW SERVICE

Client hereby wishes to retain the services of FFA to provide a _____ (quarterly, semi-annual, annual) review of Client's financial plan and/or investment. FFA will be compensated at the rate of _____ dollars per hour for such review. It is FFA's best estimate (such estimate not intended not to be binding) that _____ hours will be required _____ (quarterly, semi-annually, annually) to provide the review requested by the Client. The Client agrees to pay to FFA in advance of each periodic review such amount as may be requested by FFA. Receipt is hereby acknowledged by FFA of the sum of _____ as a retainer paid and to be applied to the compensation for the periodic review requested by the Client. FFA will refund any prepaid amounts not expended in connection with the services to be provided or in the event of termination of the Agreement.

IN WITNESS WHEREOF the parties have executed this Exhibit A and acknowledge it as an attachment to FFA's Financial Planning and Consulting Agreement dated _____.

CLIENT SIGNATURE(S):

X _____

_____
PRINT NAME

X _____

PRINT NAME _____

FREEDMAN FINANCIAL ASSOCIATES, INC.

By _____

DATE _____